The Ultimate Guidebook

All the things you need to know before and after bringing home your feathered friend

By

Kimberly Link

With Contributions by: Jennifer Garey

Majestic Waterfowl Sanctuary

www.majesticwaterfowl.org

A Happy Duck Publication™

Other Happy Duck Titles...

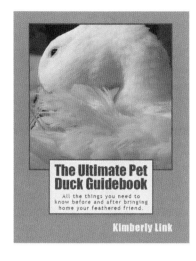 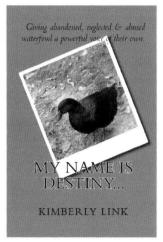 

A portion of the proceeds from the sale of Happy Duck books
Are donated to
Majestic Waterfowl Sanctuary!

In Loving Memory of Golly & Ethel

Thanks to the generosity of:

Lew, Sally, Mary, Glynis & Abby

The Garey Family

All Friends Animal Hospital

Dr. Otka, Lona, Leigh, Tara, Joanne, Amanda & Holly

Dr. Melgey

Dr. McGee & Collierville Animal Clinic

And all of our Majestic Friends, Supporters, Volunteers & Adopters

Kim also wishes to thank:

Tony, for all of your hard work and devotion

Isabel, for your endless patience

And our amazing geese who have given us so much more than we could ever give them

Jenn also wishes to thank:

Mike for always standing beside me and doing the very best for our flock

My wonderful children: Marylynne, Kristina, Elizabeth "The Goose Whisperer"
& Pancho I love you all so much and cannot thank you enough for your tireless help and support

Carol for always seeing me through

My beautiful geese… I don't know what I would do without you
You are my babies and you have brought so much joy and love to my life

Table of Contents

Goosey Anecdotes	
Ali's Bill Pouch	*28*
China Girl's Fox Bite	*59*
Egor's E. Coli	*68*
Duran's Sore Feet	*72*
Tutter's Staph Infection	*80*
Tutter's Osteomyelitis	*81*
Grampa's Bumblefoot	*83*
Victor-Victoria's Injured Eye	*93*
Ethel's Hardware Disease	*104*
Golly's Aspergillus	*110*
Ms. Donald's Plucked Feathers	*117*
Losing Ethel	*173*
Naming Ali & Chan	*191*
Taking Grampa Out of the Wild	*195*

Introduction

I remember the day we rescued our first dozen ducks from a pond and formed Majestic Waterfowl Sanctuary. Our Web Designer was a goose enthusiast and over the course of the following year she would occasionally email me to reaffirm that we were actually planning on welcoming rescued geese though our doors at some point. I kept saying yes, but I have to admit, I was silently pleased that we had not yet run into any geese that needed our help.

The following winter we discovered two ganders who were surviving on a small pond in front of a very busy parking lot that neighbored six lanes of traffic. The boys somehow managed to cross this street without being hit, but locals knew their days were numbered. This wasn't the only hazard to their health. As we prepared our pen for their arrival, I occasionally drove by to check on them and frequently found a pizza delivery truck parked next to the pond and the driver feeding the two geese pizza crust. Other visitors, thinking they were doing the ganders a favor, fed them cereal and junk food. We knew a month before their arrival that malnutrition was going to be among one of the challenges these two boys faced.

With permission from the land owners and after informing local police, we went in and rescued them the day before record low February temperatures rolled in. I remember it being so freezing that we had to buy extra gloves from one of the stores neighboring the pond and our volunteer kayaker was covered in a thin layer of ice as she herded the ganders on shore and into our arms.

That was the day we rescued Ali and Chan. I was overwhelmed to say the least. For all the fear their bills inspire, I quickly learned that the true danger lied in their wings. During their precautionary wormer treatment Ali opened and closed his expansive wings and literally beat me so hard I had black and blue marks all up my legs and he nearly broke my wrist—and through my protective winter clothing! Although I was quick to retreat out of the pen, I at least knew enough to compose myself and go right back into his pen again; that is, MY pen again. It took me a week to successfully reclaim my pen, but I did it. I earned my place as alpha goose and Ali earned his name.

I spent the next year watching these boys closely, studying their interactions and behaviors and learning everything I possibly could about them. I soon discovered that unlike ducks who will protest against and avoid anything new in their pens for at least three days, geese will immediately come over and curiously explore anything out of the ordinary. They have very inquisitive minds, enjoy playing, thrive in family groups, form very tight bonds and are excellent guardians.

Although I had once been wary about bringing geese into our sanctuary, once I got through the learning curve, I was amazed to discover that these overlooked pets are truly quite wonderful, intelligent and entertaining companion animals.

I had only one handbook to get me through the adventure of caring for geese and I can't say that I gained anything useful from it. Like so many duck books out there, it wasn't geared towards a Momma Goose, but aimed to please an audience of breeders who believe that their stock is expendable.

That's what my book is for, to walk you through the preparations that need to be made, to bring to mind the things you need to consider and to give you some enrichment ideas to make their long-term stay with you that much more wonderful. In addition, I have set up the most detailed table of contents I could possibly provide along with an index in order to help you find the information you are looking for *quickly!*

Geese are a high-maintenance pet and they require a lot of care and attention even though some sources will try to tell you otherwise. They are not an adventure for everyone, but for those of us who are drawn to them and prepared to put in the time and energy to provide for them, they are purely perfect and worth every minute of our attention. Above all else they deserve a better life than to be dropped off and abandoned on public ponds and waterways.

Many geese have come through our sanctuary, and we have learned so many things from them. I felt the need to share what we know in the hopes it helps both you and them during your time together. One thing I've discovered in handing out goosey advice is that there are some situations that have more than one solution. In these cases you may not agree with all of the options I've provided, but someone else might. What works for one family's goose may not work for another. The idea here is to find the best solution for you.

REMEMBER: Although I have written this guide book to help you, I am <u>NOT</u> a veterinarian. No guide book can replace the assistance of a certified and qualified vet. This book will provide you with the information you need to ask your vet educated questions, but it is no way intended as a substitute for proper vet care.

Rio and I have a conversation about the weather

Preparations

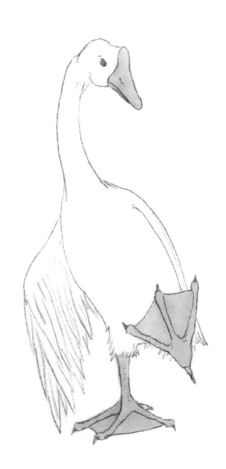

Preparations

So you're looking at that cute gosling and thinking, *"How much trouble could that little thing be."* Before you hold that tiny darling against your cheek and smell the sweet scent of their fluff and the pleasant odor of their crumbled food, consider carefully. This little fellow won't be much trouble now, but in a few weeks, you are going to have your hands full. There are many preparations that need to be considered and addressed *before* you bring a new gosling home.

As with any pet, goslings need a lot of care and attention—and *a lot* of protection from predators. You will need to find yourself a good vet, purchase waterfowl supplies and build an enclosure for your goose to live in—not to mention all the cleaning you will need to do. So, put that gosling back down, read this book, and if goose ownership still sounds perfect for you, then go back and buy a couple—one for each cheek.

Preparation #1
Vet Care

First and foremost, on the top of your list is always vet care. Finding a doctor for a goose can be extremely difficult—not at all what you're used to when finding vet care for your other animals. For this reason, I highly recommend that you call your local vet hospitals *before* bringing a goose home to make sure you have access to health care and information for your goose prior to their arrival. Just because an avian vet is qualified to see birds does *not* mean they are qualified to see geese. Birds such as parrots and parakeets require different care and medications than geese. What is safe for some birds is not always safe for your geese, and in some cases, can be quite harmful.

Finding a Waterfowl Vet

We have begun a nationwide registry of waterfowl vets on our website in an attempt to help folks find a doctor for their geese. Families who have waterfowl vets provide us with their vet information through the site, so we can contact the vet office, confirm information and then add them to our website's Vet Finder.

Another good way to find a waterfowl vet is to do an internet search for avian vets in your state. Begin calling each of these vets to determine which ones specifically handle geese.

- **Ask your vet questions**

Never assume anything when it comes to your vet care. There are questions that you will need to ask of your new vet. For example, how much training and experience do they have with geese? Do they have other goose patients? These are questions you can ask a knowledgeable staff member if the vet is not available for consultation.

Also be sure to find out what kind of service you will get after-hours, on weekends and holidays. Which vet office covers their practice when they are closed? Does that covering office have a waterfowl vet on staff? If they are the only waterfowl vet in the vicinity, will they answer their pages during off hours and under what conditions?

Keep in mind that staff changes occur in vet offices, so it is a good idea to periodically check in and confirm that the same qualified vet is still on staff and available for appointments should the need arise.

Here are some good questions you can ask your potential vet:

    * How many goose patients does this vet have?

    * How many geese does this vet see as patients in any given month/year?

* What formal education has this vet received that has directly prepared them for the special handling of waterfowl *(not parrots)*, including any training seminars attended?

* Is this vet experienced with reproductive issues that may occur in egg-laying geese and how to properly treat those issues should they arise?

* Has this vet operated on geese in the past? If so, what types of surgeries did they perform and what were those outcomes?

* What reference books does this vet recommend you read in order to better care for your geese? *(If they can't think of any... be wary!)*

* If ever in the future this vet should become stumped by your goose's medical condition, what resources will they tap into for assistance? *(Ideally, you are looking for a vet who is willing to consult with other vets. They are the best. Avoid vets who will "read up" or "surf the internet" as their sole means of research.)*

<u>HINT:</u> One tell-tale indication that a vet does not have a lot of experience with waterfowl is often demonstrated in their inability to easily open up their bills. A vet who tries to pry a goose's bill open at the TIP is demonstrating their experience with parrots and their *inexperience* with waterfowl. You want to see a vet who knows to pry the bill open at the BASE. A vet who cannot manage to open a bill within a few seconds most likely does not have many waterfowl patients.

- **Find a back-up vet**

I don't know what it is about our geese, or any of our animals for that matter, but it seems if they're going to get sick, injured, or just start acting funny, they always seems to do it after-hours, on weekends, over a long holiday, or during that particular week that our vet just happens to be away on vacation. This is why it is vital to have a back up plan if your vet is unreachable.

I highly recommend finding a second, emergency veterinarian willing and qualified to take geese into their care as patients 24 hours a day, 7 days a week. This is needed *before* you bring your goose home. You don't want to spend precious time in an emergency calling dozens of vet offices, trying to find someone willing to assist.

- **Confirm only qualified waterfowl vets will be handling your goose**

Anytime your goose is being treated while you are not right in the room with them, make sure that the vet handling them is the actual qualified waterfowl veterinarian. This is especially true in emergency situations or when operations are being performed. You don't want your goose being passed into unqualified hands after you leave the room. There's only one way to be sure that this is the case and that is to be fearless and ask.

- **Trust your instincts**

One of our vets once told me to never trust anyone, not even a vet, when it comes to the diagnosis of one of your animals. She said no matter how hard your vet tries to convince you that they can't find anything wrong with your animal, if you still don't feel comfortable—TRUST YOUR INSTINCTS and call on another vet. Keep in mind that you know your pets better than anyone else because you are with them every day and know their normal behavior. If you see them acting a bit peculiar trust your eyes and your heart. This is another reason to have a second vet contact available ahead of time—to get a second opinion when you need it.

When cared for properly and kept in clean quarters, geese tend to be very healthy and very resistant to disease. When they do become ill or injured, geese are well known for hiding their ailments as a defense mechanism, so predators won't recognize that they are easy pickings. Early recognition of subtle warning signs can be life saving. Closely monitoring behavioral changes in your geese and contacting a vet early on with your concerns can often prevent a hidden health condition from worsening.

This advice should also be shared with your family. If you sense that something is wrong with your goose and a family member tells you not to worry, take it with a grain of salt. Always trust your instincts when one of your geese is not behaving normally, no matter what anyone else tells you. Place a call to your vet and have your goose seen by a professional.

Preparation #2
Stocking Your Medicine Cabinet

Now it's time to stock your medicine cabinet. These are some of the items you want to have on hand at all times if you are going to bring home a goose. You will most likely never need these items, but if you do, it's best to be prepared.

Purchase a Pet Carrier

Have a pet carrier on hand for emergencies at all times. We have a lot of geese at the sanctuary, so I keep multiple carriers on hand. There have been times where I needed to bring a few geese in at a time, which can be simple or complicated depending on which geese need to go to the vet. Some geese like to travel together while others don't, so it is best to have more than one carrier on hand in case of a two or more goose emergency.

We have a well-stocked first-aid kit for sanctuary emergencies

Important Items to Have On Hand:

- **Needle nose pliers**

You will need these to pluck a blood feather if it breaks.

- **Blood coagulant (styptic powder)**

You may need this in the case of a feather break emergency, or to control any excessive bleeding of the bill, feet or legs. Cornstarch is an effective substitute and can often be used to stop bleeding in emergency situations.

- **Reel of gauze bandage**

You may need this in the case of a foot, leg or wing injury.

- **Gauze pads**

You may need these to control bleeding if an accident occurs.

- **Reel of adhesive tape**

You may need this to hold gauze bandaging in place.

- **Tin of Bag Balm**

You may want to use this to help remedy extremely dry, cracking or peeling bills, feet or legs. Use Bag Balm *very sparingly* or your goose will spread the oil to its feathers. Feathers may become laden with the oil and lose their waterproof effectiveness.

- **Non-sting, first-aid wound wash**

You may need this to clean out a cut or treat broken skin to help stave off infection. Try to find this in a spray bottle to help make application easier. Use wound wash sparingly around feathers since some formulas may interfere with waterproof effectiveness.

- **Small towel**

You may need this to drape over your goose's head in an emergency. Covering their eyes can sometimes calm a goose in crisis.

- **Clothespin**

You may need this to hold a towel *loosely* in place over the goose's head during an emergency.

- **KY Jelly / Lubricant**

You may need this to moisten a prolapsed oviduct.

- **Disposable rubber gloves**

You may need these for applying topical ointments / medications.

- **Baytril®**

Ask your vet to provide you with a half dozen Baytril® 68 mg pills to keep on hand. You may need this if you need a general antibiotic after-hours or on a day the vet office is closed.

- **Metacam® or Rimadyl®**

In case of a weekend accident, it's good to have an anti-inflammatory/pain medication on hand. Ask your vet for a few doses to keep on hand in case of after-hour emergencies. Metacam® is a liquid and is administered orally via a syringe marked with the weight of your pet. Try to get Metacam® that is still in its original, unopened packaging (some vets pour this oral suspension into prescription bottles, which can dramatically reduce its shelf life). We prefer Rimadyl®, which comes in 25 mg pills that are divided in half for adult geese. Ask your vet for detailed dosage information on whichever product you choose.

- **Sting Free Bacitraycin Plus®**

You may need this topical ointment if someone gets a small scratch or cut. Be careful not to get it on feathers.

- **Antibiotic Eye Ointment**

Ask your vet to provide you with a tube of Vetropolycin® eye ointment. You may need this if someone gets a poke in the eye, which is not uncommon during the mating season.

- **Saline Solution (*Sensitive Eye* formula)**

You may need this for flushing out eye injuries, which are not uncommon during the mating season. A sensitive eye formula is ideal.

- **Delousing Powder**

You may need this in case you need to delouse your geese.

- **Syringe**

You may need this to dose medication or for feeding.

- **Virkon S ®**

This is a highly recommended, safe and effective pen cleaner if used as directed.

Preparation #3
Food

Your next step is to decide what type of grain you will feed your geese and what type of feed dispensers you will use to serve them. We have tried many things, and through trial and error, have finally come up with what really works.

Choose a Food Dispenser

- **Food bowl**

Geese tend to spill a lot of their dinner, so my favorite feeders come in the form of bowls, even for goslings (of course the bowls get bigger as your geese grow). I have tried a few types of feeders and found that they all caused more spillage than the bowls. Rubber bowls (2 or 4 quart) are the best because they truly are unbreakable. *Avoid* metal bowls, which sometimes have a galvanized coating and can lead to metal poisoning.

4 quart rubber food dish

- **Automatic pet feeder**

There are various automated feeders on the market. Some are battery operated and have individual doors that open up on timers, while others are electric "gumball machines" that can be programmed to release a pre-programmed amount of food at timed intervals. These feeders should <u>not</u> be used as a substitute for a reliable goose-sitter. More often, they are used to dispense food while you are at work or when you have a goose with special dietary considerations.

- **Food bins**

Food bins are another good option for geese. They can stay out in the rain and the food remains protected and dry. Then at night they can be carried into their barn. It is not advisable to leave food bins outside at night because they may draw in raccoons and other troublesome guests.

Food bins keep grain dry even in the rain

<u>Choose a Feed Brand</u>

I remember when we were first researching our options. We read long-winded advice about percentages of this and percentages of that. We spent hours reading bag labels, flipping through guide book pages and punching numbers into calculators. I felt like a chemist. I'm going to make the process much simpler for you.

If you buy goose grain that is *specifically designed* for goslings, and later for geese, the companies have already worked out the math for you. The only thing you have to keep in mind is the age of your geese, the gender of your geese and the quality of feed you want to give them. You can choose whatever goose food you want and even change your mind down the road.

The first time you go to the grain store it may take a few minutes to review brand options with a counter person who knows their product lines. If they don't know the answers to your questions, then they are not the informed person you are looking for. If this is the case, ask them to call someone to the counter who can be of better assistance.

- **Gosling crumbles**

If you are getting goslings, then you want to get yourself some brand name gosling crumbles. Don't be discouraged when you can't find a bag with big letters across the top that say: "Goose Food." Instead you will be looking for feeds that are designed specifically for waterfowl or for ducklings; these products are also suitable for your goslings.

Most brands will recommend feeding crumbles for the first four to eight weeks, but I find it is closer to the first seven to eight weeks. When you feel your gosling can easily swallow adult-sized pellets, mix crumbles with pellets for the first couple of days and once you are sure they are eating the adult food, phase it out completely. We have made the transition in a matter of days, usually no longer than three and sometimes as quickly as one. Transitioning your geese to a new type of feed tends to be relatively simple. We have never seen a healthy goose have an adverse reaction (i.e. diarrhea, vomiting) due to the introduction of nutritional food or the upgrading of formulas.

Lynyrd & Skynyrd enjoy their crumbles

- **Avoid medicated feed**

Geese require non-medicated food, which is different from other poultry foods. Never feed your geese medicated food. Geese have a very good immunity system. If you feed them medicated food you can affect this, and it can be deadly.

- **Brand options**

1. Mazuri®

I highly recommend the Mazuri® line. It costs more, but this food is designed for long life expectancy and the maintaining of good health for your pets. We have seen it work miracles at the sanctuary, so if you can get your hands on it, it is worth its weight in gold. Mazuri® has a very helpful dealer locator on their website or you can have it shipped directly to your home. Some grain stores will special order it for you.

> Mazuri® Waterfowl Starter (0-7 weeks)
> Mazuri® Waterfowl Maintenance (8 weeks and up)
> Mazuri® Waterfowl Breeder (mature laying geese)
> For more information: www.mazuri.com

2. Blue Seal®

Blue Seal® is a less expensive option also formulated with your pets in mind.

> Blue Seal® OrganicLife® Starter Crumbles (0-3 weeks of age)
> Blue Seal® OrganicLife® Grower Crumbles (3 weeks and up)
> Blue Seal® OrganicLife® Layer Pellets (mature laying geese)
> For more information: www.blueseal.com

3. <u>Purina®</u>

And finally, Purina® has two product lines for your geese, which you can interchange depending on product availability in your area.

> Purina® Duck Starter (0-4 weeks)
> Purina® Duck Grower (4-18 weeks)
> Purina® Duck Breeder Layena® (mature laying geese)
>
> Purina® Flock Raiser® SunFresh™ Recipe (0 – 18 weeks)
> Purina® Start & Grow® SunFresh™ Recipe (18 weeks and up)
> Purina® Layena® SunFresh™ Recipe (mature laying geese)
>
> For more information: www.purinamills.com

If you have all of these Purina® products available at your grain store, this is our suggested diet:

> Purina® Duck Starter (0-4 weeks)
> Purina Mills® Flock Raiser® SunFresh™ Recipe (4 – 18 weeks)
> Purina® Start & Grow® SunFresh™ Recipe (18 weeks and older)
> Purina Mills® Layena® SunFresh™ Recipe (mature laying geese)

- **Mixing grains**

Before I went with the Mazuri® line I used to mix supplemental foods in with their grain to jazz it up a bit. It's okay to do this, but in the end I came to discover that a good name-brand formula can save you a lot of time and energy.

I used to mix crimped oats and flying game food into their regular goose pellets for added nutrition, texture and flavor. Oats have the benefit of deterring feather consumption, so if you see your geese eating feathers off of the ground you can mix some crimped oats into their food. I added a ration of *flying game food* (non-medicated) to the mixture when they were molting too. I also used to add some cracked corn (a.k.a. "goose candy") into their food because they really seemed to like it. An important thing to note is that cracked corn is not the end-all be-all food for geese; this is a common myth. It is acceptable to mix it in with their goose food, but not a sufficient diet all on its own.

Another item I used to add to their mix was black oil sunflower seeds, but I found it just encouraged unwanted guests to dine at the dinner table. This wouldn't have been so bad if they didn't leave all the sunflower husks behind in the food dish for the geese to sift through. Some guests just don't have very good table manners. I later heard that bird seed can be difficult for geese to digest; whether or not that is actually true, I do not know for sure, but I didn't want to risk it, so I pulled it from the menu.

I have to admit, once I switched them over to the Mazuri® line, my gaggle was no longer interested in any of these added ingredients and began eating around them all, so I stopped mixing them in. Going with a good bag of food designed specifically for the life and longevity of my pet geese and mixed by the professionals ended up sparing me a lot of effort, and I have never turned back. I have never needed to.

- **Determine a feeding schedule**

We keep our feeders full and available for our geese throughout the day and night. I did the same when they were goslings. Some people will advise that this discourages foraging or leads to unhealthy or overweight geese, but this has never proven true with any of our geese. More so, they won't eat their goose food if something tastier is available, even if it means they have to hunt for it. Another reason I like to make food available to them all day is many of the geese that come to our sanctuary have faced starvation and malnutrition. I don't want them ever experiencing a painful hunger pang again, so the food is always fresh and available for them whenever they want it.

Every evening we go around and top off all of the grain dishes and do a quick mix with our fingers to ensure old grain is not forever aging at the bottom of the dish.

If you would like to establish feeding times, a morning and early evening feeding is usually the way to go. Offer each goose at least two cups of food twice a day, once in the morning and once in the evening. Timed feedings are not recommended for geese who can not forage actively during the day. You don't want long intervals between feeding times.

- **Feed bag expiration dates**

Some sources will advise against buying large bags of grain, but in my area grain is only sold in fifty pound bags, so there is no choice in the matter. You want to be sure to use up the last of the grain before its vitamins and nutrients lose their potency.

The expiration date of grain is six months after the date the bag was filled as indicated by a date stamped on the bag; however, within three months of the stamped date is highly preferable. You will soon learn how quickly your geese consume their food and how to judge the expiration date on the bag, so that the food is consumed well before you reach that date.

- **Fresh grain**

It is not a good idea to leave grain outside overnight. Moisture on goose grain ruins the food. You don't want to feed your geese wet, mildewed food or they could get sick. In addition, you don't want to lure night creatures towards "the water hole," so to speak. Little nocturnal creatures looking for tid-bits attract bigger creatures looking for tid-bits. Don't teach your local wildlife where to find a snack. You don't want to host a predator, prey function around your goose pen, so be sure to pick up their food at night and bring it into their house.

Poor diet or poor quality food can lead to a number of problems with your geese. Keeping your geese healthy means throwing out any food that is of questionable quality. Don't risk feeding your pets anything but the best. Read up on goose nutrition and symptoms of nutritional problems/vitamin deficiencies, so you will recognize any warning signs early on and have plenty of time to correct them.

Elizebeth gives Ms. Donald some treats

Grain Storage

We were advised not to store our grain in metal trash cans because metal can sweat during temperature changes, which can lead to mildew growth. We tried using plastic trash cans, but the mice were relentless. Too many free meals were given away; they destroyed the plastic trash barrels and they created a terrible mess in the barn. To date, we have not found a better alternative than the metal cans, and we have never run into trouble with them sweating—and we have frosty winters and humid summers.

- **Grain and rodents**

Food draws in all kinds of freeloaders; you need to keep your eyes open. If you attract a rat, you will need to react quickly. There are many opinions regarding the best way to manage rat control, but keep in mind, rats are fast learners. If you do not eliminate the entire colony quickly, the survivors will learn to avoid your traps.

Although I am fond of all animals and think there is a place for each of them in this world, even if it's on the far-end of our eight acres, we cannot have them in our goose pens. Not only will they wipe out food at a record rate, but they can introduce parasites and diseases, so if the rats come into our pens, we have to find a way to get them out.

A non-recommended common strategy to solve a rat problem is to cut off their food supply. The theory is that as the food supply dwindles, the stronger rats in the colony will kill and eat the younger and weaker ones until there is only one survivor remaining. I don't recommend it, first because it is extremely difficult to do. A hungry and determined rat will work that much harder at breaking and entering into any food establishment in the vicinity, which results in property damage. Second, I don't recommend it because a starving rat is more likely to turn on your feathered friends. I didn't dare risk having a hungry rat looking at my geese as a food source in the absence of anything else.

If you know where the rat holes are, carbon dioxide smoke bombs are the best outdoor solution to your problem. You can pick them up at most grain stores (proving that you are not alone in having this issue). You close up all but one of the holes, light the smoke bomb, drop it in and then cover that hole with dirt as well. Just sit back and wait for it to fizzle out. I recommend that you bomb a couple more times over the next few days to be sure you've gotten everyone—especially if new holes appear. This type of bomb is safe to use in the vicinity of your geese as long as you've covered all the holes properly and your geese are not near the holes while you are doing it.

Remember, these gas bombs are for outside use only. The gas is colored and scented for your protection, so if you miss a hole, you will see and smell a stream of yellowish-green gas coming out. Cover it quickly to contain the gas and any "non-friendlies." Continue with this tactic until no more holes are found and the telltale signs of the rodents are completely gone.

Grit

It is important that your geese have access to grit in order to digest their food properly. If you don't have sand in your enclosure, make a small source of grit available to them. When they eat tiny pebbles, it goes into their gizzard and helps it to grind up and digest their food. Grit can be purchased at your grain store.

If you have a goose that is trying to eat small rocks, it is most likely because they do not have access to a good source of grit. They are attempting to find the smallest thing they can, which just so happens to be too big. Introduce grit immediately if you see this behavior.

Lynyrd does a bit of nibbling

Ali's Bill Pouch

Ali was one of the first ganders ever rescued by Majestic. He came to us with a small pouch beneath his bill. While many do-it-yourselfers tried to convince us to put a rock into the pouch and then tie it off, we knew that was not in Ali's best interests.

I'm not sure why so many people think tying off injured body parts to cut off circulation is an appropriate remedy for waterfowl because it absolutely isn't. Not only is it inhumane and painful for the bird, but it is also unsanitary and can lead to serious and often fatal infections. Waterfowl owners will often hear similar advice when one of their birds has a prolapsed penis. Think of it this way: If you wouldn't want to use one of these so-called medical tactics on your own body, then it isn't appropriate for your pet either.

We did the proper thing for Ali and brought him to a vet for some professional advice. As it turned out the advice was simple: Don't do anything. Leave well enough alone. The pouch is a genetic trait, it does not inhibit him in any way or cause him any discomfort, so don't create a problem where there isn't one.

Ali has a pouch beneath his bill

Our vet did advise that we keep clean water available for Ali at all times (which is part of caring for any pet goose), so that he can rinse out the pouch and keep food from getting caught inside and going rancid. And sure enough, our vet was absolutely right. Ali's pouch has never given him any difficulties or caused him any heartache.

<u>Feeding Laying Geese</u>

If you are caring for egg-laying geese, then you will need to supply a specialized diet just for them. Geese usually begin laying on Valentine's Day and end around Memorial Day, with eggs appearing every 1-2 days depending on age and breed. You should begin feeding them a brand name laying formula February 1st and continue until egg production comes to a complete stop.

- **Added calcium source for laying geese**

You will need to have a separate feeder with some oyster shells or calcium chips in it for your laying geese. This is also available at your grain store. Rodents are not interested in oyster shells, so they can be easily stored in a plastic, covered bin.

Soft egg shells, odd-shaped eggs or shells that have a bumpy texture are a sure sign that an extra source of calcium is needed on the side.

Laying geese should have access to their calcium supplement free choice, twenty-four hours a day, seven days a week, throughout the laying season. Do not mix this extra source of calcium into their food. Your geese have the instincts to know when they need it and when they don't. It's not good for them to consume it if they don't need it, but you do want it made available to them for when they do. Ganders will commonly ignore this source of calcium, although they may occasionally poke around in the bowl to investigate it.

Another highly recommended and free calcium source is to gather up your goose's fresh eggs, hard boil them and chop them up, shells and all. Feed the eggs back to your geese.

- **Laying formulas**

Laying geese need a special diet to support their egg-laying. That being said, I want to say something very important about laying formulas. Although they are a vital part of your goose's diet, they are not the end-all-be-all of her diet.

Laying eggs every day takes its toll on your pets, which some people believe may shorten their lifespan. Having gone through labor once in my life, I can believe that going through the stress of it every day would certainly take its toll on me after a while.

For this reason and others, I think most pet goose owners would agree that they are not interested in promoting egg production, but rather supporting their goose's nutritional needs while she is laying her eggs. In other words, we do not want to push our geese to lay more eggs than nature would otherwise intend, we simply want to promote her good health.

This is where researching your available product lines comes into play. You want a brand that supports your goose rather than demands your goose. Don't be afraid to call your grain company's customer service representative before choosing the right brand of food for your pet geese.

Once you have made your brand choice, you will find that the real trick is keeping your ganders and non-laying geese away from it whenever possible. It won't hurt them to get into it now and then or to eat it in small quantities, but you don't want them eating it on a regular, long-term basis when they could be on a diet that is better suited for their individual needs.

We have different types of gaggles in different pens, so it is pretty simple to keep laying formulas out of our bachelor pads, but in those pens where ganders are penned with laying geese, rationed laying formula is often the answer to the riddle and, as you are about to read, it is also a vital part of meeting the dietary needs of your egg-laying goose.

- **25% laying formula for laying geese**

Geese are different from chickens, and some of them have a hard time laying a healthy egg. If you spend your time talking to other pet goose owners, you will occasionally hear about some very serious egg-laying issues. Having been faced with many of them ourselves (although more often in ducks), we have found that rationing laying formulas will remedy many of these problems

Whenever our geese are laying eggs, we provide them with a mix of 75% Mazuri® Waterfowl Maintenance and 25% Mazuri® Waterfowl Breeder; that is, 25% laying formula. By maintaining a low ration of laying formula we don't force egg production, but rather give our geese just enough of what they need to cover their dietary needs.

- **Adjust the ration of laying formula as needed**

Feel free to play around with the ratio of laying formula and regular food until you find the proportions that best suit the needs of your laying geese. These ratios can be adjusted daily as you examine your goose's eggs. If eggs are looking perfect, keep the same ration. If eggs are soft or odd textured, add more laying formula to the mix. It is not uncommon to have to boost the laying formula ratio up to 50% or even higher if needed. We have had geese who did not do well with anything less than 100% laying formula throughout the laying season (as indicated by consistently odd-textured eggs).

When your goose's eggs appear normal again, stop increasing the ratio of laying formula and then slowly, over the course of a few weeks, work on reducing it again, never going so quickly or so low as to cause undesirable egg quality.

Using the Mazuri® line as an example, let's say that while on a mix of 25% Mazuri® Breeder and 75% Mazuri® Maintenance your goose lays an egg that has bumpy calcium deposits on its surface. Instantly increase her ratio of laying formula to 50% Mazuri® Breeder and 50% Mazuri® Maintenance. Now let's say that her eggs look normal for the next few days, but on the forth day, her egg comes out soft. Immediately bump her ratio up to 75% Breeder and 25% Maintenance. As long as her eggs look normal after that, there is no need to increase the ratio any further.

Wait 3-4 weeks and then decrease her formula back down to 50% Mazuri® Breeder and 50% Mazuri® Maintenance again and see what happens. If her eggs change for the worse, instantly bump her up to her 75% Mazuri® Breeder ratio and understand that this will be her ratio for the duration of the laying season. However, if you back her ratio down to the 50/50 mix and find there are no adverse effects, leave her on this reduced mixture for another 3-4 weeks and then see if you can drop her down to the 25% Mazuri® Breeder and 75% Mazuri® Maintenance mix without any adverse effects. Once you find your goose's minimal ratio, it tends to stay relatively the same during her youthful years. Levels of laying formula often decrease as geese age and lay less frequently.

Mastering the ratio of laying formula is not that difficult if you understand what you are looking for and how you need to react to it. You just need to bump the laying formula instantly up and then slowly down until you find your goose's equilibrium. Finding this balance is vital to maintaining your goose's good health. Malformed eggs can lead to serious reproductive tract issues that can be fatal. Always remember to foster nature's laying cycle rather than force it.

Feeding Geese on Public Ponds

This brings me to a good point to talk about feeding geese on ponds. As we visit our local ponds in search of abandoned domestic animals that need to be removed from a wild setting, we often see people feeding the wild and domestic geese. It is always best to let wild waterfowl forage for their own foods. Interfering can cause overpopulation issues on ponds as well as migratory delays. Over population can lead to water pollution and an increase of predators in the area. Feeding can also incline wild birds to lose their fear of people. You may be a nice person only wanting to warm their belly, but keep in mind that other people don't necessarily share your kind intentions and could use this advantage to bring harm to the birds.

We do understand the attraction, especially when children are involved, of feeding the domestic waterfowl. Domestics do not necessarily have the instincts to forage properly on their own. If you wish to feed a domestic goose on a pond at least do right by feeding them the right thing. There are certain foods that simply should not be fed to these birds, or to any animals for that matter.

- **Don't feed geese bread**

Bread is *never* a wise choice for waterfowl. Geese can choke on bread, so it is a dangerous snack; the same is true of popcorn. In addition, if a goose belly gets filled up with bread, they won't forage for bugs, worms, grass and other nutritional plants. A belly full of bread leads to malnutrition in geese, which can cause all kinds of bone, muscle and feather deficiencies.

Waterfowl should not be fed bread or junk food

We are always amazed when we see folks standing at the shores of ponds throwing chips and snack foods into the water for geese to eat. None of these foods belong anywhere in their diets and should never be introduced. They are not healthy for humans and are just as unhealthy for waterfowl. Junk food is junk food, whether you're a human or a goose.

Unhealthy snack options for waterfowl

31

If you are planning a picnic and cannot resist the urge to feed the waterfowl and do not have proper waterfowl food on hand, there is a safe and healthy alternative. Plan ahead and bring some round, floating, un-medicated cat kibble with you (no hairball or urinary tract formulas). This is a protein filled snack that is a fantastic alternative to unhealthy human snack foods. Avoid overfeeding waterfowl; only throw in what the animals will consume right then and there. It is important that excess food isn't left behind to sink and decay because this can lead to deadly outbreaks of botulism.

Round, floating cat kibble makes a healthier snack for geese at the park

Preparation #4
Drinking Water

Geese need a source of drinking water made available to them, so finding your goose a water dispenser is your next step.

Make Water Available 24/7

It is not uncommon for a goose to give you a good scare and gulp down too much food at one time and end up with a marble-sized (or larger) lump in their throat. You will see them stretch and work their necks as they try to move it down and then they tend to go over to their water bucket and take a good drink to help wash it down. Not only is it humane to have water available 24/7 for your geese, but it is also necessary to prevent choking incidents. If for any reason your geese can't pass this lump of food on their own, encourage them to drink and then gently massage the area to help break up the lodged pellets. Repeat as needed until you feel the mass break up and drift down their throat.

If you do not have heated water buckets in winter and your goose's water could freeze up for any period of time (overnight, for example), then pick up their food dish, so they won't be able to eat during that time.

- **Have multiple water sources available**

As with food, I always have more than one water source available to my geese. The reason for this is simple, sometimes your pets will have issues amongst themselves, and you don't want one of your geese hoarding the only food and water source and depriving your other goose of needed sustenance.

Choose a Water Dispensing System

If you are bringing in goslings, the number of goslings and some common sense will help you determine what you need. If you need further assistance, someone at your local grain store should be able to assist you.

- **Water fount for goslings**

Purchase a small, plastic water dispenser from your local supply store for your goslings in lieu of a bowl of water or you will soon have a big mess. Goslings grow fast, so choose a size fount that will be a comfortable fit for today and for tomorrow.

Always keep your water dispenser clean and the water in them fresh. Stagnant or dirty water can lead to diseases. Botulism is just one deadly example of a disease that can reveal itself and kill your goose within days if you do not keep their water fresh.

- **Water fount for adult geese**

Finding a water fount for your adult geese is not so easy. You will soon discover that there are double walled chicken water founts, but no goose water founts. What's the difference? Geese need to blow out the two little holes in their upper bills to keep them clean. In a perfect world, one of these poultry supply companies would recognize the fact that geese need deeper troughs on their water founts, but they don't. For this reason, I mention the founts as an option, but do not actually recommend them. I find water buckets are more durable, have greater longevity (since they don't rust), are easier to clean and provide a lot more enjoyment for your geese.

- **Water fount heater for adult geese**

If you do want to go with metal water founts, you can heat them in the winter by sitting them on top of specially designed fount heaters. This ensures that the geese always have drinking water available when their buckets freeze.

A water fount heater looks like an upside down pie pan. It has a heating element underneath it and out of reach of your geese. Be extra careful to keep the cord safely tucked away from your geese. I don't suggest using this if you are using shavings as your bedding because they can easily get under the pan. If you have hay bedding, be sure to keep the hay from going under the pan.

An added benefit of the fount heater is your geese will want to sit all around it in winter time to keep themselves warm and it does not get hot enough to ignite outer lying hay. The thermostat keeps the water temperature from dropping below 50 degrees or so. This device is for indoor use only. Be sure to read the instructions carefully to prevent fire hazards.

- **Rubber water bucket for adult geese**

I highly recommend a small 8 quart bucket of water during warmer seasons. They are very durable, easy to clean and just the right height and depth for most geese. They can also withstand a freeze without cracking and even if frozen solid, you can smack them with a hammer, stomp up and down on them or kick them around the yard to get the ice out without ever cracking or damaging them. They are priced right and have a very long life expectancy.

Again, the number of geese you have should determine the size and number of your water buckets. Keep in mind that this water will have to be changed at least twice a day, so don't make your chore bigger than it needs to be. You should also know that they are going to make a big splashing mess, so it's best to stick to smaller buckets rather than larger.

Rubber water bucket with a floating toy   *A wooden jig around our water buckets helps keep the barn clean*

The great thing about water buckets is your geese can bathe using them. They can delve their head and neck into the water and jut it back out, splashing water over their backs to assist them in their preening. This benefits them greatly in winter, when they may not have access to swimming water.

- **Heated water bucket for adult geese**

Our absolute favorite option in wintertime is a nine quart, heated, water bucket. The great thing about this kind of bucket is they are weatherproof and can be used inside a barn or in an outdoor enclosure. The heating element is protected inside the plastic bottom and the electrical cord is protected by a wire spring to help prevent your geese (or any critters) from gnawing at it. Some geese will sit around them in cold weather to help keep warm and it is completely safe for them to do so. They are durable and look and feel safe, which I know every Momma Goose will appreciate. Just be sure to read the instructions to avoid any fire hazards (you can't use them with extension cords, for example).

A nine quart, heated water bucket

If you have a lot of geese sharing one bucket, you can also find these in a 5 gallon size. If you have what we refer to as a *bucket goose* (a goose who loves to hop into buckets of water of any size) and you go with this larger size bucket, the others may find themselves waiting for a drink while they take their bath. This size bucket is not recommended for bucket geese, who may injure legs or feet while getting in and out of their hot tub.

Angelo takes a dip in his 5 gallon "hot tub"

We rely on multiple, nine quart, heated water buckets during the winter and in the warmer seasons we swap them out for the 8 quart rubber buckets. After trying everything, we have found that these two items work the best for the geese and for our sanctuary.

Preparation #5
Gosling Accommodations

Housing for Goslings

Now it's time to think about housing. How many goslings are you getting? It is not a good idea to start with more than two if you haven't had geese before. A pair of geese will keep each other company when you are not at home and it is a good place to start. Remember, you can always add to your gaggle later. I have what we call a "Ling" house for our rescued ducklings and goslings, and all of our newcomers stay here until they are old enough to make the transition to our outdoor pens. I bed it with pine shavings (never cedar, which cause irritation) and hang a feather duster in the corner for them to sleep under or against. I also give them a regular light bulb protected by a guard to keep them warm and safe 24 hours a day (you can also use a heat lamp).

Light bulb guard

You will need to find a warm and ventilated but, *draft free* place that is very safe for your little goslings. When bringing up goslings inside, the only predators you need to worry about are your other pets (cats, dogs, ferrets, etc) and your children. Although goslings are a world of fun for children, they are also very fragile and can easily be killed by unknowing little hands. Their legs, wings and necks are very fragile and breaks can be devastating and costly. Children should never be allowed to handle goslings without close parental supervision.

Our "Ling" House

Remember to keep their house clean. If you can smell it, you are not cleaning it enough. You will need to change out the shavings a few times a day, especially as they get older and poop more and splash more water around. They can make a pretty good mess around their feed dishes and water founts, leaving me to spend quite a bit of time plucking pine shavings out of their food and water.

Swims for Goslings

Goslings can go for swims in the bathroom tub a few times a day, and this is a great way to bond with them and encourage them to imprint on you. They are very messy though, so I warn you, these fabulous swims tend to end with the goslings sleeping in their house while you return to the bathroom to sanitize the tub.

As goslings grow, and they literally do grow overnight, you can begin to take them from their indoor house to the great outdoors to familiarize them with what will one day be their pen. I highly recommend getting your goslings used to their future home right away (weather providing, of course) because it's where they will be quicker than you realize. Goslings get scared without their Momma Goose though, so stay in their pen with them. Don't leave your little ones unattended; they need direct chaperoning.

In the beginning the wind is often the most frightening thing in the world to them and they will run to you for protection whenever it blows or whenever they see the tiniest little thing move. Speaking of which, their instincts are right intact when it comes to birds flying overhead; most goslings will dodge quickly towards you whenever they see a shadow fall over the land.

Don't be worried if your goslings don't want to swim in anything bigger than their bathtub at first. Big water can be very scary to tiny babies. There is just no coaxing them into water they don't want to go into. The good news is your goslings will brave the water in some secret mathematical proportion to their own size. As they grow, they will slowly crave the bigger, deeper water. Just be patient with them.

Goslings grow into geese in just eight weeks. If you think they will stay little forever, you are sorely mistaken. My husband and I are always amazed at how fast they grow, practically right in front of our very eyes. Every morning when we went in to see them, they were bigger than they were the night before—and that is no exaggeration.

Inside to Outside

Geese really do belong outside, and for me it is always very apparent when the time has come for us to move them. When they are six weeks old and can no longer fit comfortably in their little Ling house and the wafts of air coming from their room in the morning become quite offensive, it's time to make the transition.

Before you bring your goslings to spend their first night outside you MUST make sure their nighttime shelter is completely predator proof. Domestic geese have little means for fighting, running or flying away from predators. If something can get into their house, your pets will be trapped and barely stand a chance of survival. Predators are one

36

of the most common demise to pet geese. One of the number one emails we get from folks contacting us through our rescue site begins, *"My geese were attacked last night..."* It pains me to hear so many geese are dying out there because their owners don't bother to lock them up and do a quick head count. A bit of poultry wire in a circle will do nothing against predators; it will only trap your geese so that they have no means to escape from the intruders. You need to do better than this so that your geese can live out their full twenty to thirty year life span.

We have a nice, secure barn with chain link kennels inside for our maturing goslings. We move them outside along with a couple familiar items, like their light and feather duster, and we place a folding lawn chair in with them as well. The chair gives them something to cuddle under that makes them feel safe during the transition from indoors to outdoors. After all, they were used to having a roof right over their head when they were living in the Ling house—suddenly the barn ceiling can seem awfully far off. The chair makes them feel safe and gives them something to hide under—a sort of surrogate mother goose. During the first week of their move, I keep a dim nightlight on to keep them from being in total darkness at night. Once they are familiar with their new place they will no longer need this. You don't want a bright source of light in your goose's sleeping quarters because it can disrupt their sleep patterns and when they're older negatively impact their egg-laying cycles.

As the goslings grow a little bigger and become more comfortable in their new place, we open the kennel door and give them a bigger share of the barn to venture out into. They abandon their feather duster entirely and their nightlight as well.

Our barn has two windows. During the summer, I like to open them at night, but I don't dare do so without proper protection; a screen is not good enough. We nailed a piece of welded wire mesh (rabbit wire) over the entire area of the window on the inside of the barn, so you can barely even notice it from the yard. If we didn't do this, a raccoon could find its way inside, which would put the lives of our geese in danger. Again, it is vital that predators cannot get into your goose house, especially at night when they are most actively hunting.

- **Preparing goslings for their move**

Moving goslings from the indoors to the outdoors will often prove more stressful for you than for them. To get both of you used to the idea, take them on frequent visits, each lengthening in duration, to their new space well before it's time to make the move. This will give them a chance to poke around and explore what will one day become their new home. Once they are six weeks old and familiar with their new pen, and provided it's safe for goslings, you can begin to leave them alone for short periods of time.

Golly watches over little Skynyrd as he takes baby steps into the great outdoors

These practice sessions always seem to do the goslings a lot more good than they do me. Whenever the time is upon us for their first overnight stay in the barn, I'm always a wreck. It takes me hours to leave them alone on their first night. I continue to visit them throughout the course of the evening and even had a camera with full audio installed for an all-night eavesdrop. I admit, I never sleep well when thunderstorms are booming across the midnight land. I usually end up suited-up and running out to the barn to sit with them and make sure they aren't frightened.

I can honestly say that every time I check on them, they are always cuddled up sleeping or happily going about their business and absolutely fine. Rest assured, you may worry at first, but once you see for yourself that they are adjusting well to their new surroundings, you will sleep again at night. I do recommend checking in on them, especially for the first two or three days while they are getting used to their new home, but once you are certain that they are safe and sound and happy, you can relax.

Jenn holds Ms. Donald, a young Chinese goose

Upon opening the sanctuary, we actually came up with a schedule for moving indoor goslings to their outdoor pens. We do not move goslings permanently outdoors until they are at least six weeks old. In winter especially, goslings should have all of their permanent feathers before making the transition.

Lynyrd, Skynyrd and Ms. Donald enjoy chaperoned exploring

We bring our rescued goslings for brief and chaperoned, outdoor visits when they are about two weeks of age and only in positive weather conditions. Outdoor excursions begin for 15-20 minutes a day for a two-week-old gosling and grow to an hour a day, twice a day, during their third and fourth weeks of age. By their fifth week of age they are spending daylight hours outside on good weather days (again, avoiding extreme heat, cold or heavy rain) and brought back inside at night. And by their sixth week, they have made the permanent move.

If a thunderstorm comes and you have young goslings outside, you will need to teach them to go into their house until the storm is over. Just close them in during the storm and reopen their house when it stops. Avoid leaving goslings out in the rain. They can get saturated and become very ill.

Preparation #6
Building a Goose Pen

We built an outdoor enclosure for our geese to reside in during the day. You can find all kinds of plans telling you how to build a house, so how do you know what's really right? You can build a goose enclosure any old way you want, just follow these steps:

Evaluate Your Predators

If you live in the boondocks like us, count on dogs, cats, weasels, foxes, raccoons, fisher cats, coyotes, bobcats, hawks, eagles and don't forget those savvy owls. These predators are designed to dig under, climb up, bite through, fly over and squeeze through anything they can to get to a goose dinner. For us that meant fencing that goes all the way around, goes at least a foot under the ground, has a digging predator barrier around the perimeter, a strong aviary net and electric fencing around the top to prevent raccoons from climbing onto the aviary net and gnawing through it. Further provisions include motion sensor lights and some kind of surveillance system. Many over-protective Momma Geese use baby monitor systems to check in on their gaggle.

Unless you have the kind of set up described above, where there is absolutely no way in, always lock your geese up in a predator proof barn or shed for the night. You don't want your geese in plain view, taunting a hungry predator during the stealth of darkness while you are sleeping. Locking them up is also a good idea because it prevents your geese from being stressed out by predators who might be circling their pen, even if they can't get in.

SEE **APPENDIX A** "GET TO KNOW YOUR PREDATORS"

Evaluate Your Building Materials Based On Your Predators

Never underestimate the hunger and determination of a predator. You want to make sure wire can't be bitten through, holes can't be squirmed through and also that it's strong enough to take a predatory punch. Be certain that your support beams are strong and sturdy and that your wire fencing has a tight fit. Pouring concrete or using bricks underground around the perimeter along with a digging predator barrier will keep diggers from burrowing inside. Scarce winter months can really motivate a predator that would otherwise not look twice at the effort, so really think your plans through before making a final decision. Basically, chose your stronghold materials by picking components that are one step above what you need and decide on a structure that will outsmart even the most crafty interlopers.

Remember, your geese don't have much defense against a predator. Your stronghold is their best defense, so make it a really good one.

Determine the Size of Your Enclosure

I once came across information that recommended a ten square foot pen for two geese. Thank goodness we did not adhere to that. This is mass production and breeder nonsense. It will not be big enough for your pets. Small, over-crowded pens lead to trampled, hard-packed grounds (which can lead to foot injuries), poor and possibly unhealthy living conditions, boredom and un-enriched lives.

- **Minimum 500' square foot enclosure for two geese**

I suggest that an outdoor enclosure for a pair of geese be at least 500 square feet in size (250 square feet per bird). This will provide ample room for a kiddy pool, a small house and will also leave them with plenty of space to move around and enjoy their days. If you want easy access and comfort while visiting your geese in their enclosure, remember to place the pen's ceiling at an appropriate height.

Keep in mind, that the larger you build their enclosure, the less maintenance you will have as far as hosing away goose poop at the end of the day and reseeding/transplanting greenery. This means you will have more time to enjoy your geese and less time spent on chores. For this reason, many pet goose owners have larger pens that measure 700 - 1000 square feet in size.

Signs that your goose pen is too small include: a lack of sustainable vegetation (no grass), hard-packed soil, piled up feces that cannot naturally work its way into the soil, which in turn leads to smell and flies.

"Abby's Goose Run" measures W 30' x L 70' x H 6'
It comfortably holds up to six geese

We occasionally get emails from folks wanting to adopt from us who free-range their geese—letting them wander freely around unfenced property without a human chaperone present. They are adamant in their belief that it is cruel to keep animals in pens. We don't adopt our rescued geese out to these people.

Although I agree that it is cruel to keep geese in small and cramped pens throughout their entire lives, I think it is even crueler to allow an unprotected goose to be predated because it has no fencing protection. Our geese live lavishly in spacious pens. They have shelter, food, clean water, clean bedding, grass and companionship—human, and goose. They are safe from predators and are wanting for nothing.

When I ask these potential adopters why they are looking to adopt a goose, 99% of the time it is because a predator killed one of their pair, leaving the remaining goose lonely. And they say we're the cruel ones for fencing them in. I truly am sorry for their loss, but I have to advise them to build a pen to protect their other goose because that predator knows its there and will be coming back, and we are not about to put one of our rescued geese into that dangerous situation. We do not believe in treating the local wildlife to a free dinner.

SEE **APPENDIX C** FOR "HOW TO BUILD AN OUTDOOR ENCLOSURE"

- **The hazards of chain link fence**

Be very cautious when using chain link fencing around your geese. Your geese can seriously injure themselves. Geese can easily push their head and neck through the holes in the chain link fencing and become trapped. They can do this out of curiosity, wondering how the grass on the other side tastes, while arguing with geese on the opposite side of the fence or while fleeing when startled. They can even manage to push their head out one hole and get it stuck in a neighboring hole when they try to come back through.

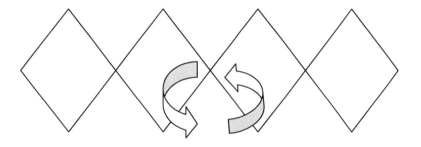

Your goose can reach its head through one hole in the chain link fence
only to have it pushed back through a neighboring hole.
This action can prove deadly.

To prevent this type of mishap you can zip-tie PVC coated, welded wire mesh to the existing fence, so that it is taught and secure and blocks any openings that a goose's head could fit through. You can either cover the entire chain link fence, or just go up about 4 feet—their head level.

Chain link fence made safe with welded wire mesh

Keeping Grass on the Ground

If your pen is too small for the number of geese inside, it will likely require constant attention to keep grass under their feet, and it is vital that you do in order to prevent serious foot afflictions. You may need to reseed from spring

41

until fall in these situations and protect newly growing grass until it is well established. Geese can wipe out vegetation at an alarming rate. This kind of upkeep can be very tedious and very frustrating, so again, larger pens are always a good idea.

We find that grass lasts all spring, summer and fall in most of our pens, but does not tend to survive winter wear, so every spring we turn over all of the grounds and reseed all of our pens. Be careful what kind of seed you use and try to avoid those coated in harmful toxins or pesticides, especially if these areas will not be sectioned off and your geese have access to the seeds because they will eat it.

My best advice for growing new grass is to try to keep your geese away from seeds and newly growing grass. They are very destructive foragers and will often wipe out new growth within hours. We section off those areas of the pen that are growing grass until it is well established.

Trying to grow grass in certain areas of your goose enclosure can be a losing battle, especially around any water sources. It is always a challenge to keep solid ground around these areas, let alone trying to get grass to grow there.

This makes for an unsightly border around your pools, ponds and water buckets. The only way we have found to prevent this erosion is to place a lip around your pond or pool, going about a foot out from the water and to set your water buckets on some kind of base. Any kind of non-slippery mat that they can't pull apart will do the trick, or you can lay cement or bricks down, which was our solution.

<u>Providing Swimming Water</u>

If you love your geese and want them to be clean, healthy and live enriched lives, you will want them to have some sort of swimming accommodations. There are some things to keep in mind when it comes to this source of pleasure.

- **Water sources must be kept clean**

In the spring, and with only two geese, you can sometimes get away with changing out the water every other day (provided they have a clean source of drinking water somewhere else in the pen), but once hot weather hits, every day is a drain and refill the kiddy pool adventure. The water becomes stinky by the end of every day and must be completely refreshed. Geese can get very sick and die from drinking dirty water. Don't confuse fresh water with clear water. Geese tend to muck up and brown their water very quickly with mud, so it will often appear dirty. This is fine; water does not have to be clear, it just needs to be fresh.

Duran Duran soak in their kiddy pool while in quarantine

42

Before installing stream-fed ponds into our pens, we used to take a big bucket and scoop out our kiddy pools every day. It really didn't take more than a few minutes to do. Nonetheless, if you don't like this kind of chore, you won't enjoy this daily event. I always saw it as time to spend with my pets. I looked forward to filling the pool again with nice, crisp, clean water. I sprayed the geese while they ran around and played.

As we progressed through our building of enclosures we replaced the kiddy pools with cascading concrete ponds, which were later replaced by preformed pond-liners. Water is pumped into the top pond, whereupon it travels down and through a couple of other small ponds. The drainage pipe is sealed with grating so predators can't gain access from outside.

- **Avoid tripping & slipping hazards**

It is very important that your geese can gain good traction around their ponds and pools. Slippery surfaces can lead to serious sprains and leg injuries. It is equally vital that surfaces around ponds are not abrupt or rocky. We often hear from people whose geese have injured themselves on the jagged rocks around homemade, landscaped ponds. The rocks that hold the pond liner in place should not be dangerous for your geese to traverse. Surfaces that provide level but textured entry and exit ways are always the best option. This type of surface should circle all around the pond, not just on one side or one area. Not only do geese have minds of their own, but when startled they could easily enter or exit their pond from an ill-intended access point.

Egor and Jack Frost contemplate a swim in their stream-fed pond

Outdoor Daytime Housing

Geese often prefer not to be outside on very stormy days, so give them a nice, cozy place to cuddle up in during bad weather.

If your goose does not have access to their nighttime barn or shed during the day, you want to be sure to provide them with some kind of small shelter in their day enclosure to protect them from the elements. You do not need to have a barn in order to have geese; a closeable shelter inside their predator proof pen will do just fine.

We built W 4' x L 4' x H 4' mini-barns and then placed a few of our spare W 3' x L 4' x H 3' duck shelters into our goose pen to give our geese plenty of places to rest comfortably on bad weather days. It also gives the geese a comfortable place to retire while laying their eggs. They have a layer of clean hay inside and shingles on the roof overhead. Our pens are completely predator proof, so the geese do not need to be locked up at night *except* in very cold temperatures.

REMEMBER, before you bring your geese to any newly built enclosures or shelters, it is *imperative* that you do a thorough visual check and remove all hardware and bits of metal from the site, so that it is not ingested. *Hardware Disease* is one of the number one causes of death in pet geese, so take your search extremely seriously and check areas more than once. Remove all dangerous debris before letting your geese explore their new pen.

Shade

If you have hot summers and your goose pen is in direct sunlight, you will want to provide shade for them, a house is not always enough. You can purchase shade cloths to put over the top of your pen, or you can plant small shade trees.

- **Shade cloth**

Shade cloth allows enough sunlight through to keep the grass and plants underneath alive while keeping your gaggle cool. The drawbacks of shade cloth may include unsightliness, seasonal installation and, if not mounted correctly, issues during wind storms.

- **Shade trees**

A non-toxic shade bush inside of their pen is another great way to keep your geese cool in the heat. We also have a few trees outside of our pens that cast shadows over the enclosures. Just remember that any trees need to be far enough away as to not become ladders for climbing predators like raccoons.

Lynyrd & Skynyrd under their shade tree

Shade trees provide a natural setting and require very little maintenance. We utilized Russian Olive trees in our pens. They are a local weed tree. They have aromatic flowers in the spring and non-toxic berries for the geese to eat in the fall. They are easy to transplant, grow very fast and can survive even a brutal pruning, which is frequently needed to restrict their height. You can train them to grow the way you want them to. A small tree only three feet high can grow to a nice six feet within a few months. So you can plant them in spring and have shade by summer.

Air Conditioning

For goose owners residing in hotter and more humid regions, I want to review air conditioning. Cool water and access to ample shade is good during the day, but often barns need to be air conditioned in order to keep geese

44

comfortable at night. If you see your geese panting in their barn it's usually a clear sign that it is too hot for them. If you have installed air conditioning in your barn, you should set the temperature to no less than 75 degrees to prevent chilling your goose, especially when they are molting and cannot regulate their body temperatures as effectively. Avoid extreme humidity variances as well.

Misting Systems

Another great way to keep your geese cool in the heat of summer is to purchase a patio misting system. Multiple systems can often be connected together to get the desired length. We mount ours to fence rails with tie-wraps, so they can be easily uninstalled in the winter and reset in the spring, but they do come with permanent mounting kits that are very simple to install. You can also purchase inexpensive filters that are simple to attach and help keep the knobs from clogging.

Misting systems connect easily to a garden hose that can be attached to a sprinkling system timer. Our system is programmed to come on for the duration of two minutes every five minutes between 11:30 – 4:00 in the summertime. The geese love it and it reduces temperatures in the pen dramatically—almost like walking into air conditioning. Timed sprinkler systems are another great option to beat the summertime heat.

Preparation #7
Bedding

Bedding for Goslings

Soft pine shavings make the best bedding for goslings. You can buy them inexpensively by the bail at many pet or grain supply stores. It will soak up messes and is easy for little webbed feet to traverse over. Goslings can easily trip over hay, making it a real obstacle. Avoid using any dyed shavings and stay clear of cedar shavings, which can cause serious skin irritations. Newspaper is also a bad idea since it can strip a gosling of its waterproofing oils.

Bedding for Geese

- **Hay or Straw**

Find a place to buy mildew and thorn-free hay or straw. Some folks prefer straw over hay because they want to avoid the risk of aspergillus / farmer's lung (caused by breathing in the dust of moldy hay). If you ensure that hay coming in is free of mold and that it remains free of mold, it is just as good a bedding choice as straw. We use hay.

If you are allergic to poison ivy be sure to ask your hay provider if their fields are free of it. You will only make that mistake once, and a horrible one it is. Keep a nice cushion of bedding under the feet of your geese. Sprinkle fresh hay over messy spots, which tend to be around their water dispensers and in the nests they've made for themselves during the night. This will keep your bedding clean and smelling fresh. It is also necessary to keep their feet healthy.

In the warmer months hay needs to be pitched and cleaned more frequently than in colder months. Fly infestations can happen quickly if you do not keep your goose quarters clean. In the winter, you get a nice long break from pitching hay. As you lay fresh hay down everyday, the old hay underneath ferments and makes heat for your geese, so in the winter you want a nice thick layer to keep piling up under them. Spring cleaning is the downside of this winter break.

- **Pine shavings**

I've read that some people use shavings for their adult geese, but I've never understood this since it can catch in a goose's throat so easily. We've had to use a bed of shavings on occasion to ensure very sanitary conditions for an injured rescued goose. I can also say it gets *everywhere*, in food dishes and water buckets. It drives me crazy. Every time wings flap, the stuff spreads all over the place.

- **Avoid litter**

Never use any kind of litter as bedding. You do not want manufactured litter in your goose's stomach. This is an invitation to disaster.

Preparation #8
Protecting Goose Feet

I don't know what it is about geese, but given two paths, a clear one and one mined with rocks and sticks, they always seem to choose the minefield. They can trip and stumble over even the smallest of obstacles making them very prone to leg and foot injuries.

Remove all sticks and rocks and fill in the holes they continually make in their enclosure to avoid any mishaps. Also be wary of plants with thorns as they can do real damage to your goose's webbing.

Webbed feet are fragile and must be protected

Preparation #9
Provisions for Separations

Sometimes your geese are going to squabble, especially in the spring. Normal pecking order stuff should be of no concern; that is, an occasional, *"Don't forget I'm in charge here."* Anything more than this, of a continual, repetitive nature, should be examined more closely. We have back up measures in place should we need to separate anyone, and you should take the same precaution.

<u>Warning Signs of Fighting</u>

Some signs that geese need to be separated include incessant honking (arguing), relentless chasing, bill and eye injuries, someone losing weight and excessive feather loss from being plucked out, especially around the back of the neck.

<u>Who Is Fighting and Why</u>

Normally, a gaggle of geese who have been together for a long time will be a close family unit and members will get along pretty well. In those instances where new geese are added to the gaggle (or in our case, as geese are adopted out) it can cause a temporary disruption in the pecking order. The onset of the mating season can also cause a bit of strife, especially as ganders mature and want to protect their laying geese.

If your geese aren't quite getting along, there are a few things to evaluate. First, you need to determine who's involved in the bickering. Ganders are usually the culprits when it comes to aggressive behavior while geese tend to be the cheerleaders. Next, you need to figure out why they are engaged in the behavior, or better put—what is causing them to behave this way. Once you understand these things, you can attempt to bring peace to the gaggle again.

Most geese begin egg-laying mid-to-late February and end in late May. It is the toughest time to control misbehavior between ganders (especially around water sources where they vie for mating rights), but the good news is things tend to quiet down relatively quickly

Although geese form very powerful bonds with their mates, they do have a wandering eye and ganders will try to mate with their own and other geese whenever possible. This can cause jealousies that result in beta ganders vying for alpha leadership. Fortunately, these battles often look worse than they actually are and tend to end swiftly with alpha ganders re-establishing their leadership authority. The more powerful your alpha gander, the less fights will break out in your pen because the other ganders will not want to risk challenging them.

- **Distraction tactics**

I have always relied first on a distraction to stop the squabbling. Introducing enrichment activities is a great way to get your ganders' minds off of one another and onto something else more fulfilling.

- **When to break up a fight**

More important than how to break up a fight is deciding when to break up a fight. Gander confrontations can look pretty frightening to the untrained eye as honking ensues and wings fully extend in display. Both ganders will aim their bills for the back of their opponent's neck feathers. The first one to get in that position and mount the other gander is commonly the winner. The loser will usually flee away very quickly. It is important that your ganders work out alpha leadership to prevent future fighting. These displays can last anywhere from three seconds to two minutes, but they tend to last 20-30 seconds. As long as the biting does not get out of hand and their confrontation is taking place on safe, flat ground, you will not commonly need to get involved. However, if you see a gander aiming for another's gander's eyes or if you see the fight escalating without one gander giving in, then you will need to step in and break it up.

- **How to break up a fight**

Breaking up a fight is best done with a helper, where each person comes up behind their gander being extremely careful of their wings. Each person grabs their gander gently but firmly by the base of the neck, closes their wings and sits over them to calm them down. Then the birds can safely be picked up and separated. When dealing with more aggressive ganders, you can take the base of each wing—one in each hand, fold the wings in and then sit over them. Once wings are under control, you can hold the head or neck gently but firmly to further control your bird.

If you are alone and need to break up a fight, always aim for the more aggressive of the two ganders. This is the bird you will need to control first in order to stop the fight.

Separating Fighting Ganders

Separations, especially initially, are hard on everyone, you included. Everyone likes to see their gaggle members getting along and it can be very stressful when they are not. There are more than one means to separating fighting ganders.

- **Portable playpens**

You can purchase tall pet playpens at your local pet store. They are expensive, but can be set up quickly and fold up nicely for storage later. One drawback is a goose can still stick their head and neck through them, so in some cases, with ganders who refuse to stop fighting, it may not put an end to the behavior. We encounter this more frequently with newly introduced ganders who were not raised up together—strangers. Ganders who are normally friends usually benefit from this type of intervention.

Mac gets a little too overjoyed by visitors, so Isabel stays behind a fence when she enters his pen

The nice thing about these fences is they connect together and you can make a large playpen out on the grass— outside of their pen on nice days. They can forage in a new area that contains them and prevents them from helping you out with your yard work. If you want to do this, though, stay very close to them because they will be exposed to predators.

48

- **Permanent fencing**

We have an infrastructure of smaller pens within our larger enclosures. This is very helpful when introducing new geese to the gaggle. The newest member stays in a smaller pen and meets the gaggle through a fence. When we see a noticeable decline in the attention and aggression the gaggle places on the newcomer, we let the newcomer out for a chaperoned meeting.

- **Temporary fencing**

Another solutions is to use four-foot high, PVC coated welded wire mesh fence (with ½ inch squares) to create a temporary fence within your pen. String the fencing across the length of their enclosure, splitting the area up the way you want it. You can hold this barrier wire in place by latching both ends of it to your pen's perimeter fencing using a few carabineers. You can put up the fencing during initial introductions and then roll it up for storage once your gaggle is cohesive. The only down fall is having to step over the fencing to get into each division.

- **Double the supplies**

Keep in mind separations instantly increase your expenditures. You immediately need additional feeders, water dispensers, swimming pools and shade/nesting houses. As we learned, you can go from one of everything to two of everything very quickly.

If you have to separate any of your geese, remember to move their food along with them. Ganders who are not penned with laying geese should have 100% Mazuri® Maintenance formula (or whatever regular formula you are feeding them) while any laying geese should have access to their specific laying rations in whatever pen they are in. It's okay if boys get into the girl mix while sharing a pen, but you don't want laying geese getting into too much regular formula or it might affect their egg-laying.

- **Separating ganders from geese**

You may also need to separate ganders from geese if your boys are getting too rambunctious. Signs of this include bruising or feather loss on the back of your goose's neck or on her back, beneath her wings. Over-mating can lead to serious medical issues including oviduct prolapse, so be sure to give your geese a break if they need it.

- **Life on the other side of the fence**

Some ganders will dread being separated from their geese so much, you might be fooled into putting them back together again. They will often stand next to each other on opposite sides of a shared fence. It can be hard to witness, but they are better off a little sad than injured. This initial reaction to the separation is often short-lived. Although they will want to be next to each other, they will begin to meander around as well.

Just remember to watch for the tell-tale signs that someone is getting picked on, and do something about it as soon as you can.

Goose Identification

It can be difficult identifying your geese if you have a large gaggle alike in breed. When we first started rescuing, it wasn't easy telling who was who—especially when it came to the Toulouse geese. It can take a few weeks to learn the subtle differences between gaggle members. We find that new owners adopting multiple geese from us also appreciate identifiers. For this reason we use colored tie-wraps as leg bands. When we run out of colors, we use a two tie-wrap color combination to identify flock members.

If one of your geese has a clone and is receiving medical attention, it is especially important to use colored leg bands. You don't want to make any mistakes when prescribing medicines of any kind. Even if you can identify the correct goose, remember that a family member or pet-sitter may not find the task of determining who's who quite so easy.

If you are sketchy at figuring out who's who from time to time and someone needs medical care, be sure to band them before administering any medications to avoid any mistakes.

- **How to put a leg band on an adult goose**

Loosely place a colored tie-wrap above the ankle and below the knee of your ADULT goose. Do *not* put tie-wraps on growing goslings. Be sure that it is not too tight, nor loose enough to slip down over or get caught on that little back toe. Cut off all of the excess plastic after pulling it through. Inspect tie wraps daily to be sure they are comfortable and in place.

Colored tie-wraps are used for leg bands

Duran Duran look a lot alike, making different colored leg bands a great idea

50

Ailments

Ailments

I learned very early on that the quantity and quality of medical information available for pet goose owners is scarce and incomplete. I'm not even going to repeat what most sources will tell you to do if your goose becomes sick or injured because you and your feathered friend deserve much better than this.

I've also found that although our vet is very well versed in goose health, many avian vets are not. Most veterinary colleges offer courses on ornithology and poultry, but not more than brief seminars on waterfowl care (if anything at all). This prepares students for a career in the poultry industry or as an avian (parrot) vet, but doesn't really prepare them for handling your goose. In addition, not all vets have a lot of goose patients, which leads to less hands-on experience with their ailments and subsequently, less experience with treatment options.

For these reasons, I have dedicated a lot of my attention to *Ailments* in the hopes that it will benefit your goose.

- **You need to know what your vet may not**

Since many vets are not very experienced with waterfowl, it is *your* responsibility as a goose owner to learn all that you can about your goose's health. Your goose may fare better if you call up your vet's office and say, *"I think my goose may have gape worm; these are his symptoms... and I've read..."* than if you say, *"Something's wrong with my goose."* Your information may give your vet a chance to do some detailed research before you and your goose come in for your appointment. It is in your goose's best interests if you have an idea ahead of time of possible treatment options. If your vet prescribes a different treatment regime than you expected, you will know just the right questions to ask.

A responsible goose owner should educate themselves about the types of ailments geese can encounter in order to better prevent diseases and recognize early warning signs. This is the best way to avoid mistakes and unnecessary accidents.

This chapter will cover the ailments that we've seen and heard of in our rescue work—a few of which we have not seen covered in other reference guides. This list is not all–inclusive, but it will give you a good starting place. Always remember to consult with your vet should any of these issues come up. Non-prescribed medicines or home remedies should never be administered without consulting a vet first.

- **Signs that your goose requires vet care**

Some obvious signs that vet consultation is needed are: vomiting (yes, geese do vomit), any kind of discharge or bleeding, the build-up of feces or fluids around the cloaca, a disinterest in their food or water, deteriorating feather condition, limping, tiredness, keeping their feathers fluffed-up or diarrhea. By diarrhea, I am not referring to the urine mixture that passes out of your goose—and could commonly be misconstrued as diarrhea by owners of other types of pets. This is how they pass urine and is completely normal. When dealing with geese, diarrhea is not judging how waste actually comes out of your goose's body, but rather, what it looks like once it is on the ground. Feces without shape or structure to it should be considered diarrhea.

Another clear indicator that your goose is not well is respiratory stress. If you can hear a raspy sound when your goose is breathing, or they are panting with an open bill, or you see their body heaving or tail pumping up and down for long periods of time, you are witnessing respiratory stress. Keep in mind, it is normal for geese to pump their tails while laying their egg, some even pant. Labored breathing is only normal during the short period in which a goose is actually laying her egg (which is usually in the early morning), but it is abnormal in any other circumstance.

There are other less obvious signs that vet consultation is needed, such as your goose behaving unusually. Perhaps they are not interested in things that normally appease them. Maybe they are not actively foraging, running up to greet you, or just don't seem as curious as normal and getting into their normal lot of trouble. You know your geese better than anyone else. Remember that, and don't let anyone talk you out of it. Trust your instincts and seek vet assistance early on.

Ailment #1
Bill Problems

Scratched Bill

Accidents can happen and you may discover a scratch on your goose's bill. Scratches can bleed if they are deep enough. Simply clean the area with an antiseptic wash a couple times a day for the first one to two days to keep it from getting infected. It will eventually heal and fade away. You will want to seek vet assistance if you see a deep, bleeding laceration as opposed to a slightly bleeding scratch. You will also want to see a vet if a cut crosses over the edge of the bill and severs into your goose's skin.

Tutter's scratched bill

Broken Bill

We have been contacted on a few occasions for advice on proper care when it comes to damaged or broken bills. If your goose breaks a piece of their bill off, save the piece (if you have it) and seek veterinarian assistance immediately. Bills do bleed when broken, so you may need to use blood coagulant to help control the bleeding until you arrive at your vet's office. If the break will not affect the goose's day to day functioning, they will often cauterize the bill to seal things up nicely.

If the break is more serious and there is still blood supply your vet may try to reset the bill and wire it together. Dental acrylic is often applied to further protect the bill and hold things together. If your vet tries this tactic, you will most likely be learning how to tube feed your goose. You will probably be doing this for a few weeks while you wait for the bill to mend. Insist upon pain medication for your goose.

Laurtrek's bill was damaged when his mother tried to help him out of his egg
Photo Courtesy of Laurtrek's family

- **Non-exposed tongue**

There are two kinds of bill breaks: those that leave the tongue exposed and those that do not. Some bill breaks will occur on the tip or edges of a goose's bill. Have your vet examine the break to determine if cauterization is needed or if filing or trimming is required to prevent future hang-ups. This is normally a quick and simple procedure. Depending on the severity of the break, vets will often send you home with a cauterizing agent just in case it begins to bleed again at home. Although the bill will mend, it will not grow back to its original shape. This kind of damage usually does not cause a goose any future difficulties.

- **Exposed tongue**

The second kind of bill break results in an exposed tongue. These can range from mild to severe depending on how much of their bill they lose. In mild cases, your goose will not have any difficulty eating once things heal up, but in more severe cases, you may need to grind their food for them and keep a water dish nearby while they eat to help them wash it down.

In severe cases it may take your goose quite a bit of effort to eat and they may tire of it quickly; if you notice this, just leave their food out at all times. They often do better if they can just help themselves to the buffet multiple times throughout the day, rather than just at one or two daily feedings.

Water should be made available at all times to any geese you have, but in the case of an exposed tongue it is extremely important, so they can keep their tongue moist and comfortable. Remember to use extreme caution in cold weather. An exposed tongue can easily become frostbitten. Do not leave geese with exposed tongues open to the elements during cold weather. They must be locked up in a barn or shed to prevent exposure to the cold and wind.

In extreme cases of broken bills, some vets recommend keeping the tongue moist by using a non-fragranced (no baby powder) vitamin A&D diaper rash ointment. This can be found over-the-counter in medication aisles, rather than baby aisles. Petroleum jelly does not tend to stay on well enough to be effective.

- **A common cause of bill injuries**

Geese are smart. It doesn't take them long to make the connection that whenever you have your shovel out and begin digging around the yard, a few tasty earthworms tend to turn up. Be very careful. Impatient geese have been known to get overly excited at the site of freshly tilled earth. A goose can quickly put its bill in the way of the blade of a shovel coming down. We have heard of it happening, so be sure to modify your digging rules.

Geese are not allowed in the work zone. When you are doing yard work, keep your geese in their enclosures or otherwise occupied. If you want to go on a special mission to dig up earthworms for your geese, be sure your geese are well out of danger's way. Be careful because *well out of danger's way* is farther away than you might suspect. Geese come in very fast when a soil turn reveals an earthworm. Keep your eyes on them; they can be quite sneaky.

Prosthetic Bills

We have not seen this personally at the sanctuary, but know of goose rescuers who have utilized prosthetic bills. Snapping turtles (and bites from other animals) can wreak havoc on a goose's limbs and bill. Many geese have survived these attacks, but sometimes the damage to their bills is extreme. Pain medication is definitely in order.

If your vet is unable to assist you, avian vets specializing in parrots, or rescuers of wild raptors often know how to create a prosthetic bill. Start calling around and asking for referrals.

Punctures or holes in a bill can be treated pretty easily. Your vet will clean it out thoroughly with an antibiotic and then the holes are commonly filled utilizing dental acrylics. Your goose will also be placed on an antibiotic to prevent infection, usually 68 mg Baytril® (which is in pill form).

*SEE **APPENDIX D** FOR "HOW TO GIVE A GOOSE A PILL"

If your goose has a broken bill and a prosthetic is required, as I understand it, if the breakage has a jagged edge, it is easier to fit with a prosthetic bill, than if it is a clean break. The prosthetic bill will not last forever and will need to be replaced as it wears out.

Deformed Bill

Some goslings hatch out with a twisted, misaligned or curled back bill that can range from a mere aesthetic difference to actually inhibiting with their eating and preening. Conditions may advance as a gosling grows and develops. When the top and bottom bills don't line up properly it is often referred to as "scissor bill." This condition may be the result of their position within the egg during incubation or it can be genetic.

Depending on your goose's particular needs you may need to either grind up their food or serve them a courser food that is easier for them to pick up. Try it both ways to see which consistency works best for your goose. If the deformity actually inhibits food ingestion, vet assistance will be immediately required. As with geese with broken bills and exposed tongues, remember to keep your goose properly protected during cold weather and vitamin A&D diaper rash ointment works very well in these cases too.

Photo of Sivey Courtesy of Barbara Collins

Pouch Beneath Bill

Some geese will have a pouch beneath their bill. This is usually caused by genetic predisposition, but it can also be caused by an injured tongue that no longer rests in the bill cavity correctly. While some sources will recommend tying off the pouch, our vet advised that we let it be. The only precaution we had to take was making sure Ali always had fresh water to wash out the pouch and keep food from collecting inside. Since this is already a vital part of goose care, there really wasn't anything else different we needed to do.

Ali has a pouch beneath his bill

Ailments #2
Skin Disorders

Frostbite

Frostbite is a real hazard for domestic geese during freezing cold temperatures. Feet and bills are vulnerable to extreme cold and real damage can be done if they are not properly protected.

If you notice your goose favoring a foot in cold weather, be certain to do an immediate examination. If you don't see any issues, try holding their foot in your hand or sitting them on your lap to see if slowly warming the limb solves the problem. If so, further accommodations may be required to keep them warmer.

Although geese control the blood circulation to their legs and feet in order to avoid the loss of too much heat, there is only so much their bodies can do when the elements grow too harsh. The appearance of black areas on their feet is a clear indicator that your bird is most likely suffering from frostbite.

Geese with frostbite need to be brought to a veterinarian for treatment as soon as possible. Treatment often involves the cutting away of damaged tissues and sometimes even a partial amputation.

Prevention is the key when it comes to the cold elements. Trust your instincts—if you think it's too cold out for them and you see ice forming on their feathers, or ice encroaching in on your pond, this can be a clear sign that your waterfowl need to spend more time in the comfort of their barn or shed. Also, if you see flock members spending too much time sitting on top of their feet and not moving, it is advisable to bring them into a cozy barn or shed where they can meander around a bit. Use your good judgment and control the time they spend outside. For their protection, it is best to keep your feathered friends inside during freezing rain, ice storms, high wind chills or temperatures beneath 15 degrees Fahrenheit.

Knobs on Chinese and African geese can succumb to frostbite in cold weather

Lacerations

If your goose receives any kind of skin laceration, apply direct pressure to stop any bleeding and bring them to a vet for immediate treatment. Surgery and/or stitches will most likely be required to mend the wound after it is flushed out. Baytril® will most likely be prescribed as a general antibiotic to avoid infection. Your vet may have you wash the area with an antiseptic solution. Lacerations beneath the feet are very serious and will require extra special care after surgery to ensure they do not become infected. In this case your goose will likely require special quarters that are kept very clean. Clean pine shavings work best at keeping things sanitary during the healing phase. Once your goose is safe and sound, you need to determine the cause of the laceration and eliminate it so no further injuries occur.

Cysts

Any lumps or bumps on your goose should be examined by a vet. Free floating bumps that are not attached to muscle or bone and are not red, irritated or weeping are likely harmless cysts. If your goose has a cyst, your vet will commonly advice that you just keep an eye on it to make sure it doesn't become irritated or increase in size. If conditions change, have them rechecked by your vet.

Abscess

An abscess can be difficult to spot on a goose as they tend to be hidden beneath feathers. Behavioral changes are an indicator to pick up your bird and give them a precursory medical exam. Have a look and feel around to make sure all is as it should be.

An abscess may become noticeable as it grows, making an area of pink skin suddenly viewable. They can get very large, sometimes as large as an egg—and they can even feel as hard as an egg.

If your goose has a large swollen area you must bring them to the vet immediately for draining. Vets will often use a syringe to drain out the fluids out and will typically prescribe a few weeks of antibiotics until it is completely healed and gone. Multiple visits may be necessary to remove fluids. The liquid drawn from the area should be clear to slightly yellow. If the liquid is yellow, thick or creamy in consistency it is a warning sign of infection, which may require immediate surgery.

A drain may need to be inserted, but this is normally reserved as a last resort (or in the case of serious infection) since geese are meticulous preeners and may pluck out the drain tube causing further problems.

An abscess can be caused by a scrape or bite that has become infected. You will want your vet to identify the cause, if possible, so you can properly address the issue. Either something in your pen poked your goose and put them at risk, or something is nipping at your feathered friend.

If an abscess breaks open, emergency vet care will be needed. If it is after-hours, do not wait until morning to call your vet. The area will need to be flushed and drained, antibiotics will be needed and stitching will be required. In some cases, a drain tube may need to be stitched into the area for a short period and then removed later. If an abscess bursts, your bird will need to be placed in a very clean pen out of reach of the remaining gaggle—to avoid any of the others causing further damage to the area.

China Girl's Fox Bite

China Girl and Bowie were abandoned on a pond in a housing development. Upon rescuing them we discovered that China Girl had a large wound near her tail where a fox had nipped her. The wound was about the size of a baseball. We brought her to the vet for an immediate exam.

When a goose survives a predatory attack it is vital to get them on antibiotics as soon as possible to prevent an infection. Animal bites in particular can become seriously infected and even fatal if proper precautions are not taken.

Our vet prescribed China Girl 68 mg of Baytril® once a day for 14 days. The wound itself had already scabbed over and sealed itself, so no bandaging was needed. In cases were the wound is still open, your vet will need to flush it out and do some bandaging. They will teach you when and how to change the wrapping and then schedule a follow-up appointment to check up on things.

When you take your goose home you will want to put them in a clean and stress-free environment. When we take in rescued geese with injuries, we put them in our 8' x 4' basement infirmary pen, which is bedded with pine shavings. Because geese form tight bonds, we often bring their partner inside to visit with them for the night. We usually place a portable playpen fence between them to prevent any further injuries.

In China Girl's case, the antibiotics prevented any infection and a few weeks after rescuing her, the scab began to flake off, revealing healthy pink skin underneath. China Girl's feathers grew back and she was soon as good as new.

China Girl was dumped on a pond with Bowie after a fox bit her

Follicular Cysts

Follicular cysts tend to appear on the wings of birds, but they can occasionally turn up in more vulnerable areas. A follicular cyst is when a feather follicle is facing the wrong way and the feather is aimed, and grows, inside of the bird's body instead of outside. The tiny vestigial feathers grow, break off and then form into a knot around the follicle. New feathers will continue to grow and break off, and become embedded in a fatty mass. From the exterior, this hard mass is strikingly similar in appearance to an abscess. As with an abscess, vet intervention is required.

When the follicular cyst is located on a goose's wing it is commonly recognized by a good vet and a simple surgical procedure will be required to remove the misdirected feather follicle and the mass surrounding it. Your goose will likely be placed on Baytril® for a week or so and recovery tends to be quick and easy.

When a follicular cyst is located on a goose's body, it can easily be mistaken by a vet for an abscess. If this occurs, your vet will drain the area and most likely prescribe a round of Baytril® to remedy the infection. The liquid drawn from the area may be slightly yellow, but should be rather clear and uninfected. Since Baytril® is a safe, general antibiotic, this slight misdiagnosis should not cause your goose any harm; in fact, if the follicular cyst is infected, it will help reduce the swollen area.

If misdiagnosed, your goose should return to the vet's office on a weekly basis to have liquids drawn from the *mock abscess* and although the swollen area may reduce significantly in size (we have seen them as large as an egg, reduced to the size of a marble), it will not completely diminish. At this time, the vet will probably recommend surgery to clean out the site and during this surgery they will discover the real culprit is a reversed feather follicle. The vet will remove it, clean the area and stitch it up. They will most likely prescribe Baytril® for 7-14 days.

Behavioral, appetite, activity or temperament changes during treatment of the *mock abscess* is an instant indicator that vet intervention needs to be stepped up. Additionally if thick, yellow liquid with a creamy or pasty consistency is drawn from the site, this is a warning sign of infection. If they appear, your vet will most likely recommend immediate surgery to see what's going on inside, at which point they will quickly discover the abscess is actually a follicular cyst and they will remove it.

As with any surgery, you will want to keep your goose in very clean quarters and fenced off from other geese who might poke at them. They should not be allowed on ponds or streams. Any bathing should be in freshly filled pools and should not be allowed to continue for any length of time, as fresh water doesn't tend to stay fresh for long with geese. To help prevent infection, you can gently spray the area twice daily with a non-stinging wound wash.

Although a singular follicular cyst is quite treatable, geese with multiple, reoccurring or masses of follicular cysts may be suffering from a high level of estrogen, which may in turn be caused by some form of lymphoma of the reproductive system. High estrogen levels also result in liver damage and may result in retained fluids in the abdomen.

Bruises

Lumps that come on suddenly—not there in the morning, there in the evening are injury based and they often occur on the neck or wings when one goose nips at another. Lumps in the neck can also be caused by a goose eating too fast and jamming his throat with food. An experienced owner can easily distinguish the difference. If it's food, gently massage the lump to see if the food can be broken up and eased down and encourage drinking.

If you discover a bruise on your goose, do a careful examination of the area to confirm the area is not bleeding and that no bones are broken. Cold packs or an anti-inflammatory medication can be utilized to reduce swelling. Keep a close eye on your goose to make sure the swelling has stopped and the injury is not worsening and call a vet if needed—especially if the bruise is on the neck and is causing any difficulty eating, drinking or breathing.

Ailments #3
Parasite Problems

If your goose is not maintaining a healthy weight, has a body so small that it is ill-proportionate to the size of their neck and head, or has chronic diarrhea, these are some symptoms that may be indicative of worms. The best thing to do is bring a sample of your goose's poop to the vet to be tested for parasites.

There is no such thing as goose wormer, so cattle, horse or dog wormers are commonly used to remedy issues. The difference between the dosages for a 300 pound horse listed on an over-the-counter wormer package and a 15 pound goose is vast. There are a lot of resources providing conflicting dosage information for wormers and many of them are *wrong*. Do not worm your own geese. Let a vet help you with proper dosing. You could easily kill your goose if you do this incorrectly.

Be sure to provide the weights of all of your geese to your vet. The entire gaggle will need to be treated. If you are worming a female goose, do not eat any of her eggs for at least eight weeks following her last dosage.

If your geese have worms, you will want to take the added step of cleaning out their barn and pools and hosing down their enclosure. Worms can sometimes be a sign that you are not keeping your pens as clean as you should be. If it is difficult to keep their pen clean of fecal matter it's likely that you have too many geese in too small of a space. Either increase their pen size or clean their pen more frequently.

In rescue work, it is not uncommon to bring in geese with parasites, so we've learned a lot about how to remedy situations before introducing newcomers to our existing gaggle.

Roundworms: Capillary Worms

Capillary worm or *Capillaria* is a type of nematode (or roundworm) that can be found in the esophagus, gullet or small intestine of waterfowl. They are very similar in appearance to whipworm and are found in the respiratory tract and transmitted from bird-to-bird through fecal exposure. They can be introduced via the consumption of earthworms or naturally through drinking water in nature. Symptoms may not be apparent except in large infestations or in younger birds.

- **Symptoms**

Symptoms of the presence of this parasite may include bloody diarrhea, weight loss, weakness, chronic coughing, anemia and in severe cases, pneumonia.

- **Treatment**

Our vet prescribes a dose of 10 mg of fenbendazole (Panacur®) for every 2.2 lb. of goose weight. Liquid Panacur® is ideal for measuring out this small dosage.

We administer this dosage of liquid Panacur® orally via syringe, once a day for 5 days. Then we wait two weeks during which time no treatment is administered. After the two weeks waiting period, we gave the goose one <u>single</u> and final dose of liquid Panacur®. Three days after this second treatment, a follow-up fecal test is done to ensure the parasites have been successfully eradicated.

If your vet does not have access to liquid Panacur® or if you are uncomfortable dosing via syringe, you can also get powdered Panacur®. Just put a little leaf lettuce (or other favorite treat that your goose will consume in entirety) into your goose's food dish and then sprinkle the prescribed amount of powder over the top.

If follow-up fecal testing reveals the infestation is not cleared up, a <u>single</u> dose of 200 micrograms of Ivermectin® for every 2.2 lbs of your bird's weight can be given orally to resolve the issue for good. This should be done under your vet's guidance as well.

- **Pen Cleaning**

Thoroughly clean infected pens and houses and remove any contaminated top soil. Once this is done, remove and replace any bedding (hay) every day throughout the entire treatment period. Sometimes geese have favorite places to sit. If you can, clear away any piles of goose poop at least once a day. Roundworms are vulnerable to sunlight and drying; use this knowledge to your advantage when fighting them.

For best results, after your birds are free of worms, remove them from the pen and turn over the infected soil to a depth of 8-12 inches. Seed new grass and allow it to grow in, giving the pen a few weeks resting period. When the grass is fully re-established, return your birds to the area.

Roundworms can be very contagious, so be sure to clean all tools, gear and equipment thoroughly with a 10% bleach solution and adhere to a strict quarantine routine until the problem is thoroughly resolved.

Keep in mind, Panacur® effectively removes capillary worms from your goose's body, but it does not necessarily kill all stages of these parasites. It mostly helps your bird to expel them. Practice caution to avoid re-infection of your bird or spreading these roundworms to other pens and animals, or to yourself.

- **Prevention**

As always, prevention is the best measure in preventing this sort of problem. Keep your goose pens clean and dry. You don't want pens that are frequently muddy because they lack poor drainage. Always avoid overcrowding your geese and change around the locations of your water buckets.

Even when precautionary measures are taken, natural exposure is entirely possible. Don't take prevention so far that you deny your geese those things that make them happy (i.e. feeding them worms). Just try to keep the grounds of their pen clean and dry.

Cecal Worms

Heterakis gallinarum is an intestinal worm or cecal worm. Cecal worms are a type of roundworm that spend most of their time in the lower intestine or the ceca.

- **Symptoms**

Symptoms may include lethargy and reduced egg production. Large numbers of these worms can also cause thickening of the cecal walls, which can eventually lead to hemorrhaging.

Rarely, a goose can become infected by a protozoan carried by cecal worms, which can cause serious damage to their liver and ceca. This is called Blackhead Disease or *Histomoniasis*. Symptoms include: decreased appetite, lethargy, yellow droppings and an infected goose will sometimes avoid other geese and normal routines. This condition is very uncommon in geese (who tend to be immune to it), but it is deadly without treatment.

- **Treatment**

Our vet prescribed a Strongid-T® liquid suspension in the dose of 1 cc per 20 lb bird *(each 1 ml contains 50 mg of pyrantel base as pyrantel pamoate)*. Strongid-T® is a milky, yellow liquid that is loaded into a syringe and simply given orally. A single dose is administered based on weight and then two weeks later, a second, single dose is given. Three days after the second treatment, a fecal sample can be brought to your vet again to confirm that the parasites have been effectively removed from their system.

- **Pen Cleaning & Prevention**

Follow the same steps and precautions as when dealing with Capillary worms, which is the same for all types of worms.

Gizzard Worms

Gizzard worms are another type of roundworm and a fecal exam can confirm their presence in your goose. As their name implies, they are a parasite of the gizzard. They are not uncommon in geese and are more likely to be found among malnourished gaggles that are kept in unclean pens. The presence of this parasite can lead to decreased immunity in your goose as well as death depending on the level of infestation. Symptoms of gizzard worms include lethargy, loss of appetite and emaciation. If tested positive, your vet will most likely prescribe Levamisole® or Panacur®. Doses are often spaced 2-3 weeks apart to eradicate any newly hatched worms. Treat all flock members and retest fecal samples to ensure they have been thoroughly exterminated.

Gape Worms

If you see your goose continually opening its bill and gasping, like it's trying to get something out of its throat, this could be gape worms, which is also a roundworm. Geese most commonly get gape worms from eating earthworms. Don't take this as a sign of poor hygiene if it comes up. Just call your vet and tell them you think your goose has gape worm *(Syngamus trachea)* and let them know what you're seeing as far as behavior. Your vet will have a look down their throat and may be able to see them, or they can confirm their presence by fecal exam, so be sure to bring them a sample. If positive, they will commonly prescribe a one-time treatment of Ivermectin® solution, which your vet will need to prepare for you. Be sure to treat all of your flock members.

Intestinal Fluke

Fluke worms *(Cyathocotyle bushiensis)* are a type of flatworm or trematode. Even mild Fluke infestations can lead to cecal hemorrhaging and death. Although uncommon among domestic geese, they can become infected after eating snails that are usually found around the Great Lakes in the U.S. The presence of fluke worms can be confirmed by fecal exam. Symptoms of fluke worms include weight loss, lethargy, fever, diarrhea and dehydration. Praziquantel found in Drontal Plus® is commonly prescribed to treat fluke worms.

Tapeworms

Tapeworms are a type of flatworm or trematode. Your goose can become infected upon eating earthworms, bugs, flies, slugs, ants or beetles. The presence of tapeworms can be confirmed by fecal exam. Symptoms of tapeworms include weight loss, loss of appetite and diarrhea. Praziquantel found in Drontal Plus® is commonly prescribed to treat tapeworms.

Trichomonas

Trichomonas are one-celled protozoa that geese can get when they drink water contaminated with saliva or droppings from an infected host bird (especially pigeons or raptors who eat pigeons). Symptoms, if noticeable at all, include diarrhea, lethargy and excessive gulping or swallowing motions, especially while eating. Metronidazole (Flagyl®) is prescribed twice a day at 25 mg for each 2.2 lbs of your bird's weight for 7 days. It tends to come in 250 mg tablets, which can make administering it difficult. After cutting the pill appropriately, you will likely need to crush it, mix it with a small amount of water and then give it to your goose via syringe.

Coccidiosis

Coccidia are another one-celled protozoa found in ponds, streams, lakes and other natural bodies of water all over the world. They are deposited in the feces of wild ducks and geese and since waterfowl love to dabble in water, they can easily ingest these parasites. The smaller the water source and the more wild waterfowl visiting it (and pooping in it), the higher the risk of a coccidia infection.

Coccidia infect the lining cells of the intestine of geese. Some symptoms include bloody diarrhea and weight loss. Your vet can confirm whether or not they are present by testing a stool sample and looking for their eggs. If you are bringing in a fecal sample for routine testing be sure to specifically ask for it to be checked for coccidia or your vet may not look for it. If the test shows positive, your vet will most likely prescribe Albon® or Amprolium (which is mixed with their drinking water) to your entire flock. As with worms, thoroughly clean out all of your shelters and pools and begin giving your outdoor enclosures a daily hose down to remove fecal matter.

Harmony & Melody, Pilgrim geese, were both rescued with Coccidia

Vets who are inexperienced with waterfowl sometimes assume that for a goose to get coccidia their living conditions must be the same as when dogs get it. When dogs get coccidia it's often because they are stressed and living in filthy conditions (often in dirty kennels) where they are ingesting fecal matter. Such vets might assume that your goose is being kept in similar adverse living conditions, which may incite warnings about contaminated and ruined soil. This is when it's important for you to understand (and perhaps clarify with your vet) that geese are different than canines.

First, geese who have access to water that wild waterfowl are also frequenting can be exposed to coccidia without filth being a factor.

Second, whereas dogs tend to be in "fowl" conditions in order to be ingesting fecal matter, it's part of a goose's natural tendency to dabble in puddles. All it takes is a little rain and grounds frequented by wild waterfowl can become dotted with puddles that embody fecal matter. Even the cleanest of geese cannot resist a good puddle and may become incidentally infected. This is why it's a good idea to do periodic fecal exams on your birds if they are at risk of exposure.

If your grounds are deeply infected with coccidia you can either turn over the soil or arrange for a *safe and legal* burning of the grounds to eradicate them. In barns/houses a 10% bleach / 90% water solution often does the trick. Be sure to let closed structures air out completely before allowing your geese access back into them.

Geese in closed flocks who do not have access to "community" water or grounds frequented by wild waterfowl are not likely to be exposed to this parasite (unless you track something in). Also, waterfowl coccidia cannot transfer to humans or other pets. It is species specific.

Dearth

If you have a goose with a positive fecal you should have your vet prescribe medication for quick control and to prevent their spreading. However, if you are looking at prevention, Food Grade Dimeacious Earth or *Food Grade Dearth* is a good option (especially if you're concerned about an area being contaminated with parasites). It is safe and effective provided you use *Food Grade* Dearth. Do <u>NOT</u> give your geese Dearth unless it is Food Grade.

Food Grade Dearth has to be fed daily as 5% of your goose's diet for 7-60 days to eliminate hookworms, roundworms, pinworms, tapeworms and whipworms. If fecals still show positive, the amount of Dearth may need to be increased. It is *always* advisable to consult with your experienced waterfowl vet before beginning any dietary regime.

Another means of using Food Grade Dearth to help decrease parasite populations is to sprinkle it over the grounds of your goose pen. This can be easily done by pouring the Dearth into a salt shaker and then dusting it in the areas of their pen that are of most concern. Do *not* do this while your geese are in the pen to avoid accidental inhalation. When parasites try to cross the Dearth it causes them serious injury and in many cases, kills them.

Lice & Mites

Mites and lice infestations should not be an issue if you are keeping your geese in a clean environment with plenty of access to fresh water. If either of these pests appears in numbers, as indicated by damaged feathers, listlessness, excessive scratching, a visual sighting or vet confirmation, then this should be treated as a warning that you may not be keeping things as clean as you should be or providing enough clean swimming water for your geese to bathe in. Lame geese tend to have more difficulties preening than healthy geese, which can make them more vulnerable to these pests, so be sure to do routine examinations. Chickens are also more susceptible to these parasites and can be a source of their introduction.

- **Three common types of waterfowl lice**

Head lice are found close to the skin, near the base of head and neck feathers. This is the most common type of lice seen in our rescues.

When a goose gets a little stressed, their skin temperature rises a bit and the lice around their head and upper neck tend to migrate out to get away from their skin. On a white or light-colored goose this leads them into plain sight. Unless you have a really friendly goose who loves to be held (in which case examinations are easy), you can commonly flush the lice out just by catching and holding your goose for a moment while feigning an attempt to look for them. Lice are easiest to spot around the head and neck of your white goose. Gently flip through their head and neck feathers with your finger and look for tiny critters moving over the skin or crawling on feathers.

Shaft lice are like small body lice and they tend to hang out on feathers, and run inwards toward the goose's skin when feathers are parted. We occasionally see these in the wings of our rescued geese and most birds who have them have deteriorated wing feathers because the lice have been eating them.

Body lice move around on the skin, commonly on the belly, around the vent or under the wings. They can commonly be seen running for cover when you part your goose's feathers.

Lice chew dry skin scales and feathers. They don't actually bite the goose, but their movements over the skin cause discomfort and irritation. Since humans don't have feathers, there is no concern about catching them. Mites are different from lice in that they bite into the skin and suck blood. Treatment for both is the same.

You can purchase poultry powder at your local grain store. The label should indicate that it is appropriate for the removal of lice and mites on waterfowl. Sprinkle a bit in your hand and work it into the goose's feathers. Although you want to powder all over (avoiding the well around the eyes) focus the delousing at the base of the back of the neck, under the wings and on their underside, especially around the vent. Goose feathers need to be treated very carefully to avoid them from losing their waterproof effectiveness, so be very careful in administering these powders and use them sparingly. Delousing powder labels often have instructions on how to apply them to the goose's bedding, but we have never found this useful since lice die soon after falling off of their hosts and therefore tend to cling tightly, rather than thriving in hay or bedding.

If you discover lice or mites on any one of your geese, assume they exist throughout the gaggle. Treat all flock members according to the instructions on the label. Be careful not to over do it, so the animal does not ingest excess amounts of this pesticide. It is always advisable to double check dosages with your own vet before administering treatment. Lice commonly fall off within 24 hours of powder treatment (we've actually seen them begin to drop off within minutes). Access to clean water and bedding are also necessary until all eggs have hatched and all lice have been eradicated.

Whenever newcomers arrive at our sanctuary, they are given a precautionary delousing treatment on day 1, day 7 and day 14 to avoid contamination in our existing gaggle.

Tutter & Angelo get deloused on the day of their rescue

Maggots

Finding maggots anywhere on your precious goose can mean any of these things:

1) There is too much poop on the ground, drawing in excess flies.
2) Your goose is not cleaning themselves properly.
3) Your goose has a hidden wound somewhere that needs attending.

In any case, bring your goose to the vet for an immediate examination. Your vet will likely advise three courses of action:

- **Clean bath**

Place your goose into a fresh, clean water source (kiddy pool or tub) and encourage them to clean frequently with frequent water changes. You can use a very, very diluted Betadine® (diluted to the color of weak tea) in a syringe to flush out the affected area over and over again.

- **Tweezers**

All maggots must be removed using tweezers and flushing. If any maggots are in the vent further vet care will be required.

- **Medication**

Your vet will likely prescribe .3 ml of Ivermectin® to give to your goose orally via syringe to help eradicate any missed maggots and eggs. Have your vet help you with this because it is easy to overdose and this kind of error can be very dangerous.

- **Fly Predators**

Preventative care can include reducing your number of flies. Fly predators are a great way to do exactly this. These tiny wasps predate on maggots and dramatically reduce fly populations. We have them sent every month from May through August. We sprinkle 5000 around our pens each month and house flies are no longer an issue. For more information you can visit their website: www.spalding-labs.com.

All of our incoming geese have fecal exams to confirm they are parasite free

Egor's E. coli

Egor was a rescued Pilgrim gander who came to us extremely weak and ill. He was literally at death's door. Over the course of about a week a family noticed that he was no longer able to hold up his neck or eat properly. We were called in for an immediate assist. An x-ray was done to ensure nothing was lodged in his throat (fishing lure) and that no bones were broken. Limberneck is symptomatic of botulism, so we began immediate treatment including a heavy dose of antibiotics while we awaited test results. Extensive blood work ruled out botulism as well as a number of other suspected causes. In the end, the answer came from researching the beach where Egor was rescued from. The lake had been closed multiple times that summer due to an outbreak of *E. coli* in the water caused by human fecal matter.

Egor on the day of his arrival

After three months on potent antibiotics administered twice daily and follow-up blood tests to monitor his progress, Egor finally made a full recovery and was able to hold his head up high and join the gaggle.

Egor a few months later

Ailments # 4
Leg and Foot Problems

Swelling

After we began to rescue waterfowl it became important to be able to discern healed broken bones from infections. This information is handy should you notice a knot or swollen area somewhere on your goose's legs or feet.

- **Indications of an infection**

When examining an infected leg or foot, the swollen area will feel soft and fleshy. When compared to the same region on the opposite leg, the swollen area will feel warmer. Infections are warm, bad infections are hot. Infections are treated with antibiotics, clean pens and sometimes surgery and drain insertion. If caught and treated early on, most geese will make a full recovery.

- **Indications of a healed broken bone**

A healed broken bone feels like a hard knot under the skin. It is not fleshy or squishy—there is no pus filled areas or infection. It literally feels like fused bone. When examining the swollen leg/foot area and then comparing it to the same area on the opposite leg, you will not feel a difference in temperature. There is no remedy for a fused and healed bone. They may or may not result in any lameness or limping depending on where the break occurred and how serious it was.

- **Indications of a broken bone requiring attention**

A newly broken bone is pretty easy to spot—especially in your own pet goose because it comes on suddenly, usually looks broken and is also swollen and hot; even more so as time continues to pass. A broken bone can lead to further infection and things can get pretty nasty if not attended to quickly, so be sure to rush your goose to the vet for an exam.

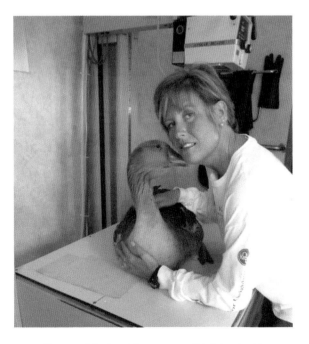

Grampa visits the vet for an x-ray of his injured ankle

Broken toes will sometimes heal themselves and fuse together provided antibiotics and pain medications are administered and the goose is kept in a relaxing setting in a small pen (to reduce their urge to go exploring). A pond with a sloped bank and easy access is a good idea to give them some time off of their feet and floating.

In some cases, broken toe bones can be reset by a vet using an acrylic splint that consists of a precise mixture of super glue and baking soda. This should *never* be tried at home and should *only* be performed by an experienced and qualified veterinarian who knows *exactly* what they are doing.

In still other cases, a broken toe may be so bad that splinting is not an option and toe amputation becomes necessary. This is only an option if the break is on one of the outer toes.

Bumblefoot

Bumblefoot is the most common affliction we see in our waterfowl rescue endeavor. Geese that are abandoned on ponds often walk rocky shores and slip on rocks. They get cuts on their footpads and these cuts get infected.

We also commonly see bumblefoot in neglect cases, where geese have been confined to dirty, un-bedded cages, forced to walk on concrete or on hard-packed or unsanitary ground for extended periods of time. The bottoms of their webbed feet become swollen and black calluses appear on the pressure points of their foot pads and toe joints. Left untreated, bumblefoot can lead to osteomyelitis (infection of the bone) and become fatal, so vet intervention is required.

Baytril® is the most effective and safe antibiotic for remedying this ailment. Many of our Majestic rescues have come to us with this type of foot ailment. One 68 mg Baytril® pill is administered daily until the swelling disappears and any black scabs are no longer prevalent. This can range from a few weeks to a few months of intervention. Some vets will also recommend foot washes/antiseptics (Tricide-Neo® & distilled water). It is vital that grounds remain soft, dry and clean in order to prevent recurrence. Access to *clean* swimming water is highly recommended to expedite recovery. In really tough cases, vets will commonly add a prescription of 150 mg of Clindamycin to the routine. In severe cases, they may have you administer these doses twice a day along with a weekly injection of Adequan® to prevent joint damage. In the most severe cases, surgery may be required, but this is frequently used as a last resort since it can further spread the infection.

In stubborn cases, where the scabs don't fall off on their own, your vet will painlessly peel and remove the black calluses—only peeling them back as far as they will go without causing bleeding. Be sure your goose only swims on *clean* water during the 24 hours following a peel or have them stay off the water for an entire day. As added treatment, keep them on soft grass or very thick bedding. Lots of swim time is highly recommended because it helps the calluses fall off on their own.

The best way to prevent Bumblefoot is to maintain clean pens for your gaggle. Do not keep them on hard-packed surfaces. Pens should be kept clean and their grounds should be soft with grass, hay or sand. Avoid constantly wet surfaces—they should have free access to dry areas.

In warmer months, and in spacious pens, fecal matter tends to naturally work its way into the soil and decompose. In winter, however, it tends to hover on top of snow and ice. In cold weather it can be impossible to remove frozen and piling fecal matter making it necessary to use plenty of sand to bury it every day—especially around water buckets where it really tends to build up. On those days when you are blessed with a temporary thaw, take advantage and shovel out whatever you can and then bury any remainder under sand.

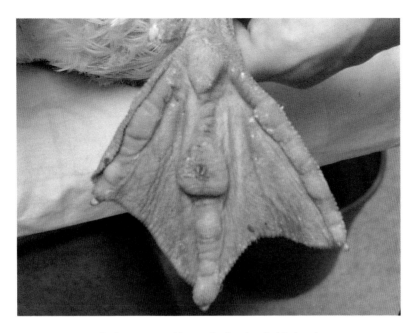

Rosie was rescued just as the first dot of a black scab
was forming in the center of one of her calloused toes

Geese are more prone to getting tiny cuts on the bottoms of their feet when the ground is covered with snow and ice. Having exposed fecal matter hovering on top of this wintery blanket further increases the risk of infection. It's a tough battle, but be as diligent as you can, and keep a close eye on your birds' feet and legs. Watch for any signs of swelling or limping, and if you do see them, intervene quickly.

- **Avoid housing chickens and geese together**

This is probably a good time to mention chickens. Although some people will say that chickens and geese can be safely housed together, I'm going to take the side of housing them separately whenever possible for precautionary reasons. This is especially true in large gaggles or in small pen areas

The bacteria *staphylococcus aureus* tends to be more prevalent among chickens. When geese get normal little cuts or scratches on the bottom of their webbed feet and tread through chicken excrement it can lead to staph infections, which in turn can lead to bumblefoot. In addition, chickens are less resistant to parasites and disease and can spread them to your geese. They don't have the powerful immune systems that your geese have, which is why chickens are often fed medicated food, while geese should never be given medicated food.

As much as I love chickens, they really should have their own space to avoid these risks. If you do want to keep both together, at least be sure that pens are spacious and kept very clean.

Footpad Injury

If your pet goose gets a visible cut on the bottom of their foot, it is vital that they get medical treatment right away in order to avoid a serious infection, which can potentially lead to bumblefoot. Treatment must be rapid and aggressive. Our vet has us clean injured footpads with a mixture of 3 cc of Betadine solution and one 12 fluid oz bottle of sterile saline solution (contact lens solution). In addition, they are prescribed 150 mg of Clindamyacin twice daily for 7-10 days or until the wound is fully healed along with a regimen of probiotics (more on this in a moment). Silver Sulfadiazine 1% topical cream is applied twice daily to the injury for 10-14 days. For pain management, 12-25 mgs of Rimadyl® are administered every 12 hours for 5-7 days. It is vital that your goose is kept on extremely clean and dry grounds during their recovery. We achieve these conditions in our infirmary, which is bedded with pine shavings that we clean frequently.

Duran's Sore Feet

Duran Duran are two Toulouse ganders who came to us during their middle-aged years. The boys got a bit out of hand in their previous home and their owners needed to surrender them. For clarity, we named one of the boys Duran Rio and the other Duran Moon. Duran Rio began limping one wintery day and upon closer examination, we discovered he had a toe infection. This kind of infection is not uncommon in winter when webbed feet can be easily cut or scratched on ice and snow. Afterwards, all it takes is one step into what we refer to as a "sugar bomb" and the toe can become infected with bacteria.

Rio's infected and swollen toe

Fortunately, treatment is pretty straight forward. Our vet prescribed Baytril 68 mg and 150 mg Clindamycin once a day in addition to cleaning the area with a Tricide-Neo® / Distilled Water solution. We just put the solution into a squirt bottle and then picked him up and quickly saturated his toe. Treatment continued until the issue was resolved and Rio made a full recovery.

Lots of swim time on clean water is highly recommended. If the condition is prolonged add weekly Adequan® injections to avoid permanent joint issues.

Duran Duran in the snow

Osteomyelitis

Osteomyelitis is a bone infection that is usually caused by the bacteria *staphylococcus aureus*. Bacteria can travel into the bone through the bloodstream from other infected areas in the body or by direct infection through a wound that reaches into the bone. When the bone becomes infected, it produces pus, which usually creates an abscess in the joint. The abscess then deprives the bone of its normal blood supply.

In severe cases, a pus filled cavity develops inside the bone and new bone can form around this area. Your vet may advise surgery to help drain the pus out, so that the bone can heal up properly. Your vet will likely want to surgically remove any damaged or infected tissue during this operation. In very severe cases, amputation may be required, but this should only be performed when the infection has reached life threatening stages.

Symptoms of osteomyelitis include: lameness, abscess, fever, lethargy, nausea, appetite loss, behavioral changes and depression.

Treatment of osteomyelitis depends on the severity of the infection and how quickly it is discovered. It is vital that vet treatment be sought out immediately because this condition can get worse very quickly. Prognosis is highly dependent on the timeliness of medical intervention.

Vets will often recommend an x-ray for your goose to determine whether an infection in the bone is present; however, the infection may not appear on the x-ray if it is in its early stages (which is why a safe and general antibiotic like Baytril® may be prescribed while your vet is in the process of determining the cause of symptoms in your goose).

Once osteomyelitis is diagnosed, your vet will remove a sample of bacteria (via a needle) from the site of infection in order to choose the correct antibiotic treatment. If the infection is in an advanced stage, injected antibiotics are often utilized until the condition improves; then, oral antibiotics are substituted.

We have seen osteomyelitis once at our sanctuary and there was no warning that there was an infection—the bird was fine one day and suddenly not walking the next. Our vet prescribed a strong dose of antibiotics: Baytril® and Clindamycin, which may be needed for up to 6-8 weeks, sometimes longer. He also prescribed Metacam® (anti-inflammatory) for the first week, to offer pain relief. We x-rayed every two weeks to confirm progress, but you may not see any for at least 30 days. Osteomyelitis can leave permanent arthritis in its post recovery wake; to help prevent this, Adequan® can be administered intramuscularly upon diagnosis. It is injected once a week for 6-8 weeks, and positive results can often be seen very quickly. As an added precaution, we keep our geese off of pond water for 24 hours following their injection to avoid the risk of further infection.

Many vets are accustomed to injecting Adequan® into the leg and switching which leg is used every week in order to prevent soreness; while this may work well with a four-legged pet, it is vital to protect *both* legs when remedying a two-legged pet. You don't want to make the injured leg any more sore than it already is, nor do you want to weaken the leg that is already taking on the bulk of the workload. Our vet always chooses the muscles of the breast as an injection site. I gently hold in the goose's wings and then slowly and carefully roll them onto their back. While they lay on the vet table, I normally cover their eyes with the bottom of my shirt to help calm them down.

Some geese may require the occasional Adequan® injection down the road and provided they aren't administered too close together, they can be injected directly into the leg muscle if you prefer.

The easiest way to prevent osteomyelitis is to maintain good flock hygiene. If one of your birds receives a cut or wound clean it thoroughly using an antiseptic wash. Be sure to keep the injury clean. Take your goose to the vet if the wound is deep, becomes infected, is not healing properly, if they are in pain or exhibiting any of the above-listed symptoms.

NOTE: Exercise caution when using Metacam®. If not used in moderation it may lead to long-term liver damage. Our vet advises that we use Metacam® for no more than 7 consecutive days except in extreme circumstances or when the benefits outweigh the risks. Rimadyl® is a better option during extended treatment periods.

Equally, the administration of Clindamycin for extended periods of time may interfere with the balance of the colon, which may lead to more serious issues. For this reason, our vet exercises caution when prescribing Clindamycin and recommends starting with a low to moderate dose and increasing the milligrams only as needed, if you are not seeing noticeable improvement. In addition to treatment, you can give your goose Lake's® Lacto-plus probiotic powder with *L. acidophilus* to protect intestinal flora.

As an example of Clindamycin dosing, we once had a 20 lb. gander named Tutter who was diagnosed with osteomyelitis. He could not walk at all and he was treated successfully on a dose of 75 mg of Clindamycin and 22.7 mg Baytril® every 12 hours for 6 weeks. This and a once weekly injection of Adequan® (which was dosed according to directions and is safe for waterfowl) did the trick. This dosage of Clindamycin is much less than what is suggested in many publications, but it worked very well.

Broken Toenail & Torn Webbing

Protecting webbed feet is a vital necessity when you have waterfowl. Geese can be quite accident prone and tend to stumble easily over small obstacles in their paths. In order to prevent injuries keep their yard free of sticks, rocks and nuts. Fill holes as they appear.

Avoid requiring your geese to step up and over objects (especially through doorways); instead build up the ground to make broader, more natural ramps whenever possible. This solution is often safer than constructing ramps out of wooden boards. Geese have been known to fall sideways off of board ramps or hop off the ramp when they get near the bottom; either of these actions can lead to injuries.

Kiddy pools are a great swimming option for geese, but it is always best to dig out a hole and sink the pool into the ground rather than just placing it on top of the ground. Sinking the pool into the ground is much safer than asking your geese to jump up over the lip when hopping in or out. This simple step can prevent leg, foot and toe injuries.

If your goose breaks a toenail, which results in bleeding, the bleeding will most likely be minimal and stop all on its own, but you can utilize a blood coagulant (or cornstarch if you don't have coagulant on hand) to help things along. Excessive bleeding is rare, but if this does occur, you will want to call your vet for emergency assistance.

Once bleeding is controlled, you will need to address any damage to the goose's toe or webbing. If the toenail was not completely severed and you can avoid any further damage to the quick (inside vein) you can cut the remaining portion off with clippers. Do not do any trimming yourself if you suspect it could cause any additional bleeding; take your goose to the vet for further care instead. This is also true if your goose has dark toenails and you can't see the quick inside.

Torn webbing does not normally require vet intervention as long as it is minimal (a straight tear, less than a ¼ inch in length), but it can't hurt to call your vet and double check. Some situations do require stitching or the removal of the entire triangle of webbing to avoid further mishaps.

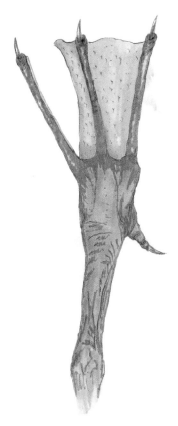

Diagram of webbing torn all the way back to the crook of the toe

To prevent infection, put the bird in freshly drawn, clean water and allow them to swim in it for a few minutes to cleanse the wound. Remove the goose and disinfect the injury using wound wash (preferably a spray). Spritz the toenail/webbing area 3-4 times daily until the wound appears completely healed. Torn webbing does not mend or grow back, so afflictions are permanent.

Clean your goose's pen and house and put down fresh bedding. Keep quarters as clean as possible to prevent infection while the toenail or torn webbing heals. If the bird is limping, you will want to keep them in smaller, more confined quarters—preferably sectioning them off in an area measuring around 4' x 4'. This will encourage them to rest and stay off it for a little while. It is best to keep other flock members in sight, but outside of this penned area until the injured goose is feeling better again.

Watch the injured area closely. If an infection occurs at any time, continue to use the wound wash and call your vet for immediate assistance. Unattended foot and leg injuries can result in lameness. When in doubt, call your vet.

- **Toenail Filing**

Some geese have fast growing toenails that don't seem to wear down on their own. Geese with leg injuries that don't walk with both of their webbed feet flat on the ground may have a couple of toenails that do not naturally wear down. Geese have pretty thick toenails, so it is advisable to bring them to your vet for filing rather than clipping them especially if they have dark toenails and you can't see the pink quick inside.

Our vet files down some long toenails. Do __NOT__ try this yourself at home.

Lameness

It takes a lot of time and attention to try to get a lame goose on its feet again, and it isn't always possible.

- **X-Ray for broken bones or dislocations**

The first thing we do in the case of a lame goose is bring them to the vet for an x-ray to ensure there are no broken bones or dislocations. Abandoned or neglected geese can freeze into their ponds and dislocate hip and knee joints while attempting to free themselves. There is often no safe treatment for this condition, and euthanizing is a common vet recommendation, especially when the animal is experiencing pain.

- **Systemic Infection**

When systemic infections occur it is vital to treat them immediately to avoid serious and permanent damage. It is not uncommon to discover a swelling knee or ankle joint on your goose as the internal infection fills the area with pus. A round of Baytril® and Clindamycin are often used in combination to address the issue. If there are no changes in your goose or if conditions worsen within the first two weeks, your vet will likely draw a sample of the fluid inside and send it off to a lab to determine exactly what type of bacteria is inside. It is best for your goose to be on antibiotics for a week or two before doing a fluid draw in order to reduce the risk of further infection. It usually takes a week to receive the test results and the lab will often list the types of medications that will be effective to resolve the issue. Just be sure that the medications prescribed are safe for waterfowl. Once weekly injections of Adequan® can prevent permanent joint damage during your goose's recovery, so this treatment is highly recommended and very safe.

A systemic infection that is not attended to may resolve itself in time, but the end result is often a lame goose. Geese can lose their freedom of mobility due to a former infection in their joints. During the infection the joint fills with pus and after healing, this pus hardens to a fingernail-like consistency. This hardened material locks up the joint and prevents a normal range of motion. There is no medical procedure for a goose who is struggling with this sort of lameness. It is best to give them as much time on water as possible to keep their legs strong and to alleviate the stress of walking and holding up their own weight. Periodic Adequan® injections may improve your goose's mobility in these situations.

- **Arthritis**

Another cause of swollen joints is arthritis. Arthritis in geese is actually quite common. Vet examination will determine if this is the case. If a round of Baytril® doesn't bring on results, your vet will most likely draw a sample from the area and send it off for a culture. If the culture comes back negative, arthritis is a likely culprit. If caught in early stages, monthly/quarterly injections of Adequan® may prevent further damage to the joints and prolong happy days. Joint supplements also sometimes reveal results.

- **Option 1**

  Our vet recommended a couple Usana® products for joint care. Usana® (www.usana.com) products are FDA approved and so unlike many over-the-counter joint care products, their ingredients are guaranteed.

  Each bottle of Procasa II® contains 120 tablets. Each tablet contains 75 mg of Vitamin C, 1.25 mg of Manganese, 500 mg of Glucosamine Sulfate, 125 mg of Turmeric Extract and .75 mg of Silicon. Our vet advised a 1 tablet a day for adult geese.

  Each bottle of OptOmega® contains 237 mls of oil that include Omega 3, Omega 6 and Omega 9 fatty acids. Our vet advised a 3 ml per 2.2 lbs of body weight, once a day for adult geese.

- **Option 2**

  Other vets recommend giving adult arthritic geese 1000 mgs of Omega 3 fatty acids every day to help their joints. In addition they can be given a combined daily total of 500-1000 mgs of glucosamine and chondroitin. These supplements are administered daily for the duration of your goose's life to help foster healthy joints. NSAIDs (Non-steroid Anti-inflammatory drugs) like Rimadyl® can also be given on particularly bad days to help reduce any joint pain and swelling.

Rosie holds still for her x-ray

- **Staph infection**

It can be very difficult to prevent staph infections in lame geese. They have a tendency to sit in the same place, basking in the sun, for long periods of time, which exposes them to higher risk. Advanced staph infection can result in necrotic tissue and the sudden loss of your goose's feathers, but be careful not to confuse this with the normal molting of feathers, which can also appear quite sudden and drastic.

If your vet aspirates a sample of fluids from an inflamed leg and discovers staph bacteria (*Hemolytic staphylococcus*), they will likely prescribe an antibiotic like Clindamycin and an anti-inflammatory like Rimadyl®. The lab will provide a list of suggested antibiotics for your vet to choose from and an experienced vet will know which of these are safe for waterfowl. Always ask your vet for copies of any tests performed on your geese and keep your own medical files at home.

When you review test results, "S" means the bacteria is Susceptible to the antibiotic listed. "R" means the bacteria is Resistant to the antibiotic listed. If you see that the isolated bacteria is Susceptible "S" to ALL types of antibiotics, this could be a sign that the sample drawn from your goose was contaminated. It is rare that an infection is susceptible to all types of treatment, which is why this is a warning sign. If you see this type of result and your vet doesn't catch it, be sure to ask them for a retest to confirm results. Prescribing the wrong antibiotic can often lead to zero results and the worsening of your pet's condition. Below is an example of a contaminated sample since the infection shows susceptibility to every type of antibiotic on the list. If it sounds too good to be true, it probably is.

Test Results:

AMPICILLIN	S
AUGMENTIN	S
CETIOFUR	S
CEPHALOTHIN	S
CLINDAMYCIN	S
ERYTHROMYCIN	S
GENTAMICIN	S
ENROFLOXAC	S
OXACILLIN	S
PENICILLIN	S
TRIBRISSEN	S
VANCOMYCIN	S

Staph infections are very difficult and slow to treat. Do not expect to see external improvement for at least 6-8 weeks and count on treatment continuing for up to 2-3 months.

In severe cases, surgical intervention may be required to flush out the infection and insert a drain into the swollen area. The port remains in the affected area and twice daily flushing is required at home for the next five days. Following this, the goose returns to be rechecked and to have the port removed and the leg re-closed.

Surgery is usually not performed until the goose has been on antibiotics for 2-4 weeks without the desired results. Tricide® (used when an operation is being done near nerves) and Tricide-Neo® (used when an operation is not being done near nerves) is a recommended flushing agent for staph infections. Your vet can obtain Tricide or request further information by emailing tricideinfo@yahoo.com. It comes in a small, instructional packet that includes preparation details. Tricide® can be mixed with a variety of antibiotics making it ideal for flushing out staph infections.

Because geese have a diving instinct and will commonly try to hold their breath while going under anesthesia it is vital that they be intubated. Most vets will mask waterfowl down with sevoflurane and then utilize injectable butorphanol and/or midazolam as anesthetics.

Depending on severity, post-surgical plans may also include a sling that can be height-adjusted, so that you can fluctuate your goose's position from setting their feet flat on the floor to suspending them off of the ground—and everywhere in between.

Joint care products (like those used for arthritis) can be utilized during recovery periods.

- **Osteosarcoma**

Osteosarcoma is a type of bone cancer that tends to occur at the end of long bones, usually around the hip or knee joints in geese, but also in ankles. From the outside, osteosarcoma appears as swelling that can become very extreme as the cancer progresses. Since the treatment of osteosarcoma involves limb amputation and chemotherapy, there is no suggested course of action for geese. Although pain medications can be utilized in the short-term, in the long-term euthanasia is the common veterinary recommendation.

Tutter's Staph Infection

Tutter was rescued from a parking lot where he and his best friend Angelo were pushed out of a moving vehicle. They both were rescued and brought to our sanctuary with foot and leg injuries from the ordeal. We started them both on two 22.7 mg pills of Baytril once daily for 14 days and cleaned the wounds meticulously. Both boys healed up nicely and moved to their new pen once their quarantine period was complete.

Many months later, during a Christmas Eve snowstorm, Tutter completely stopped walking one day. He never exhibited a noticeable limp before that day or gave us any other indication that something was wrong. He just sat down abruptly and refused to get up. We picked him up and found that one of his ankles was a little swollen and warm, but that we could flex all of his joints without causing him any discomfort. We brought him inside to our infirmary and then called our vet. Feeling confident he had not broken any bones, but likely had a staph infection, we started him on two 22.7 mg pills of Baytril® and 150 mgs of Clindamycin once a day. In addition, we gave him Metacam® to help alleviate any discomfort.

We also gave Tutter Lake's LACTO-Plus® probiotic powder (www.lakesbirdfood.com), to protect his intestinal flora from the Clindamycin and Metacam®. Although you can sprinkle the appropriate amount of powder over their food, Tutter's appetite came and went, so we often dissolved anywhere from 1/8 to ½ of a teaspoon of the powder into a couple mls of water and ground Mazuri and then administered it to him via syringe twice a day (He ate more often than this, but we only added the LACTO-Plus twice a day). Geese with compromised immunity systems who are on more powerful medications receive a higher dose of LACTO-Plus than stronger birds who are on less potent medications. Your vet can help you with the proper dosages.

When our vet office re-opened a couple days later, we brought Tutter in for an x-ray and discovered that he had osteomyelitis—a bone infection. At some point, he had likely received a tiny cut on the bottom of his foot and it had become infected. The course of action remained the same and we were forewarned that Tutter had quite the battle ahead of him.

Despite continued medical treatment and hydrotherapy, any attempts to encourage Tutter to put any weight on his foot came without result. And then two weeks later a vet friend of ours advised us to begin weekly Adequan® injections to help protect his joints from any further damage and to speed up his recovery time.

Tutter has everything he needs, nice and close to him

Tutter's Osteomyelitis

After two weeks of medications and hydrotherapy to address Tutter's osteomyelitis, we began taking him to the vet for weekly Adequan® injections. Three days after his first injection, Tutter stood up on his good leg while keeping his injured one tucked up underneath him—it was a day I'll never forget. He received further injections for a total of 7 consecutive weeks (while continuing his other medications) and there was marked improvement in his behavior and abilities within days of each treatment.

Tutter spends time in our sunroom during his recovery

An integral part of Tutter's therapy was keeping him acquainted with his best friend Angelo. As friendly as Tutter was, like most geese, he preferred the company of his friends over we humans. On sunny days we would carry Tutter out to the goose pen, encircle him in protective fencing and give him some time to say hello to his good friends.

Tutter takes his first steps towards a full recovery

It wasn't too long before Tutter was hopping along and using his wings to help with momentum and soon after that he was walking again. Today, Tutter is enjoying a complete recovery, without even the tiniest limp.

- **Malnutrition**

Lameness is often the result of malnutrition, so our first tactic has always been the introduction of the Mazuri® waterfowl diet. Specifically, *niacin deficiency* is often the culprit in these problems, so we lightly spray some water on the Mazuri® food and shake it up in a container. Then, we add a tablespoon of powdered Brewer's Yeast (which you can find at your local health food store) to the container and shake it again. This process coats the Mazuri® grain with a layer of Brewer's Yeast, which is very high in niacin. Prepare this mixture in the morning and again in the evening, throwing away any uneaten portions.

Malnourished goslings (usually those not on a brand-name gosling food) can lose their ability to walk, and it can literally happen overnight. Immediately upgrade their diet to a brand-name formula and sprinkle some Brewer's Yeast over their crumbles. If caught early enough and remedied immediately, you should see results within the first 24-48 hours and your gosling will often make a full recovery.

- **Sprains**

Lameness can come on quite suddenly and for unexplained reasons. We once found rescued gander *Joop!* limping around his perfectly flat pen. The first thing I did was pick him up to have a look at the leg. There was no swelling anywhere in any of the bones or joints. I had my husband hold him while I held his feet in each of my hands to compare their temperature—both legs and feet felt the same. I proceeded to slowly flex each of the joints from his hip down to his toes. He displayed no discomfort, so it was clearly a sprain. I continued to inspect the leg and flex it similarly 2-3 times a day to be sure nothing changed.

It is not uncommon to have an x-ray come up clear on a limping goose and as with any pet, it usually means good news. When a suspected sprain lasts more than a week, it is always advisable to bring your goose to the vet just to be sure there is nothing more serious going on.

- **Stress**

The occasional goose has been known to react to stress with sudden lameness. It is relatively rare and should only be concluded, if the goose suddenly and near miraculously gets on their feet again soon after stressors are removed. Otherwise, assume something else is wrong.

Mademoiselle Fifi experiences anything but stress while tending to her gorgeous feathers

Grampa's Bumblefoot

Grampa is a Dewlap Toulouse gander who was discovered limping along the shore of the lake where he had been abandoned. The bottoms of his webbed feet were exposed to hard concrete, broken glass and bottle caps. It wasn't long before he sustained an injury that lead to infection and resulted in a serious case of bumblefoot. Because Grampa didn't have anyone to take him to the vet for treatment, the infection went unattended and eventually entered his toe and ankle bones. Without rescue and intervention, Grampa would have lost full use of his leg and eventually died of advanced bone infection (osteomyelitis).

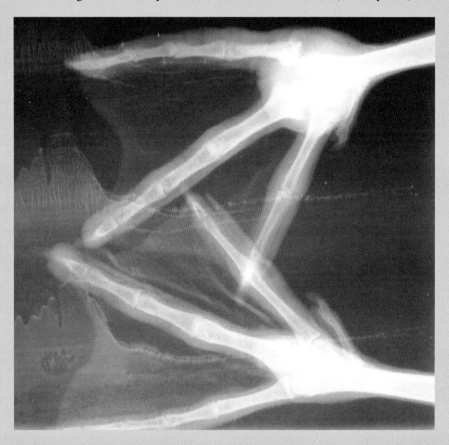

X-ray of Grampa's injured foot (above) compared to his normal foot (below)

Upon his rescue Grampa was taken to the vet for x-rays and to aspirate some of the fluid from the site to determine the best course of treatment. After being prescribed alternate courses of Baytril® and Clindamycin along with weekly injections of Adequan®, the infection was eventually halted in its tracks.

While further impairment was prevented, plenty of damage had already been done. The infection resulted in deteriorated cartilage and had caused the bones in his foot to separate leaving him with a debilitating limp and a foot that turned inwards.

Attending to Lameness

- **Hydrotherapy**

It is vital that a lame or limping goose have access to swimming water every day (even if it's in your bath tub) for maximum effectiveness in curing sprains. Without hydrotherapy to re-strengthen muscles the goose will either lie in the same spot all day long not getting the exercise they need to improve, or they may injure themselves further trying to get around on a weakened leg.

Lengthy daily swims enable a goose to take the weight off of their injured leg while working and strengthening their leg muscles again. It is vital to keep them swimming and moving around during these sessions of hydrotherapy, rather than just resting and floating.

Tutter during his daily hydrotherapy treatment

It is important, especially during cold weather, that your goose has ample time to dry before going back outside. We usually drain the tub and set down a thick layer of towels for them to lie down on, so their bellies will dry. Swap out the wet towels with dry ones every 15 minutes until they no longer become wet. Then, allow your goose to dry thoroughly before bringing them outside again.

- **Stretch therapy**

A lot of exercise is needed for the goose who is permanently lame, either in part or in full. This is the best way to keep them healthy and strong. A little bit of stretch therapy can go a long way.

Without the mobility of their legs, some lame geese have difficulty reaching their oil gland, which in turn may compromise their feather quality. You will want to coax them into improving their reach. Stretching is encouraged with their favorite snack—lettuce is usually the big winner. Hold a leaf near the left side of the goose's oil gland and encourage them to turn their head to the left and reach back for it. You may have to slowly work your way back if they can't reach this far at first. Next hold the leaf to the right side of the goose's oil gland and entice them to turn their head to the right and reach back for it. This should be a daily activity and can be repeated with any favorite snack the goose may have as long as the snack is healthy.

- **Weight management**

Lame geese need plenty of exercise to avoid becoming overweight. Ration food carefully and allow plenty of swim time to keep your goose as fit as possible.

- **Keep flock mates close**

It is imperative that an injured goose spends at least some time in the company of their gaggle during their recovery, even if separated by a fence for their own protection. If you have a gentle friend that can be on the same side of the fence as your injured goose, place those two together. Geese are motivated to get on their feet again by other geese, so don't deprive them of this natural source of encouragement. If the injured goose does need to spend time away from the gaggle, it is best to give them a mirror to accompany them, so they don't feel all alone. Remember, they are a flock animal and are often unhappy when they are not in the company of other geese.

Angelo and Ali check in on Tutter during his visit

- **Clean bedding**

Be certain to keep a lame goose's bedding very dry and clean while they are getting well to prevent the onset of other medical problems. You don't want your goose sitting in the same messy spot all day. While your goose is not walking, they may have a great deal of trouble cleaning their underbelly and as a result the condition of their underside feathers may wane a bit.

- **Goose wheelchair**

When pet geese go permanently lame or have very limited mobility, many families improve the lives of their feathered friends by constructing a goose wheelchair. We discovered that a simple mesh laundry sorter contained most of the parts needed to assemble a goose go-cart, including the wheels and the mesh for sewing their sling. The only additional parts we needed to purchase were six buckles with straps that we found in the camping department of the same large, chain department store. The PVC pipes included in the laundry sorter will need to be measured and cut down to size and you will also need to do a bit of measuring, cutting and sewing to make your goose's buckled sling, which will hold them in place. The alternative to sewing a custom made sling is to order them from Jorgenson Labs (www.jorvet.com). They sell both carts and slings and you can order them separately.

Homemade Goose sling for post-surgical care

Keep in mind, your goose is only allowed in their cart on flat surfaces and while under direct supervision. Geese in carts also wear diaper harnesses to keep from messing on their sling.

Lame geese still make wonderful pets. In addition to time in their carts, it is also important to give them plenty of swim time because most of them can experience full movement and freedom from their affliction on the water.

Ailments #5
Eye problems

Healthy eyes appear shiny, bright, clear and clean. Anything outside of this is not normal and requires vet examination.

Skynyrd demonstrates the appearance of a healthy eye

<u>Sticky Eyes</u>

Geese with certain types of disabilities, including those with neurological issues or those afflicted with various levels of lameness, can sometimes experience sticky or runny eyes. The reason for this has to do with coordination. Many disabled geese cannot successfully use their toenails to assist in the delicate preening of the feathers around their eyes. As a result one or both eyes can get a little messy.

As often as needed (which can range from daily to weekly, to every now and then) get a lukewarm bowl of water and a clean facecloth. Dip the facecloth into the water and get it soaking wet. Sit over your goose to hold them in place while very carefully wiping the feathers around the eyes, being careful not to touch their eyes. Motions should be slow and gentle. Do *not* scrub the feathers and always move the facecloth in the direction of feather growth.

If feathers are caked down or hard, hold the water-soaked facecloth in place over the eye and allow the warm water to permeate through the build up. As the feathers start to feel soft again slowly begin wiping the feathers. Be sure to turn the facecloth to a new and clean area of the towel as frequently as needed and re-dip it into the water bowl whenever necessary to keep it generously wet.

In some cases, you may not be able to get the eye completely clean in one sitting and may have to come back to it over the course of a day or over a couple of days. Sometimes if you get your goose started, they can finish up the job on their own. In more severe cases it is highly recommended that you bring your goose to a vet to see if an antibiotic eye ointment is needed as well.

<u>Eye Infection</u>

Although rare, Geese may occasionally get eye infections in one or both eyes. We tend to see this in rescues who come from polluted ponds or who are malnourished. To clear this up our vet prescribes Vetropolycin® eye ointment to be applied directly onto one or both eyes 2-3 times a day until their eyes are cleared, which usually takes about 7–10 days. This has worked successfully on a handful of geese who have come to us with eye infections. It is easy to administer and it offers them immediate comfort as well.

<u>Eye Trauma</u>

From time to time you may walk out and find one of your goose's eyes swollen or foamed over with tiny bubbles. This is usually the result of it being impacted either by their surroundings or quite commonly, another goose.

Look around their pen and be sure there is nothing dangerous sticking out around eye level that could be causing the problem. Although eye injuries may be caused by a stray piece of hay or straw it is usually brought on by a squabble with another goose that results in a poke.

We flush the afflicted eye out 2-3 times a day with sterile saline contact solution (we prefer to use a *sensitive eye* formula) for as long as the tiny bubbles continue to appear in the eye, which usually only lasts for the first day or so. After flushing, we immediately apply Vetropolycin® eye ointment twice a day to the injured eye until the eye is completely healed. The eye will normally clear up in 3-7 days. If there is any swelling you can also give your goose an anti-inflammatory like Metacam® or Rimadyl® for a day or two. Be sure your goose has very clean water available to help prevent it from getting infected. Separations may be in order to prevent future mishaps, which can lead to serious permanent damage and blindness.

<u>Swollen Tear Duct</u>

It is always a good idea to have a vet look at your goose's infected or injured eye to ensure you provide the best care possible to your feathered friend. Vets will take a closer look at your goose's eye by flipping down the lower eyelid. Sometimes vets will discover that your goose has a swollen tear gland. This can be caused by infection or injury. Our vet prescribes Vetropolycin® HC antibiotic eye ointment for swollen tear glands. It is usually given twice daily for 3-7 days. If improvement is not seen, it is important to bring your goose back to the vet for a follow-up exam.

Long term use may result in a partially-closed or squinty eye, so your vet may switch your goose over to regular Vetropolycin® eye ointment and have you continue with that for a longer period of time until the issue is cleared up.

Sinusitus

Bubbles that appear in the corners of the eyes on a regular basis that are <u>not</u> caused by an impact injury may be an indication of a sinus infection. *How do you tell if the bubbles are caused by an impact injury?* If your goose is squinting or if there is any swelling or obvious signs of eye injury than you are witnessing bubbles brought on by trauma. However, if your goose has bubbles, but their eyes look healthy and open, you may be seeing signs of a sinus infection. Sinus infections tend to affect both eyes, which can be another indicator. In some cases, the corners of the eyes may appear a darker pink than usual or even red.

Your vet will likely prescribe Tobramycin 0.3% (which usually comes in a 5 ml bottle). Most vets will advise two drops per eye every twelve hours.

Cataracts

Even the most attentive pet owner may not recognize what is usually a slow onset of cataracts, especially since they tend to develop in one eye long before the other, preventing any noticeable change in behavior. To avoid this oversight (no pun intended), it is important to take a once-a-month look into the eyes of your geese.

Cataracts are the result of lens deterioration, irritation or disintegration. Cataracts can cause blurry vision, poor night vision and even blindness. An eye with cataracts will usually have a cloudy, grayish-white, opaque discoloration in the pupil. Cataracts begin small and may grow to cover the entire pupil over time.

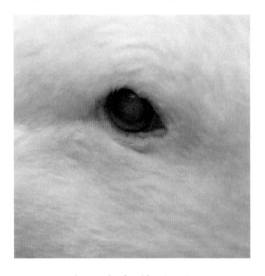

An eye cloudy with cataracts

There are Age-related Cataracts, Congenital Cataracts (inherited), Traumatic Cataracts (impact or injury) and Secondary Cataracts (brought on by malnutrition, exposure to toxins or bacterial infection). Beyond this, cataracts are classified by the location of lens affliction. There are various levels of Anterior, Nuclear and Posterior cataracts. Operability depends on which kind of cataract your goose is diagnosed with. Some types progress rapidly and require timely diagnosis and treatment to avoid blindness while others progress more slowly. No matter what the case, when you notice cataracts in your goose, a trip to your vet is in order for closer examination and to determine exactly what is going on in one or both eyes.

As a first step, your vet will most likely advise blood work to rule out any kind of infection that might be causing the issue. They will also be asking you questions about your goose's diet. Provided that your feathered friend is on a healthy, waterfowl-designed menu, your vet will be able to rule out malnutrition as a source of the problem.

If diet is the issue, corrective measures may stop the progression of the condition, but are unlikely to reverse it. The same is true of cataracts caused by infection, the infection may be remedied through proper medical treatment, stopping the progression of cataract formation, but things will not likely improve.

Surgery, when possible, should only be performed by an experienced avian veterinary ophthalmologist. Blood work should be done first to ensure your goose is a good, healthy candidate for surgery and anesthesia. Surgery should only be performed if it is expected to restore your goose's vision to an effective degree.

Patients are usually operated on within an hour or two and tend to return home the following day. Surgery in waterfowl does not include the implantation of an artificial lens, so birds tend to have blurry or far-sighted vision in their eye afterwards.

Your goose will likely go home with an anti-inflammatory and special eye drops following surgery. Try to avoid medications with steroids whenever possible; ask your vet about safe alternatives.

- **Holistic options to discuss with your vet**

As with any medical regimes, never proceed with holistic options without first discussing them thoroughly with your vet. Often, holistic options are incorporated into a vet-prescribed treatment regime.

Raw carrots and dark green lettuce consumption may result in the reduced risk of cataracts caused by old age. They may possibly even slow the progression of existing cataracts caused by age. Other healthy foods that may help are: oranges, grapes, raisins, figs, dates, cauliflower and ground almonds.

A quality supplement (like Vionate®) can be measured and sprinkled over your pet's food to increase their intake of vitamins, which may help slow progression, but this must be done under vet supervision to avoid vitamin overdoses, which can be fatal.

Blindness

Blindness can be the result of age, injury (especially from other geese or birds poking at eyes), genetics, cataracts or disease. After an initial vet examination to properly assess the situation, you should continue to visually inspect any injured eyes on a daily basis. If you see inflammation, swelling, moving cataracts or any other changes, contact your waterfowl vet. Your goose may be experiencing pain and require further assistance or medication. Cataracts can sometimes be removed surgically by an experienced veterinary ophthalmologist, but it can be challenging to find a qualified vet of this sort who is willing to work on waterfowl.

- **During the transition**

Geese may demonstrate signs of fear, aggression or depression during the onset of blindness—or if blindness is sudden, during the period immediately following their loss of vision. You will need to be their support system during this time by offering love, companionship, stability and security. It is vital that you maintain/establish trust during this time. Your feathered friend needs you. Remember your birds need the same thing you would: time, patience, love and security.

- **Creating a safe pen**

Like healthy geese, blind geese should not be let out of their pens without direct supervision. Assuming your goose is already in their predator-proof pen, you will want to enhance it to make it safer for them. As with any pen, make sure there are no pointy objects. Remove any rocks, sticks and tripping obstacles or anything they can stub their toes on (including a door jam leading into their house). Inspect their pen daily and fill any small holes in the ground that they can stumble into. Try to keep ground surfaces smooth and free of debris. Additionally, ramps are not safe for a blind pet; remove them. Remove anything your goose can bump their head on or fall off of. You may need to modify/enlarge entryways leading into their house.

- **Routine & consistency**

Geese thrive on routine—blind waterfowl rely on it. Drinking water should be made available 24/7 to all geese. We highly recommend making food available 24/7 for blind birds as well, so they consistently know where to find it.

Food and water should be easy for them to get to. If you do insist on a feeding schedule, keep to a strict schedule. If they eat all of their food, leave their empty food dish in their pen—do <u>NOT</u> remove it. Environmental consistency is vital. Always keep food and water bowls in the same location in their pen. Furthermore, keep <u>EVERYTHING</u> the same in their pen. Do not move things around or you will disorient them. Try to keep your interaction with them on a schedule as well—including topping off food and water bowls, so they know when to expect you and what you will be doing.

- **Rubber mats to guide them**

One tactic you can use to help your goose learn their way around their pen is by using textured rubber mats. You can make a trail that leads to their food and water bowls or create a path into their house. These will act as tactile signals for them as to where they are in the pen. Be creative and help them utilize their sense of touch. Just remember to keep the mats in the same place; do not change them around.

Mats can also be very helpful around trees or bushes that you do not want them to bump into. Speaking of trees and bushes; be sure all plants are well pruned. You want a tall trunk, so that any branches and foliage reach well over and above the head of your blind goose. You don't want a branch sticking out that can poke an eye or cause injury.

- **Water safety**

Pond safety is vital to avoid drowning. Remember geese trapped on water can drown. Blind geese can easily become injured while stepping out of a small pool or trapped in a small pond (especially during the molt when they drop their primary wing feathers and lose their flapping power). Even small ponds can be unsafe for an un-chaperoned blind goose. There are two solutions to this problem, either gate off their pond so that they cannot access it unless you are present, or build a specially designed pond just for them.

To build a quick pond, you can dig out a small cavity into the earth with a slightly inclined ramp at one end. Then use a thick mix of concrete to seal the pond with a two inch surface all around. Now your goose can safely walk into their water source and get back out. Close monitoring is vital until your goose has mastered the pond's location and can enter and exit it with ease.

We highly recommend placing a one foot cement lip around all edges of the pool to prevent your goose from pulling dirt into their pond while they are sitting on it. This sort of goosey fun will quickly make a muddy mess of things. This lip will also will give them a reliable signal when they are stepping close to the water's edge.

The great thing about this pond system is you can easily cement a small PVC outtake pipe in place at the deep end of the pond to create a drain. Then, to clean the pond, simply run a hose down into the deep end of the water and turn it on. The fresh water will flush out and replace the old water.

The one drawback of a concrete pond made in this fashion is, in colder regions, the pond will crack over the course of winter and will need a quick re-facing every spring. Also keep in mind that geese should not be allowed to sit on a small pond that can freeze over while they are in it. Sunk-in kiddy pools and small non-circulating, freezing ponds should be drained in winter and filled with hay or safely covered / fenced off over to prevent a flock member from falling inside of them.

- **Companionship**

If your goose is alone, you should highly consider giving them a companion to offer them company and reassurance. If your goose is completely blind, new flock members should not be welcomed in until your blind bird has completely adapted to their new situation and environment. If your goose is slowly losing their vision, it can help to introduce a newcomer while they can still see. Try to find a docile or shy goose (or duck) that is smaller in size than your blind bird. It is highly recommended to add a goose rather than a gander as a companion to a blind goose. Boys can sometimes get a little overzealous during the mating season and accidentally cause injury to a special needs bird.

- **Exercise and stimulation**

Your blind goose will need exercise; you do not want them spending their day sitting in the same place without any stimulation. If you notice this is occurring, you will need to go out and visit them more frequently and coax them to move around. Healthy green snacks can be a good way to reward them for moving around. Blind geese can forage too—encourage them to keep up this behavior. This is where a companion for them can really help. Blind flock members will often follow sighted ones to avoid being alone. A good friend will keep them happily entertained, provide security and keep them moving around.

- **Harness and leash**

Use extreme caution when taking your blind goose outside of the safety of their pen. If you insist on taking them for walks in the yard, you should invest in a high quality, well-fitted goose harness and leash. When blind geese get spooked, they tend to flap quickly across a yard and can put themselves into immediate danger; you will need to have constant control over them outside of the safety of their pen. Once you have your harness and have trained and made them familiar with it inside of their pen, you can begin to take them outside of their pen. Start out small. Don't go far and don't stay out long. Remember to keep to a routine. Walks should be on a timed schedule and the walk should be directed on the same path every day. You can go further along the path as your goose becomes more comfortable, but do not stray from the path.

Skynyrd walking on his harness and leash

- **Signal sounds**

When approaching the pen of your blind goose use a familiar sound to offer reassurance, so they know that it's you coming. You can talk—call out a familiar phrase like, *"Mommy's coming!"* or you can whistle or even sing a song (my personal favorite!). This tactic works well with partially blind geese as well. Additionally, when dealing with blind feathered friends, some people tie a small bell around their belt loop or bootlace so their goose can hear them moving around in their pen. This works when taking them on leashed walks as well. Be careful to choose large bells, so if it happens to fall off it does not pose a choking threat to your gaggle.

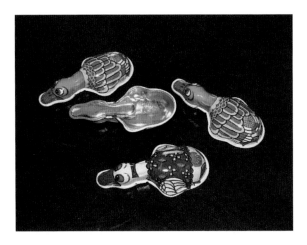

Duck Clickers for making sounds

Be creative with sounds. You can signal any number of things as long as you are consistent. Other ideas include a specific signal for meal times, treats, when a visitor is coming into their pen and signals that tell your goose when they are about to be petted or picked up; this way, your goose expects the physical contact before it actually happens and isn't frightened.

Remember, small steps are best when working with blind geese. Be consistent and adhere closely to routines. Blind geese can live enriched and productive lives; you just need to help them to do it. The time you spend with them can be rewarding for both you and your flock mate.

Victor-Victoria's Injured Eye

Victor-Victoria came to our sanctuary following an altercation with a wild Canada goose that ended with a serous jab to his left eye. In order to prevent any infection, we applied Vetropolycin® antibiotic eye ointment to the socket 2-3 times daily. The application procedure was simple and painless and performed in a matter of seconds. We continued this for 7 days. Although we were able to prevent any infection to Victor's injured eye, we were not able to save his vision on that side.

Jabs to the eye can result in an eye actually becoming pushed inside the skull. Should this occur, Vetropolycin® must be administered right into the eye socket for 7-10 days. Anti-inflammatory medication to control pain is also a vital part of healing. Vets will rarely remove a damaged eye in these instances since they tend to heal on their own in time and with the right medications. In the case of infection, however, the eye may need to be removed and the lid stitched closed. Surgery should only be performed by an experienced ophthalmologist. In cases like this where a specialist is required, we have our waterfowl vet (who understands the special needs of waterfowl and anesthesia) present while a qualified ophthalmologist performs the actual surgery.

The good news in Victor's case was that his right eye was perfectly healthy and he was able to get along fine and live a completely normal and happy life in our sanctuary and eventually in his new home.

Victor-Victoria keeps his injured eye closed

The only consideration we really had to keep in mind was staying on Victor's "good side." You don't want to startle a half-blind goose by standing on his blind side and having him suddenly turn his head and realize you're there. Be sure to use sound signals or talk while meandering through the pen of a visually impaired goose, so they are aware of your location and won't become panicked—especially if you welcome a goose into your home following this kind of trauma, while they are still getting to know you and are easily frightened.

93

Ailments #6
Reproductive Issues

Egg Binding

Egg binding occurs when a goose cannot pass her egg normally through her oviduct. This is often the result of a soft shelled or misshapen egg that cannot be easily passed due to its shape or texture. As with other reproductive issues, egg binding is often the result of a nutritional problem (including overweight issues) or genetic predisposition.

Some signs that your goose is having trouble passing her egg are open bill panting and her tail feathers bobbing up and down for extended periods of time. Sometimes they will not want to walk, or they may do so stiffly.

As soon as you notice your goose having trouble passing her egg, call your vet immediately. They may suggest that you give her a little more time and place her in warm bath in a warm room if she is not in too much distress, but we have never had the good fortune of this being of any help. In fact, if your vet will be closed in an hour, do not take this tactic. Egg binding can be fatal.

If the egg isn't passed within the hour, or if your vet will be closed by then, they will normally have the goose come in for a shot to help her contractions along and they will lubricate her oviduct to help the egg to pass. You then take your goose home and give her some quiet, alone time in a warm and comfortable place to try to pass her egg, checking on her frequently (every 10-15 minutes).

Geese will often lay soft eggs at the onset of the laying season. First eggs from new layers are often very large and double-yoked. If you see either of these, the risk of egg binding is increased. Immediately and significantly bump up your goose's *breeder / layer* formula ration to get her on track quickly. Over the coming weeks, slowly reduce the ratio to a level that maintains healthy eggs.

- **Discuss after-hours plan with your vet**

Passing the egg can take a long time and your goose can easily end up in trouble after your vet's closing hours. Before you leave your vet's office, be sure to ask them what the plan is should the situation worsen and even more importantly, what to do if it worsens after normal business hours. You need to verify that they will be on call after-hours and how quickly they can respond if things begin to go downhill fast. If they are not on call and they give you the number of another vet who will be available, call that covering vet right then and there—while you are in your vet's office. Explain your goose's situation to them, make sure that they can handle this problem should your goose's health deteriorate, and confirm that they are on call for emergencies after-hours. This way, if the situation does not improve, you will both be prepared for it. You may find that the covering vet cannot help in your particular situation; this is a very good thing to discover while you are still present in your vet's office. This knowledge will enable you and your vet to rethink things through and come up with another plan.

- **Re-evaluate your goose's diet**

Once the egg is passed, you need to immediately examine her diet. Her ratio of laying formula may need to be increased and, if you don't have one already, she may need an added source of calcium made available to her free choice.

If after adjusting your goose's diet, she is still passing abnormal eggs or having trouble laying her eggs, some people have had success with hormone injections to stop egg-laying all together. Others have had short-lived success in halting egg-laying by changing their goose's environment. This can be done by placing the goose in a different bedtime kennel in the barn at night, by decreasing the time she spends in the daylight, by having her stay the night with different goose companion or even by introducing a new goose to the gaggle. Routine changes will often pause the egg-laying cycle for a couple days, but long term results are unlikely and all the changes can be stressful on your goose.

Geese imprinted on humans will sometimes lay more frequently when handled by their owners. Some people will suggest limiting your hands-on time with your goose to help decrease her egg-laying, or similarly to remove geese from the presence of ganders. We have not heard of this being very successful, but if you're desperate, you can certainly give it a try.

Obturator Paralysis

Although more common in ducks, Obturator Paralysis can also occur in geese. A goose that is found with its legs paralyzed and splayed out behind them for a few hours during egg-laying is likely suffering from this condition.

Obturator Paralysis occurs when an egg passing through the oviduct applies pressure on the obturator nerve, which runs just inside the pelvic canal. Compression of this nerve results in the goose's legs splaying out behind them. This condition usually occurs when the egg is soft, larger than usual or malformed, which results in it rotating at a slower-than-normal rate down the oviduct. The result is an egg that remains pressed against the obturator nerve for a longer-than-normal period of time, which leaves the goose basically paralyzed for a few hours until the egg moves further along the oviduct, at which point the symptoms are relieved and the legs can move normally again.

Provided the egg is moving along the oviduct, there is nothing really to be done other than keeping your goose safe and comfortable, which includes protecting them from other members of the gaggle. Keep a watchful eye without disturbing them to be sure the symptoms pass. The condition usually lasts two to three hours and then the goose slowly begins to regain control of their legs again. It's usually a few more hours after that before the egg appears although it sometimes won't appear until the following morning—at normal egg-laying time.

Obturator Paralysis is more common in geese that have just started laying for the first time or in geese who lay soft, large or malformed eggs. Veteran layers will occasionally experience this at the start of their annual egg-laying season. More often than not, a particular goose will be prone to this and experience it on a re-occurring basis (usually not more than once a year).

Oviduct Prolapse

Sometimes when a goose is laying her egg, her oviduct (internal egg laying tube) comes outside of her body. This can happen in varying degrees, ranging from the minor protrusion of the oviduct to up to 4-6 inches coming outside of her body. Over-mating is a common cause of this condition although not the only cause; geese can have a genetic tendency for this condition.

Immediate vet care is needed when this happens. Remove the goose from the company of other geese to avoid them injuring the oviduct. Do not attempt to push the tube back into their body by yourself. Keep the oviduct clean and moist until you get to the vet. A tube of plain KY Jelly is a good item to have in your waterfowl medicine cabinet. A small amount can be placed on the protruding tissue to keep it moist. Sprinkle a little sugar on the exposed oviduct to take down the swelling. This helps the vet when it's time for them to push the organ back in. Wrap your goose in a towel to prevent her from poking at her own injury.

Your goose will need surgery to stitch the oviduct back into place. Sutures need to be tight enough to hold the oviduct in place, but they should in no way prevent normal egg-laying. The egg must be able to pass through the oviduct normally. A hormone injection is highly recommended to stop egg production during the healing phase of this surgery.

Once an oviduct prolapse occurs, it will most likely happen again as normal egg-laying continues. In order to prevent this, injections to prevent egg-laying are often prescribed until healing is complete. Once laying begins again you will want to be around while your goose is laying to be sure that her oviduct does not prolapse again. In extreme cases, where risk of reoccurring prolapse is present, a salpingohysterectomy may be recommended.

Salpingitis

Salpingitis is the inflammation of the oviduct (the *upper* reproductive tract). The oviduct becomes lined with pus filled cysts that are often brought on by infection—commonly *E. coli*. As with egg binding, it is more common among overweight or malnourished geese, or among geese who are pushed to lay excessively utilizing laying formulas.

Geese suffering from Salpingitis often pant excessively and have a routinely difficult time passing their eggs. This makes it extremely easy for a misdiagnosis. As with egg binding, geese with Salpingitis may also exhibit lethargy. Other symptoms include: redness or swelling around the cloaca, discharge or odd-shaped, malformed eggs. Sometimes the goose's abdomen may actually appear enlarged or she may even experience weight loss, but many geese show neither of these traits, hiding their affliction.

If your goose is exhibiting abnormal panting or stress during egg-laying, seek vet assistance immediately. Vets will commonly do an x-ray to get a closer look and then advise a salpingohysterectomy to remove the infected oviduct as no other treatment is effective.

Metritis

Metritis refers to the inflammation of the *lower* reproductive tract (the uterine portion of the oviduct). It can be brought on by a systemic (bacterial) infection or by damage caused by egg binding or peritonitis. Visible symptoms of Metritis and Salpingitis are the same.

Metritis can effect contractions during egg-laying as well as having a negative impact on actual shell formation. A salpingohysterectomy to remove the infected oviduct is commonly recommended.

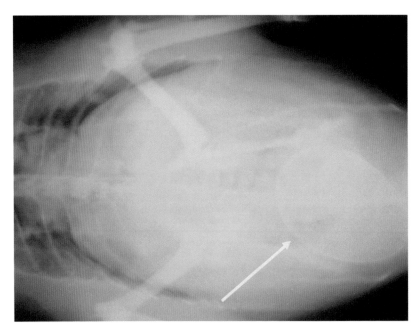

An egg appears on Ethel's x-ray

Peritonitis

Sometimes when a goose is egg bound (especially when multiple eggs are trapped in the oviduct) egg components can move incorrectly through her body and end up deposited in her abdomen. Peritonitis is more common in overweight geese, those with a genetic predisposition and among those who lay eggs excessively—commonly brought on by over-mating or excessive quantities of laying formulas.

Symptoms of Peritonitis mimic other aforementioned reproductive ailments, except that you may also witness yolk colored droppings. An immediate trip to the vet is in order and an x-ray needs to be done.

If an egg has slipped into the abdominal cavity, immediate surgery will be required to remove the egg and clean out the cavity. Post operative care includes: antibiotics, tube feeding and often fluid injections to prevent dehydration. Because there is a risk of reoccurrence, many vets will advise continual injections to prevent egg-laying or a salpingohysterectomy as a means of preventative treatment.

<u>Treatment of Reproductive Disorders in Geese</u>

Two common vet choices to temporary halt a goose's egg-laying are Human Chorionic Gonadotropin (HCG) and Luperon (Lupron®).

- **HCG injections**

HCG causes deterioration of ovarian follicles, which inhibits ovulation. The benefit of this drug is that it *works quickly* and has few side effects if used for short periods of time. This drug is an option for first time/one-off reproductive incidents. Three treatments are often given at 48 hour intervals. Long term side effects may include ovarian tumors, so it is only recommended for intermittent use.

- **Luperon injections**

The most widely used hormone therapy being utilized at present time to stop the egg-laying cycle is Leuprolide or Lupron®. It represses the release of gonadotropin (a hormone that regulates reproductive activity) into the body, which brings egg production to a stop.

Side effects, if any, are minimal, so vets consider it very safe. One problem with Lupron® is it may take up to several weeks to begin taking effect. This time delay can be a real issue if your goose needs an *immediate* break from her daily egg-laying routine. In addition, some geese become immune to the treatment within a short period of time, making it only a temporary solution. It seems to have the greatest effect on those geese who have only been laying for a short period of time.

- **Utilizing both injections**

Many vets will administer HCG to *immediately* stop egg production in addition to a Lupron® shot for a *longer lasting* effect. A shot of Lupron® may be repeated about every three weeks, if a longer break in laying is required. Combined together these two therapies are an excellent way of preventing egg-laying during the waiting period before a salpingohysterectomy can be performed and then afterwards during your goose's recovery.

- **Salpingohysterectomy**

The only permanent solution to put a stop to chronic reproductive disorders or prevent repeat reoccurrences of prolapsed oviduct or peritonitis is via surgery. The procedure in which the left oviduct (the functioning oviduct) is removed is known as a salpingohysterectomy.

An abdominal incision is made and the left oviduct is removed. The operating vet should inspect the vestigial right oviduct to verify that it truly is non-functioning. There have been rare instances of the right oviduct being operative and functional; if so, it will need to be removed as well. The ovary is not normally removed because it can be difficult to reach and can bleed heavily.

A salpingohysterectomy is often left as a last resort because it is a complicated, extremely risky and costly procedure, but it is commonly necessary to prevent reoccurring and life-threatening medical issues. It can be especially risky if your goose is still recovering from prior surgery. Be sure to research this option *thoroughly* with your experienced waterfowl vet before making a decision.

Confirm your vet of choice has performed this surgery successfully before on waterfowl—not just on birds (parrots, etc.). Ask them about their surgical and post-operative experience, mortality rates, anesthesia risks, pain-killers, antibiotics, post-surgical care requirements and expense. Be sure to inquire about after-hours and weekend emergency situations. Plan out your options in advance should your vet be unavailable during these times. You may need a back up vet who is fully versed in the situation and can assist you and your goose post-surgically if your vet is unavailable.

Exposed Penis

This question has come up since our inception and it continues to make its rounds. The corkscrew shaped body organ dangling from your gander is not his entrails falling out, but rather, quite normally, his penis.

It is not unusual, and perfectly normal, to see this appendage outside of your gander's body (especially after mating rituals) *unless* it does not return all the way back inside again soon after making its appearance. If you see the tip of your gander's penis continually exposed over the course of a few hours or more, something is most likely wrong.

An exposed penis (penis paralysis or phallus prolapse) most frequently occurs when a gander is not given ample access to clean swimming water. If one of your flock members exhibits this trait, serious considerations to the availability of swimming water in his living environment should be taken—now and going forward. If you are certain that lack of water is not the issue, over exertion during the mating season, genetic tendency, illness and old age can also be factors.

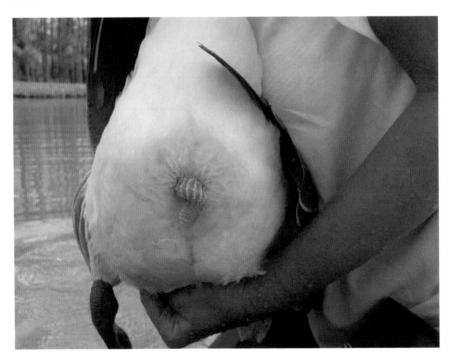

Photo of a goose's penis (for the sake of privacy, I won't say whose!)

In any case, you will want to make it immediately possible for your gander to have ready access to clean swimming water—a kiddy pool is perfectly acceptable. You will also want to give him a break from courtship in case overexertion is part of the problem.

The more time he spends relaxing on clean water, the more likely the situation will remedy itself quickly. During this time, it is *vital* that swimming water and grounds are kept exceptionally clean to avoid an infection of the penis. Change out water frequently and hose down yards a couple of times a day in addition to laying down fresh bedding frequently.

Vets have varying opinions on this matter; some suggest no medical intervention, while others recommend a round of antibiotics (Baytril® 68 mg, once daily for 7 days) to rule out any possible infection. We highly recommend this general antibiotic treatment since it is not harmful to geese and can help your gander towards a quick recovery. In addition, a topical antibiotic that will help keep the area moist can also be helpful.

If your gander is exhibiting a visible infection (redness, irritation, dark necrotic tissue, etc.) he should be brought to the vet for immediate examination and treatment.

In most cases, if attended to immediately, the penis will not become infected and it will retreat back into the gander's body within a couple of days. It is not unheard of, however, for the penis to remain exposed for months before returning inside the body. Some ganders exhibit the trait for the remainder of their life. Vets can surgically remove the tip, but this is not recommended unless there is a serious infection that requires drastic medical intervention. Only experienced vets who know how to do this properly should perform surgery to ensure it is done correctly. An exposed penis is very rarely fatal when properly attended to.

Lots of time on clean water is just what the doctor ordered

Inflamed Vent

If your goose has a red, inflamed or bleeding vent they should be brought to a vet for examination. An inflamed vent can be as serious as a reproductive tumor or as minor as an irritation remedied with some ointment. In the case of irritation your vet will probably prescribe Animax cream (Nystatin-Neomycin Sulfate-Thiostrepton-Triamcinolone Acetonide). Just put on some disposable gloves and administer a small amount on your finger and apply to the outside of the vent every 12 hours.

Ailments #7
Neurological Problems

Seizures

Seizures are most commonly caused by genetic defects, poor hatching technique, age or exposure to poisons including plants, fertilizers and pesticides. Do not apply poisons anywhere near areas your geese have even remote access to; in fact, I highly recommend avoiding poisons all together. Poisons have a notorious way of spreading. They can be washed through rainfall, snow melt (ice melting chemicals), made airborne by wind, or treaded by foot into other areas of your property. They can be seriously life threatening to your pets.

If your goose or gosling is experiencing seizures you need to bring them to a vet immediately. Vets will sometimes admit the patient; other times, when conditions are less severe, they will send the goose home and advise you to wait out the seizures.

To keep up your goose's strength, some vets will advise a dose of Karo® syrup (dextrose) immediately after each seizure (6 ml dosage for geese over 3 pounds). Some people have also reported success by adding powdered Brewer's Yeast to their goose's meals until they were well again. Geese can often survive environmentally caused seizures with little or no permanent damage if the source is removed and they are immediately treated by a vet.

Carefully inspect the grounds that your geese frequent for poisonous plants. Toadstools and many flowers are poisonous and are good examples of plants that should be removed. Different areas of the country have different types of foliage. Research the types of toxic plants that are prevalent (or even not-so-prevalent) in your area and be sure to remove them. Before buying or transplanting any foliage into your enclosures, be sure to read up on the species and ensure that it is non-toxic and safe for your geese.

Hardware Disease

One of the number one killers of pet geese are the beautiful and shiny objects they find lying in the grass, glittering in the sunshine. They ingest these tid-bits completely unaware that they may have just sealed their fate. These objects are screws, nuts, bolts, nails, staples, bits of wire, coins, bits of aluminum foil or jewelry… you name it. If it's shiny, they will try to pick it up and eat it. These pieces of metal remain inside their body and are slowly absorbed into their bloodstream. The result is called Hardware Disease. The sad thing is, although there are symptoms, by the time they appear it tends to be too late to help your goose.

Some symptoms include difficulty standing or walking, fatigue, decreased appetite, seizures or watery green, almost fluorescent, droppings. If your goose displays any of these symptoms take them to the vet immediately for an x-ray and blood test to check for traces of metal. I must confess, Hardware Disease is nearly always fatal. We have been contacted by quite a few folks who have lost their geese either during or after the invasive surgery that needs to be performed to try to save their feathered friends. Laparoscopy alternatives are currently being explored by some vets to remove objects from the gizzard. This is much less invasive and can be successful especially if the object is removed soon after ingestion.

Although Hardware Disease is extremely difficult to treat, it is entirely preventable. Avoid wearing jewelry in your goose pen whenever possible and make weekly inspections of your waterfowl enclosures, barns and pools. Search for and remove any small metal objects that can be picked up or pulled out and eaten by your geese.

In addition to visual inspections, whenever possible, we highly recommend that barns, enclosures and outer-lying yards be periodically swept with a metal detector. This is especially vital when any building or maintenance projects are underway or have been completed. Sweep any area your geese have access to as well as any outer-lying property. It is always a good idea to sweep outside of the area your waterfowl have access to because objects may drift within their reach through rain wash, children's hands or being tracked in.

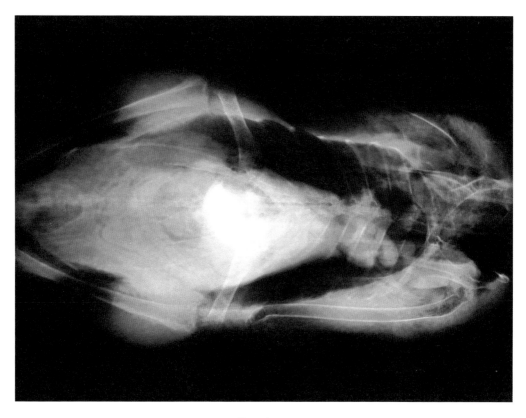

Normal x-ray

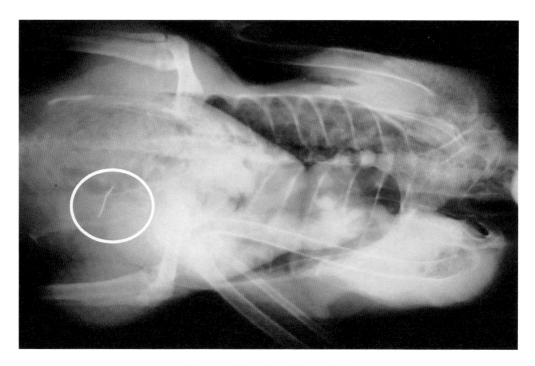

X-ray revealing a piece of ingested wire

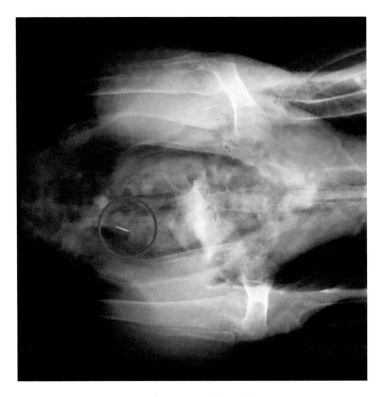

Hardware disease is a common killer of domestic geese

Do not run lawn mowers, weed-wackers, chainsaws, etc. in the vicinity of your geese. I never understand folks who put on all their protective gear, eye goggles and all, and then proceed to work right next to their goose enclosures, while their geese are in it. They fire shrapnel right into the direction of their geese as if feathers are protective gear. In addition to putting your geese at risk of injury, it's also an effective way to shoot unsafe objects into your goose pen. Always point your lawn mowers away from the goose enclosure when doing a pass, so that grass blows outwards and away from your goose enclosure. Geese should be housed safely elsewhere whenever you are mowing near their pen.

Lucy's x-ray reveals that she is perfectly healthy

Vets find the vein for drawing blood in a goose's "armpit"

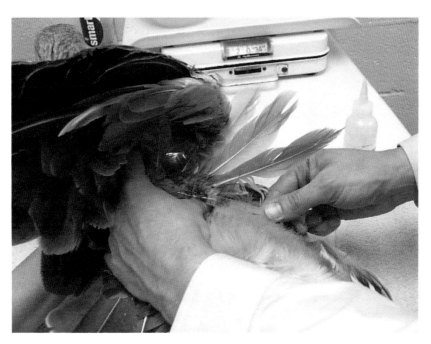

Our vet draws a little blood from Rosie

Ethel's Hardware Disease

Ethel and Lucy are two Toulouse geese who were removed from a home whose grounds were scattered with garbage and debris. When we brought them to the vet for their baseline exams, we knew we should check them both for Hardware Disease to see if they had ingested any bits of metal that had been lying on the ground. Ingested metal can lead to serious medical issues and often result in death—especially if left untreated.

Although Lucy's x-ray came up clear, her sister Ethel was not so fortunate. Her film revealed a piece of wire embedded inside of her intestine. Because of its risky location, our vet advised that surgery to remove the wire should not be attempted *unless* it came down to a life or death situation. We also learned that this kind of surgery should not be performed during the laying season when eggs in the oviduct could interfere with the operation and further complicate things.

Ethel

In order to determine if Ethel was suffering from any metal toxicity as a result of the wire, our vet drew some blood and sent it off to the lab for testing. Results from the blood work revealed that her levels of zinc were abnormally high. While treating her with Ca-EDTA injections for zinc poisoning, we patiently waited and hoped that the wire was newly ingested and might pass all on its own.

Follow up x-rays confirmed that the wire had not moved along her intestine and upon closer examination they revealed that her body had encapsulated the wire. This ended up being helpful because it prevented any more metal from leaching into her system. The ball of tissue surrounding the wire shielded it away from the rest of her body, which meant that once her initial high zinc levels were alleviated, she had no further related problems.

Ethel's follow-up care included periodic blood tests and x-rays to confirm there were no new changes and she went on to live a normal and happy life.

Lead Poisoning

Lead paint chips and lead shot from guns are not the only sources of lead poisoning. Because so many domestic geese are abandoned to public ponds, they are in real risk of ingesting fishing gear, such as lead sinkers and lures. When lead is ingested, it gets into the gizzard and begins to erode. As it erodes, lead enters the bloodstream and stores in a goose's body.

- **Test your water**

Have your pond and any water sources your geese will frequent tested for lead toxicity prior to building your pen around them or allowing your geese access to them. If lead levels are high, you can often consult with the testing company or a local university about remedying the problem.

- **Test Your Soil**

Have the soil of your pen site tested. If lead levels are high, you will not want to build your goose pen there. It is wise to test your soil before building your waterfowl enclosure to avoid any issues down the road.

- **Symptoms**

A goose suffering from lead poisoning (confirmed by a blood test) may exhibit seizures, weakness, weight loss, drooping wings and bright green diarrhea. It can also lead to reproductive problems and increased susceptibility to disease or infection.

- **Treatment**

We have heard from a few people who have lost their pets to lead poisoning despite veterinarian intervention. Even when it is discovered in very early stages, it can be difficult to remedy. Lead needs to be removed from the system with the aid of forced vomiting (emesis), laxatives and/or injections. If not discovered in the very early stages, euthanizing is most likely the course of action your vet will recommend to avoid any further suffering of the animal.

Surgery may need to be performed if the discernable, lead object is inside the goose, although this tends to be very invasive and equally risky for the goose. Most vets will suggest euthanization as the appropriate course of action. New endoscopic surgeries; however, are proving effective if you can find an experienced vet.

- **Prescription**

Edetate Calcium Disodium (Calcium EDTA or CaEDTA) is a heavy metal chelating agent. It is injected into the animal or given as an IV treatment. So as not to encumber you with complex chemistry, suffice it to say that it will go into your goose's body and bind with heavy metals. The agent then leaves the body through the urinary tract, taking some of the heavy metals along with it.

Side effects include diarrhea and vomiting. Since it also removes other minerals from the body, excess loss of calcium (hypocalcemia) can result.

Calcium levels should be closely monitored—especially in laying geese, who rely heavily on calcium to produce their eggs. Calcium sources (such as oyster shells or calcium chips) should be removed during treatment and for a couple hours afterwards, and then reintroduced again.

Zinc Poisoning

Zinc poisoning is different from lead poisoning in that zinc is able to work its way out of your bird's system, provided the source of contamination is successfully and completely removed. Zinc poisoning is entirely preventable if you understand its causes. In addition to keeping foreign objects out of your pens (zinc plated nuts, bolts, etc.) there are other things to consider.

- **Galvanized wire**

Zinc is used in the process of making galvanized wire fencing. You can use non-coated galvanized wire for applications entirely above ground where it will not be in contact with any water sources. This will prevent the zinc from leaching into the water or soil where it can be digested by your geese. For those applications that will be underground or near water you will want to go with a PVC / vinyl coated wire.

- **Avoid metal feed & water dishes**

Zinc can be found in the coating of metal food and water pet dishes. Avoid metal food dishes at all costs. Always use plastic or rubber dishes to feed your pets.

- **Test your water**

As with lead, you can have your pond tested for zinc toxicity to ensure the safety of your geese. This needs to be specifically requested since zinc levels are not normally tested by all companies offering water testing services.

- **Test Your Soil**

Have the soil of your pen site tested. Remnants of paint or chemicals poured into the soil can cause zinc toxicity. Fertilizers are also high in zinc.

- **Grain mixture mistakes**

A bag of feed mixed improperly can also lead to high zinc levels. If an x-ray confirms no metal was swallowed (Hardware Disease) and you cannot determine the cause of zinc poisoning among your gaggle, you will want to examine their grain.

Although uncommon with name brands, grain companies do make mixture mistakes. The zinc levels could be too high in a batch of food. Your best bet is to stop feeding them from the bag on hand and purchase a new bag. Be sure to compare lot numbers on your current feed bag and purchase a new bag from a different batch. Contact the manufacturer if you need help finding this information on their packaging. You may wish to actually have a sample of the feed tested at a local university for confirmation. If it comes up positive, follow up with the manufacturer. Be prepared to fax / email them the label from the bag, information stamped on the bag and the lab's test results.

- **Symptoms**

Symptoms are lethargy, loss of appetite and seizures. Unfortunately, once they appear the condition tends to be too far gone to treat. This makes *prevention* your best defense. Test your water and soil before building waterfowl enclosures to avoid future mishaps.

- **Treatment**

In addition to isolating and eliminating the cause of the zinc poisoning, you will need to treat your effected flock members. Medication and follow-up blood tests will need to be performed once treatment begins to verify that zinc levels are being reduced effectively.

- **Prescription**

If your goose's zinc levels are high enough to warrant intervention, as with lead poisoning, a chelating agent is commonly prescribed to bring their levels back under control. Injections of C-VT Calcium EDTA solution is the most common and effective treatment.

Vets will commonly prescribe 200 mg/ml of C-VT Calcium EDTA solution. They inject 1.0 ml intramuscularly twice daily for five days. After this, they stop the treatment for four days. On the fifth day, they begin the treatment again for another five days. After two weeks they retest your goose's zinc levels by drawing more blood.

A less effective treatment is D-Penicillamine (or Cuprimine). It is dosed orally and also helps draw zinc out of the body. The trouble with this drug is it can be near impossible to get your hands on. You have to go to a human pharmacy to get it and most pharmacies don't stock it and will not special order it due to the low demand and high cost.

If neither of these treatments are readily available where you are, your vet may instruct you to purchase over-the-counter DMSA (dimercaptosuccinic acid). Our vet prescribed a dose of 25-35 mgs daily for every 2.2 pounds of goose weight. This means a 15 pound goose with high zinc levels would do best on a dose of 245 mgs daily, while a goose with lower zinc levels might do better on a dose of 175 mgs daily. This is also a good option to get your goose started while you wait for a special order of C-VT Calcium EDTA to come in.

All of these treatment options draw calcium from the body, so again, calcium levels in laying geese should be monitored closely. Calcium sources should be removed at dosing times and then re-introduced a couple of hours afterward.

In cases where zinc toxicity is low and the source has been removed, vets may attempt to increase your goose's urine flow with a crystalloid solution to flush the zinc out.

Ailments #8
Respiratory Problems

Heat Stroke

For those regions of the country that experience temperatures over 90 degrees, remember to provide your geese with access to plenty of shade for everyone and cold water for drinking and bathing. Kiddy pools get hot quickly in summer and need to be changed out frequently to help your gaggle beat the heat.

Toulouse geese in particular seem to have the most difficulty in hot weather and tend to be the first to start panting. Geese can't perspire, so panting is a means for them to cool off. Feathers are designed to help them cool off in summer and keep warm in winter, but sometimes the heat is just too much for them. If you see your goose panting, make sure their water source is cold enough.

Excessive panting can be a sign of the onset of heat stroke. If your goose overheats bring them into a cool barn or basement and apply ice packs beneath their wings for 60 seconds and then remove them again. Continue to place on-and-off as needed every few minutes without leaving them in place for too long or else risk frostbite.

Aspergillus

Aspergillus is a group of molds. If breathed in, a few of these molds can be a health risk to both you and your geese. Immunity deficient people, the elderly and children are most susceptible to the fungus *Aspergillus fumigatus* a.k.a. "farmer's lung."

It is not uncommon to turn over wet hay and discovery a bluish-white mold growing underneath, especially in humid seasons. Clear your geese out of the area, ensure proper ventilation if you're indoors and then thoroughly clean the location. Disposable face masks (painter's mask) are commonly viewed ineffective against the tiny mold spores, but they certainly can't hurt. Be more careful going forward to ensure wet hay is removed promptly and bedding is kept dry.

Avoid using mulch or wood chips in your pens because as these items naturally decay, they can lead to the growth of Aspergillus fungus right in your goose pen.

If you discover this Aspergillus mold growing in your goose's food source, immediately discard all of the food, thoroughly clean, safely disinfect and thoroughly dry contaminated containers.

Symptoms of Aspergillus may not be readily apparent in your effected goose until the fungus has actively invaded their air sacs. Respiratory issues, lethargy and fever are some common symptoms.

If your goose succumbs to this ailment, anti-fungal prescriptions will need to be administered. Vets will usually prescribe itraconazole (100 mg twice a day for 14 days for an adult goose) because it has the least side effects, including NOT interfering with feather growth. Anti-fungals are very potent and can make your goose very ill and can even cause death if the doses are too high. Frequent vet visits and follow up x-rays will be needed to closely monitor the healing of your goose's air sacs. Close attention to your goose's blood chemistry is also necessary to prevent liver damage. Blood is commonly drawn every two weeks to monitor levels and make comparisons.

Pneumonia

The onset of heavy or difficult breathing or wheezing should be taken extremely seriously. Call your vet immediately. Upper respiratory infections and pneumonia require antibiotic intervention. Vets may actually inject Baytril® into your goose along with prescribing pills for the next 7-14 days.

An x-ray will commonly be performed to see what's going on in your goose's lungs. If the film reveals your goose has pneumonia, antibiotics will be prescribed. It will be vital to keep your goose warm and dry. During colder seasons especially, you do not want your goose expending vital energy keeping warm; you want all of their energy focused on healing. It may be necessary to bring your goose into your home and allow them time to heal in a warm and controlled environment where you can monitor them. Swims in a warm tub can also be instituted to raise your goose's body temperature if they are cold.

Goslings especially tend to have hot legs and a hot bill when they have pneumonia. Fever can also keep them panting. Sometimes, in extreme cases, you will feel heat emanating from their skin beneath their body feathers. It is vital that you take them to the vet right away.

Vets will commonly prescribe Amoxi Drops® (a common antibiotic for birds under 4 pounds) to goslings and Baytril® to birds over the 4 lb marker (discuss the risks of using Baytril® in younger birds with your vet).

The tricky thing about medicating goslings is their rapid growth rate. You will need to weigh your gosling *every day* and your vet will need to give you a dosing chart that tells you how much medicine to administer as your hatchling grows.

Fever is the body's means of fighting infection. Cool baths should be used with discretion. Always ask your vet for advice. It is *vital* to keep your gosling eating and drinking. Swimming activities are often a means to this end. Goslings that won't eat or drink will often do so in a tub filled with an inch or two of water. Just sprinkle their food in the water while they're swimming.

Golly gander's drooped wings are a clear indicator that he's not feeling well

Air Sac Injury

Your goose does not have lungs, but rather multiple air sacs in their body that help them disperse oxygen into their bloodstream. An injured or ruptured air sac will often change the buoyancy of your goose, so if you see them floating rather crooked and unbalanced in the water, it would be a good idea to bring them to the vet for an x-ray. If your vet discovers a punctured air sac there is not much to be done but prescribe antibiotics to prevent any infection. 90% of all air sac injuries in adult geese tend to remedy themselves on their own (provided antibiotics are prescribed). Sometimes they return back to normal other times they may remain collapsed. As long as your goose is breathing without difficulty however, there is usually no need for further intervention.

About 10% of air sac injuries require more invasive intervention. Younger birds usually have more trouble recovering than mature birds. In these more difficult cases an open catheter is usually inserted and sutchered into place to assist in your goose's recovery.

Chronic Respiratory Disease

CRD is a respiratory infection that tends to invade geese weakened by environmental stressors, which can include a car trip to the vet, a sudden change in diet or the loss of a flock mate. Basically, it is a goose's version of a cold, and it is treated with antibiotics.

Geese that are having difficulty breathing, are exhibiting lethargy, fluffed feathers, appetite loss and a "runny nose" may have CRD. You will need to get them to your vet for an examination and antibiotics. Baytril® is commonly prescribed.

Golly's Aspergillus

Golly was rescued from a feed store where he and his mate were crammed into tiny cages, each to be sold separately and not as pets. Unfortunately, Golly's mate was sold and he was left behind. Two weeks later we found and removed Golly to prevent him from sharing the fate of his companion.

When he first arrived one of his wings always drooped lower than the other and he seemed to have a little more difficulty breathing in hotter weather. When the heat of summer hit, Golly always panted more than our other geese, but in all other regards, our vet confirmed he was a perfectly healthy gander.

We went into the barn one night and found Golly panting excessively. His tail was pumping and a clear liquid was coming out of his nostrils. We immediately rushed him to an emergency vet for an after-hours examination. The vet listened to his heart and lungs, did an overall health exam and then followed this with an x-ray to see what was going on inside. The x-ray showed Golly had some fluid in his lungs and the vet suspected pneumonia and gave him an injection of Baytril® to rapidly flood his system with antibiotics and then sent us home with a prescription.

We kept Golly in an environmentally controlled infirmary to keep him out of excess heat and humidity. The next morning we brought Golly to our regular vet. Our vet looked over Golly's x-rays, did a medical exam of his own and performed an ultrasound. Strongly suspecting aspergillus, he drew blood and sent it off to the lab. In the meantime, we started Golly on aspergillus (anti-fungal) medication.

Golly was prescribed itraconazole, which is a very potent medication. Unfortunately for Golly there is no database of blood work for domestic geese. This made it impossible to compare Golly's blood chemistry to any kind of norm. Although frequent follow-up visits and x-rays were done, the itraconazole caused liver damage and ultimately we lost Golly.

One thing we never do at Majestic is give up on any duck or goose. Even though we lost Golly we began the *"Golly Project,"* and began compiling a database of blood work for domestic ducks and geese, which will eventually be made available to veterinarians everywhere.

One great gift you can give your pet goose is to have their blood work done while they are healthy, so if anything happens later, your vet has a basis of comparison. Remember to keep your own copy of your goose's blood work, so YOU have it on hand whenever you and your goose may need it.

Golly

Cardiomyopathy

It is important to know that there seems to be a wide variance in heart rates of geese. We still don't understand why so many geese have more regular heart rates while others have more rapid rates. Because this is such an unknown, be sure to have your vet give your goose's heart a good listen when they go in for their check up to find out where your goose falls. Try not to get too upset if your vet mentions that your pet's heart rate is a little on the quick side because this is not at all uncommon. What you want to know is if your goose's heart rate is slow or if there is a murmur.

We once had a rescued gander named Lewy who was diagnosed with cardiomyopathy (deterioration of the heart muscle) and a faulty valve. It was originally discovered when our vet listened to his heart and heard a slight murmur. Further testing, including an ECG, atropine response test and an ultrasound, by his adoptive family provided the actual diagnosis. Because Lewy's heart is not as effective as it should be in pumping his blood he needed medicine to help him.

Lewy the gander has cardiomyopathy

Lewy's doctors prescribed Pimobendan capsules to be taken twice daily and his new family reported that it rapidly and significantly improved his level of activity.

Another treatment option you can discuss with your vet are Taurine and Carnitine supplements. They can be given to an adult goose in the dose of 500 mg per day to help improve their situation.

Whistling

Some geese are whistlers; that is, when they breathe you can hear a bit of a whistle through their bill holes with every breath. When this endearing little quality is ever-present, it tends to be just a harmless trait. Sudden whistling, however, can be an early indicator of a respiratory issue, so pay close attention.

Remember, it is always advisable to seek out vet assistance at the onset of any symptoms since geese are masters at masking their illnesses. By the time symptoms appear, ailments tend to already be well on their way. A safe antibiotic treatment of Baytril® for a few days will often address any hidden infections.

Ailments #9
Feather problems

Understanding Feathers

Your goose's feathers are one their greatest assets. Feathers provide insulation and protection from the environment. When preened and oiled properly, they maintain waterproof effectiveness and they make it possible for your goose to float. When they are not working properly, your goose is not as protected as they should be from the weather and the elements and they may not be able to swim or float properly. Some geese have even been known to drown while trapped on water because of poor feather quality.

Generally speaking, your goose has body feathers and "flight" feathers, but for the sake of clarity, we refer to them as "wing" feathers (since domestic geese are non-flying).

Your goose's bill is equipped with a make-shift comb that they use to preen and comb their feathers into place. Feather components are held together by tiny interconnecting hooks and barbs. Your goose zip locks these hooks and barbs together, which seals the feather and helps make it waterproof.

Oil Gland

The oil gland is located just above the tail of your goose. You will frequently see your goose tucking their head and bill there while preening to gather the oil that they will then spread over their feathers using the combs inside their bill. On a white goose the base of the feathers growing over the oil gland can vary in color from white to dark yellow.

- **Overactive oil gland**

Overactive oil glands are not all that common in geese. The only risk of having an overactive oil gland is the increased risk of it becoming clogged, but aside from that, it really shouldn't impede your goose at all.

The way to inspire a goose with an overactive oil gland to pay more attention during preening is to add a potential mate to their pen—not to mention the happiness it can inspire! More frequent preening both improves feather condition and helps remove the build-up of excess oil around the gland.

- **Inactive or blocked oil gland**

Occasionally the oil gland can become blocked and will stop producing some or all of its oil. If you notice a decline in the appearance of your goose's feathers, and have ruled out molting and parasites, you want to verify that their oil gland is not blocked. Part the feathers over their oil gland and check for obvious swelling that indicates an impacted oil gland. If you don't see this, use your fingers to gently feel along the base of the feathers growing from the gland. Move your fingers from the base of the feathers upward (moving in the direction of feather growth). Now look at your fingers and rub them together. If you see or feel ample oil on your fingertips, your goose's oil gland is working fine. If it is difficult for you to collect a decent amount, their oil gland may not be functioning properly or may even be blocked.

When an oil gland becomes blocked, you can try these remedies:

1) Oil glands can become blocked because of infection. Your vet will likely prescribe a round of Baytril® 68 mg, once a day for 7-14 days. If this does not jump start your goose's oil gland your vet will can usually try to collect a small sample of oil and make a slide to check for the presence of bacteria.

2) It is important to evaluate your goose's diet. An improper diet is a common cause of a malfunctioning oil gland. Is your goose on brand named food? What kind of snacks are you giving them? Can their diet be improved upon? These are the questions you want to ask yourself and act upon if needed.

3) Vitamin A deficiency can be another cause of a blocked oil gland. Under the consultation of a vet, a vitamin supplement may be added to your goose's diet. Gimborn Vionate® Vitamin Mineral Powder for Pets is a very good supplement if used according to the label and it is available for purchase on the internet. You can add it directly to your goose's food, but again, only under a vet's direct advice. Your vet will need to review the Vionate label as well as the nutritional label from their waterfowl feed, so bring both along with you for your consultation. Vitamin A overdoses can cause liver damage, so prescribing proper vitamin dosages is *vital*.

4) Hot packs (not too hot!) can be used to provide moist heat therapy directly to the oil gland. Warm, gentle massages to the gland 2-3 times a day can also be effective in getting it working again.

5) Stress can also be the cause of a failing oil duct. If one of your geese is being picked on by another flock member or if they have recently experienced some kind of stress, they may need a quiet reprieve. If you think this may be part of the problem, try giving them their own separate accommodations, where they are still in sight of the others, for some downtime.

6) The implementation of wheat into your goose's diet can also help their oil gland to recover and produce more oil. Some vets also advise adding a little bit of fish oil to your goose's diet. Be careful, you don't want to add too much oil. If the oil gets in the comb of their bill and they preen, you will just make matters worse. Another option is to feed them a small, round cat kibble with fish oil in it.

Jetti preens using her oil gland

- **Impacted oil gland**

An impacted oil gland is usually clearly visible by the time you notice a difference in feather quality. If you part your goose's feathers and see that the gland is very swollen, you are probably witnessing an impacted oil gland. The same therapies used for inactive or blocked oil glands may be attempted. Some vets may suggest lancing the gland to empty it out, but if the source of the problem is not resolved, the gland will likely just refill.

If your goose does not respond to any treatment options, surgical removal of the gland is a ***last resort***. Your goose's ability to waterproof will be directly affected, so consider this carefully when discussing this option with your vet, and it would be highly advisable to seek out a second opinion.

- **Ruptured oil gland**

Ruptured glands must be surgically removed immediately and your goose will require antibiotics. A drain may need to be inserted for a few days. Following surgery, your goose will no longer repel water the way they did prior to the operation.

Wet Feather

When a goose's feathers are no longer able to properly repel water, the condition is referred to as *wet feather*. Sometimes wet feather can be repaired, other times it is in a chronic stage and only a full molt will repair the situation. Even in a chronic situation, it is often possible to at least improve their feather situation and aid in their waterproof effectiveness until the next molt.

- **Poor feather quality**

If your goose's feathers appear tattered and are not properly "zip locked" together, they will not likely be waterproof. The first part of treatment is to determine the cause of this condition.

  o **Parasites**

  The first possible reason a goose's feathers are in poor shape may be that your goose has lice or mites. Have a vet examine your goose to see if there are parasites present. Treatment may be as simple as a powder treatment. However, if the parasite problem has been long-lived, your goose's feathers may be damaged and they may not recover from wet feather until the parasites are removed and the next molt arrives.

  o **Bath water shortage**

  The second possible reason a goose's feathers are in poor shape may be that you are not providing enough fresh water for your goose to bathe itself. If your goose doesn't have the opportunity to keep clean and oil up, its feathers will lose their ability to repel water. Provided the condition has not gone on for so long as to cause feather damage, the re-introduction of water should lead your goose on the road to recovery.

  o **Malnutrition**

  The third possible reason a goose's feathers are in poor shape may be malnutrition. A healthy diet is your main defense against this problem. This explains why you are more apt to see wet feather in geese who have been dropped off and abandoned on ponds and who are being fed bread as a main staple. They aren't getting the vitamins and minerals they need to keep themselves and their feathers healthy. Once a proper diet is restored, feathers will improve, although full waterproofing may not be accomplished until their next molt.

  o **Illness**

  The fourth possible reason a goose's feathers are in poor shape may be illness. A sick goose can get dirty and fall behind, so to speak, on the preening and oiling of its feathers while not feeling up to par. Once health is restored, the goose's feathers should return to their clean and natural state. During times of illness, it will really help your goose if you carry them to the tub and let them float for a bit and then allow them time to dry on a soft bed of towels.

o **Failing oil duct**

A failing oil duct can definitely lead to poor feather quality. Refer to information in prior sections for treatment options. Once your goose's oil gland issue is remedied their feather quality should improve.

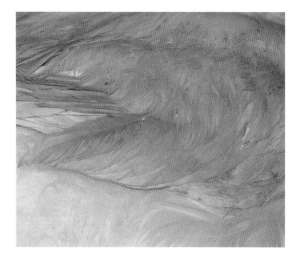

Some geese come to us with feathers in horrendous condition

<u>Wet Feather Corrective Procedure</u>

The following procedure should *not* be followed until you first try to give the goose the opportunity to remedy the problem on their own. Keep your goose in very clean conditions and allow them access to a clean water bath every day or two and see if the situation improves. It is always advisable to visit your vet before administering treatment.

1. **Wash the goose with Dawn® dish soap (plain formula)**

Place your goose into a lukewarm bath, soap them up with regular Dawn® dish soap, and gently wash them all over. Do not scrub their feathers, but gently work the soap through the feathers, *always working in the direction of their feather—**never** against.*

2. **Rinse the goose thoroughly**

After bathing commence with a thorough rinsing. You will need a flexible shower head that you can bring down to the goose's level to do this. You want to get *all* of the soap out of the goose's feathers.

3. **Dry the goose**

Now comes the somewhat tedious part of blow drying. It will take a LONG time to dry and fluff up your goose's feathers, but you don't want them to catch a chill on cold days or get their feathers dirty again, so it is necessary. Remember to keep the blow dryer far enough away from your goose and don't keep it blowing on one spot for too long, or you will burn them. Your goose will most likely actively help out with the preening as they begin to dry off.

What you've just done is removed all of the oil from your goose's feathers. This means they can no longer repel water. This gives them a starting place to begin preening. Your goose no longer needs to struggle to get on top of the cleaning of their feathers; you have just done this for them. Now your goose can focus their energy on re-oiling their feathers, which is a slow but steady process.

4. Keep the goose dry and very clean for two days

After the bath, keep your goose in a very clean and dry place for a day or two. They should have access to a *small* bucket of water—just large enough so that they can keep clean by splashing and oiling and preening, but not so large that they can swim or immerse themselves in the water.

5. On the third day, give the goose access to clean bathing water

On the third day *do* allow your goose to immerse themselves in a clean pond or preferably a tub (without soap) and let them swim for about 10-15 minutes. After that, place your wet goose back into a dry, clean pen to preen and oil (or blow dry first if necessary). Continue to do this every day or two for a week or so until you begin to see an improvement in their feathers.

6. Be patient

It is important to remember not to worry if you do not see an immediate improvement. It can take a week or two before you begin to see results. Improvement may only be very slight at first, if noticeable at all, but it can slowly improve over weeks to come. You may not be able to determine right away whether or not this soaping did the job.

Do *not* repeat this procedure. If it's going to work, it will work with one soaping. This procedure requires time, cleanliness, patience and devotion in order to have any chance of effectiveness.

This procedure does not restore actual feather quality, nor does it work in every case. If your goose's feathers are damaged, full waterproof improvement will hinge upon their next molt.

Ms. Donald's Plucked Feathers

Ms. Donald was only a week old when she was removed from a cage containing at least sixty other goslings. They were actually standing on one another's backs they were so overcrowded. Without enough water for everyone or enough space, Ms. Donald's future was bleak.

Ms. Donald then

When we removed her from the trampling situation most of the fuzz from her back and crown had been plucked out by the other birds. We brought Ms. Donald home and set her in the sink for a gentle, warm water bath (no soap) to remove any saliva left on her skin from the other bird's bills since it can be an irritant. Once she was clean we wrapped her in a fluffy towel to keep her warm and then put a small amount of soothing, no-sting Neosporin ointment on her pink and broken skin.

The main thing in getting Ms. Donald healthy was getting her clean and then keeping her out of the sun to avoid the risk of sun burn. We also needed to ensure that the other geese and goslings didn't peck at her and cause any further damage. This meant when she wasn't in her own private area, she needed constant supervision.

Ms. Donald soon began to sprout new fluff, which later was replaced by her adult feathers. She went on to become a beautiful lady much adored by all of the ganders.

Ms. Donald now

117

Angel Wing

Angel wing is a condition where the muscle in the wing tip flips the wrong way during development, and as a result, a few of the primary wing feathers do not fold up and tuck in the way their other wing feathers do. Angel wing is harmless in non-flying geese. It can be corrected in goslings when you first begin to notice one or both of their wings initially drooping and then turning outwards. It can be caused by genetic predisposition or too much protein in their diet. If you begin to see this in your gosling, your vet can give corrective dietary advice and teach you how to bandage the wings correctly in place with non-adhesive gauze. Do *not* cut feathers as a means to correct angel wing. If you adopt a goose that has angel wing in one or both wings, it won't bother them at all and you don't need to intervene in any way. It is merely aesthetics.

Angelo "The Airplane" has Angel Wing on both sides

Wry Tail

Lewy and Grampa show off their crooked wry tails

118

Some geese hatch out with crooked tails. While this can be the result of a mother goose not rolling her eggs properly during incubation, it is more often a genetic tendency that is caused by two inherited recessive genes. This condition is known as wry tail and it is completely harmless to the goose.

Molting

The first time you see one of your geese molt, it can be quite alarming. Rest assured, you will soon see new pin feathers pushing through, and their new plumage will be restored within 2-3 weeks.

Baby Skynyrd's new feathers protect him from the rain

- **Why do geese molt**?

Feathers become damaged and wear out. It is vital that your goose grows new replacement feathers to keep them insulated and protected from the environment.

- **When do geese molt?**

We get a lot of questions regarding molting. The most common question is, *"When do geese molt?"* In our experience, in our Connecticut climate, most of our geese and ganders molt their wing feathers in June and fully sprout new ones by July, but there are exceptions.

Our sanctuary looks like a big pillow exploded when our gaggle molts. You may see feathers everywhere, but your goose will still appear fully feathered; in other words, you should not see any bald spots or thin areas. Molting is also symmetrical, which means that their feathers drop out equally on the left and right sides of their body.

Keep in mind that many geese live by their own schedules. Some geese don't molt "on time," some geese molt early and others late. Some geese molt a lot—feathers everywhere, while others drop fewer feathers. When and how heavily your geese molt may depend on their breed, biology, genetics, your regional climate, lighting and their diet.

If your goose has healthy, waterproof feathers do not worry at all about molting. Just let nature take its course. If you are feeding anything other than Mazuri® Waterfowl Maintenance, some people recommend mixing a non-medicated *flying game feed* (which you can ask for at your local grain store) into their food during the dropping and re-growing of feathers, but this is not necessary.

- **A goose who has not molted**

If your goose is not molting and their feathers are in good condition, our vet has advised us not to worry, provided the bird is on a proper diet.

If your goose is not molting and their feathers are in poor condition, the problem is most commonly a nutritional issue. Evaluate your waterfowl's diet. Are you feeding your feathered friend unhealthy food; that is, food not designed for waterfowl? Nutritional deficits are the most common cause of feather problems, so if you answered, *"yes,"* this is most likely the source of the issue.

We have always noticed that new geese coming into our sanctuary often molt their wing feathers within two weeks of their arrival. This is because they go from starving on ponds (or, in many cases, trying to sustain themselves on bread) to coming into our care and being immediately placed on a highly nutritious diet of Mazuri® waterfowl feed. Their bodies quickly respond to the sudden influx of vitamins and minerals and they drop their old wing feathers (at a minimum) and re-grow new plumage. Starving geese tend to molt when they are suddenly placed on a nutritious diet.

If you read the directions for a forced-molt, you will find that it is a not-so-cleverly disguised starvation tactic. They advise you to put your goose through a fast and then slowly offer them small portions of oats and water over the course of the next month or so. What this does is puts your pet in a state of malnutrition and once this has gone on for a month; they tell you to follow this up with a sudden influx of grower ration. This results in a molt.

Forced-molt instructions follow a frighteningly similar pattern with abandoned domestic waterfowl that suffer malnutrition and starvation. Our vet does not recommend any forced-molt tactics for your feathered friends, and we are in agreement. They are unhealthy for the bird and should not be attempted.

- **Things to consider during the molt**

It is important to keep a few things in mind during the molting season. First, your goose's skin can become very sensitive during this time. Geese who normally like a good stroke on the feathers, don't want to endure a painful petting when they are feeling so tender, so don't feel bad when they shy away for a few weeks. In addition, petting or over-handling a molting goose can result in the formation of follicular cysts (inward growing feather follicles) and should be avoided.

Second, even though none of our geese are flyers, they all flap their wings to hop in and out of their ponds. Because they don't have their primary feathers, a molting goose can find themselves without the flap power needed to give them that extra *umph* to help themselves out of a pond. Be sure your geese can get out of their swimming holes and pools during the molting season.

At no time should bald spots ever appear on your goose—not even during a molt. Missing feathers on the back of the neck of female goose indicate over-mating issues. Featherless areas anywhere else on your goose should result in a trip to the vet for an exam.

Feathers and Sunshine

Be wary of the breeder or author who advises you to keep your geese out of the sun to avoid the changing or fading out of the colors of their feathers. Don't deny your geese the sunshine for the sake of their plumage. Your geese are better off happy and healthy, and that includes a good dose of sunshine. Bill coloration can also change or fade with sun exposure.

Gray Feathers

Some people (especially breeders) will advise you to pluck out feathers that are unsightly—heaven forbid! You may see random white feathers appear on your gray Toulouse or Pilgrim geese as they get on in years, but let them age with dignity and grace and avoid pulling out any feathers.

Wilma sporting her white facial feathers

Wing Clipping

Most domestic geese originate from wild Greylag Geese except for Chinese geese who originate from wild Swan Geese. Domestic geese have been breed to have heavier bodies that do not support flight. While domestic geese cannot fly up into the sky and migrate, they can get lift off of the ground.

Daisy glides over the water before her rescue

If you need to clip wings to keep your goose from gliding out of safe areas and into trouble, it is vital that you learn to do it from a professional. Have your goose-qualified vet, or a qualified local waterfowl breeder teach you how to do this. Never clip your goose's wings during times of molt. Feathers with pink centers are still growing and are referred to as blood feathers. They have an artery and a vein inside. If you cut them, your goose can bleed profusely, so it is very important that you learn to clip wings at the right time and from someone who knows exactly what they're doing.

You will find that wing clipping is more easily done with two people. One person holds the goose with one wing extended. The second person uses blunt tipped scissors (bandage cutting scissors work very well for this) to cut the appropriate primary wing feathers.

Domestic goose wings rarely need clipping because they normally can't get more than 5-6 feet off of the ground. If this is higher than your fence, you may need to do some wing clipping. Wing clipping usually only needs to be done once on a flighty goose and it's usually upon the original introduction of the goose into their new home. Once they bond with their new family, geese will rarely attempt to leave (especially if well cared for), so their wing feathers can usually be allowed to grow back during the next molt. If you have reservations that the bird will stay close with the gaggle, wing clipping should be repeated annually to keep your goose safely home.

Plucking a Broken Blood Feather

The base of the feather, where there are no side branches, is called the *quill*. When the feather is alive the quill has a vein in it that carries nutrients to the growing feather. At this stage of its growth it is called a *blood feather*. When growth is complete, the quill becomes hollow.

A broken blood feather can be deadly. If a blood feather breaks for any reason it will need to be plucked out. The ENTIRE feather shaft must be removed for the bleeding to stop. This won't necessarily be an easy task, nor will your goose appreciate it, but it will need to be done.

1. **Get your emergency medical kit and a helper**

If you can, it is preferable to get a helper to hold the goose during this procedure. You will need a pair of needle nose pliers to do the plucking, a dish towel to cover the goose's head and possibly a blood coagulant, cotton swab, and gauze pads, so have them ready just in case.

2. **Cover the goose's head with the towel**

Place a dish towel over the goose's head to block their vision and keep them calm.

3. **Mental preparation**

Give the goose and yourself a moment to relax. Read through your instructions a couple of times. This is a mental task, not a physical one. You will not want to discomfort your pet goose, but I promise you, they will be fine and so will you. The procedure is quick and the results are instant.

4. **Locate the broken feather(s)**

Body feathers are smaller in size and easier to pluck out than wing feathers. In the case of a broken body feather, just put the fingers of your non-dominant hand on either side of the broken feather and press slightly down against the skin and then skip forward to STEP 5.

If your goose has a broken wing feather, the person holding them will need to extend the goose's wing for the person who will be plucking the feather. The person doing the plucking needs to carefully examine the wing in good lighting to locate the troubled feather and the exact spot it enters the skin. This is the place where you will want to grip the feather with your needle nose pliers—at the base of the feather, and as close to the skin as possible—but not yet. Just find it visually first. Some resources will advise the person plucking the feather to feel around and find the base of the feather, which is a bump under the skin, but in our experience some regions of the wing have feathers too thickly layered to accurately find this bump, so if you can't find it, don't worry.

The person plucking the feather will need to hold the extended wing with their non-dominant hand. In other words, hold the wing gently but firmly in place with one hand, pluck the feather with the other (dominant) hand. This way, when plucking the feather, you don't yank the whole wing.

Estimate where the hidden base / root of the feather is located under the skin (about an inch back from the plucking point). Hold the wing firmly just *behind* this area. Remember to hold the wing with a secure grip, but not so tight as to hurt the goose.

5.   Pull & guide the feather out

Pliers need to grip the feather as close to the base as possible, as close to the skin as possible. Keep calm, take a deep breath and give it one firm, smooth pull, being sure to pull the feather STRAIGHT OUT of its hole, in the direction of feather growth. Do not hesitate or you will only hurt the goose. Make a decisive pull. Pull with your dominant hand; grip the wing with your non-dominant hand. It's only a feather, so a strong, clean pull will take it out without a fuss. Your goose may give a little honk, but that's about all. If for some reason the feather does not come completely out, you will need to bring your goose to the vet for immediate assistance.

6.   Apply blood coagulant with a cotton swab

Once the feather is out, the bleeding will normally stop *instantly*. If not, you can use a small amount of blood coagulant applied with a cotton swab to stop the bleeding. Apply a sterile gauze pad over the wound and apply mild pressure for one minute. If bleeding does not stop, add another layer of gauze over the first and continue to apply pressure and head for your vet's office right away.

The alternative to pulling the feather out yourself, is to put blood coagulant right on the feather break to temporarily stop or at least control the bleeding while rush your goose to the vet to have *them* pull out the feather.

Most geese will never run into this problem, but it's a good idea to familiarize yourself with this procedure should it happen. Next time you are visiting your waterfowl vet, ask them for a demonstration, so you will be properly prepared for an emergency.

A broken blood feather seconds after pulling

Ailments #10
Fever

A goose's bill often gets noticeably hot when they have a fever, especially a high one. A fever is a clear indicator that something is wrong with your goose. Some causes of fever are: infections, inflammations (often related to the reproductive organs in female geese), tumors (cancerous or benign), abscesses or parasites.

Whenever your goose is exhibiting a fever, they should be brought to your vet for an immediate examination. In addition to a physical exam, your vet will ask you questions that will help determine the cause of the fever. Be sure to mention any recent behavioral changes you have noticed in your goose, including those relating to egg-laying and appetite. If any other flock members are exhibiting uncharacteristic traits, be sure to mention these as well.

Baytril® is often prescribed to immediately address the fever and any infection that might be the source of the problem. An untreated fever can lead to weight loss, lethargy and dehydration. Failure to seek treatment also allows the underlying issue causing the fever to continue un-prevented on its course—which can be fatal.

You will want to ask your vet if your goose needs to be quarantined from other flock members and the duration of any such quarantine periods. If your goose's ailment is contagious and you are approaching a weekend, you will be wise to ask your vet for extra Baytril® tablets. This way, if any other flock members exhibit symptoms and need treatment while your vet is off duty, you will be fully prepared.

Also be sure to ask your vet about after-hours and weekend emergency care, in case your bird needs additional assistance when their office is closed. Be certain that the covering vet practice will treat waterfowl.

Unexplained Fever

Blood is often drawn to help reveal the cause of an unexplained or extremely high fever—especially if your goose does not respond well (or quickly enough) to antibiotics.

When the cause of a fever is unknown, an x-ray or other therapies may be explored, including anti-inflammatory drugs (Rimadyl®) or other antibiotics (Clindamycin or Clavamox®).

Nature has designed fevers as a natural reaction to help the body counteract infectious diseases. For this reason, feverish geese should not be put into cool baths as a home remedy. Forcibly cooling your goose's body can interfere with their regulatory mechanisms and should be avoided *unless* prescribed by your vet. You can, however, provide your goose free access to cool, clean swimming water, giving them the option to self-cool if they want to.

Ailments #11
Appetite Issues

Appetite loss is a clear indicator that your goose is not feeling well and many ailments can result in the appearance of this symptom. If any members of your gaggle exhibit an unusual disinterest in their food—especially a sudden one, you should take them to a vet immediately for an exam.

Seasonal Appetite Changes

Any sudden increases in appetite should also be monitored closely. We do see appetite changes seasonally. Geese tend to eat more near the end of fall, preparing themselves for winter. Once winter is upon them, many will eat substantially less. Many geese also eat noticeably less in the heat of summer. These seasonal appetite changes tend to be gradual.

Appetite Loss from Medication

Some medications can lead to appetite reduction. Antibiotics like Baytril® or Clindamycin are common culprits.

- **Dose in the evening**

If your goose has been prescribed Baytril® once a day, it is best to dose them in the evening, after they have eaten. This way, by the following day, they should have their appetite back again.

- **Make food available 24/7**

If your goose is experiencing a loss in appetite, be sure to have food out at all times rather than serving times. This way, if your goose is feeling good at any point during the day, they can help themselves.

- **Measuring food consumption**

If your goose is losing weight in response to medication, try to measure how much they are eating. Separate quarters may be in order, so you can measure their food in the morning and re-measure in the evening to see how much they have eaten.

- **Syringe feeding**

Sometimes geese need a jump start to coax them into eating again. We put their Mazuri® feed into a small food processor and powder it. Then, we add just enough water to draw the liquid food into a syringe. A few small feedings throughout the day can often be enough to bring back their appetite.

- **Tube feeding**

If your goose is experiencing weight loss because of appetite loss, you will want to discuss tube feeding with your vet. Tube feeding is not as difficult or frightening as it may sound. It is actually quite simple and quickly becomes routine for you and your goose. Ground food and water are often used (the same as with syringe feeding) unless your goose is emaciated, in which case your vet will prescribe special formulas.

- **Energy water**

Sometimes substituting water with electrolytes with your goose's drinking water can give them a well needed energy boost. If your goose is eating well, do not introduce this water, or it may cause nutritional imbalances.

- **Healx® Booster**

If your goose is not eating properly while taking medicine some vets will advise you to give them a product like Healx® Booster. Healx® is a liquid dietary supplement that can be administered orally via syringe. It is prepared similarly to baby food which has to be warmed in water first. Be sure to get proper dosages from your vet.

Dehydration

You can check to see if your goose is dehydrated by lifting one of their wings. In the crook of their "armpit" you will find a flap of skin. If you press this skin between your fingers and it does not spring back into place, your goose may be dehydrated. Take them to the vet right away for immediate assistance.

Digestive Issues

When your goose eats, food travels down their throat and into their gullet. From this sac, the food then moves downward into their gizzard. Gullet or "crop" issues are rare among geese that are cared for properly and maintained on a healthy diet; they are more likely among abandoned geese.

- **Sour Crop**

Sour Crop is a bacterial infection in the crop, and you can normally detect it by smelling your goose's breath. A vet examination is urgently needed when your goose has a crop issue. They will commonly x-ray to ensure the source truly is bacterial. They will flush out the crop and then prescribe antibacterial medication. Additional flushes and a special crop diet will be prescribed.

- **Blocked Crop**

Blocked Crop is when a large stone, object or mass of grass blocks the passage leading out of the crop. It prevents food from properly leaving the crop and moving downward to the gizzard. Avoid letting your geese forage on a freshly mown lawn as this is a common cause.

After performing an x-ray and confirming the crop is blocked, your vet will determine whether the object is small enough to be flushed back up the throat or whether surgery is required. A special crop diet will be prescribed for before and after surgery. Sometimes a pea-sized amount of cat hairball remedy (molasses) will clear grass that is blocking the crop.

- **Slow Crop**

Slow Crop is when the crop functions at a decelerated rate. This can be caused by illness, Hardware Disease or by lead/zinc poisoning.

Your vet will perform an x-ray to confirm your goose has not swallowed a metal object (Hardware Disease) and a blood test to rule out possible lead and zinc poisoning. Vets can sometimes remove a metal object, depending on its location, via surgery. Endoscopic procedures are recommended.

If the bird shows positive for lead/zinc poisoning with no metal object showing up on the x-ray then the object has already passed through their body. A chelating agent will often be prescribed to bind and flush the remaining metals out of their body.

If both tests come back negative then you've at least ruled out a worst-case scenarios. Your vet may want to flush out the crop and check for bacterial presence and prescribe a general antibiotic to address any unseen infections.

- **Pendulous Crop**

Pendulous Crop is a chronic condition. It can be the result of genetics, neurological issues, starving/gorging behaviors (a hazard faced by abandoned waterfowl) or an improper waterfowl diet.

If a crop issue is not attended to early enough the muscles surrounding the crop can become stretched out and lose their effectiveness over time. This leads to a permanent condition in which every time the bird eats, the crop distends abnormally. Food will move to the gizzard, but at an improper rate.

The only treatment for a pendulous crop is a controlled diet. Teaching your goose to eat small quantities in intervals rather than gorging is a vital part of this plan. Sometimes a slow recovery can be expected, other times partial recovery and in some cases the condition remains for the lifetime of the bird.

- **Special Crop Diet**

While attending to crop issues, your vet will give you dietary advice depending on which crop issue your goose is experiencing.

Dietary care often involves grinding their grain into a powder utilizing a food processor and then feeding small amounts at frequent intervals throughout the day. This limits the amount of the food in the crop at any one time and it allows the grain to move more freely into the gizzard. Make sure clean water is available 24/7. Be sure your bird has ample access to grit or sand to help with their digestion.

Depending on whether the condition is temporary or chronic, this diet may need to be maintained for the short term only (slowly transitioning them over to whole pellets), or for the rest of their lives.

- **Automated feeders**

Interval feeding can be very difficult for the working family. Fortunately, you can purchase automated feeders for your goose that will dispense specific amounts of food at pre-programmed times.

Automated feeders are especially effective for geese with severe starvation anxiety and who tend to gorge themselves whenever they see food. Because this behavior can be very unhealthy, automated feeders are a great way to teach your goose better eating habits. They will soon learn that food is available regularly and reliably while limiting the amount they can eat at each interval.

- **Friendship**

Remember, geese are flock animals and one of the best things you can do to help them through a non-contagious medical issue is to be sure they have a good friend to keep them company.

Lynyrd and Skynyrd are the best of friends

Ailments #12
Disease

Cancer

Sadly, cancer is not uncommon among geese, especially reproductive strains in females. There is not much that can be done in these instances except manage pain. As long as your goose appears to be going about their normal business and they aren't experiencing any loss of appetite or discomfort, you can just let them live out their last days in peace.

If your goose is experiencing any discomfort, anti-inflammatory medications like Metacam® or Rimadyl® can be utilized to help keep them comfortable. If this is the case, you won't need to be too concerned with long-term health risks, which will give your vet a little more leeway in prescribing effective dosages.

Symptoms of reproductive cancers can include an irritated cloaca as tumors inside the oviduct grow and expand. The vent may appear red and swollen or sometimes dark scabs will form a crust around the edges. In addition to an anti-inflammatory medication your vet will likely advise a topical, twice daily external application of Sting Free Bacitraycin Plus® around the vent to keep your goose comfortable. Be sure to keep the vent clear of any feces and schedule follow-up visits to your vet to monitor your goose's condition.

Although tumors can sometimes be felt externally, often times they are entirely invisible from the outside. Breathing patterns that worsen over the long-term are sometimes a symptom of cancer. Lymphoma of the internal organs can result in large pockets of fluid around them that appear as rapid weight gain from the outside. If your goose suddenly gains weight without a change in diet, you will want to take them to a vet. X-rays sometimes are unable to permeate the fluids and see underneath, in which case your vet will either order an ultrasound or aspirate a sample of the fluid and send it out to a lab for testing.

A positive result does not always require immediate euthanasia; it depends on the health and happiness of your goose when you discover their ailment. Just be careful not to wait too long so as to cause your goose undo suffering. This being said, it is not uncommon for geese to live comfortably for a year (or more!) beyond when the symptoms of their cancer first become noticeable. We have had birds surprise us and live happily well after their original diagnosis and far beyond our vet's expectations. It is important to watch diagnosed birds very closely, so you can determine when pain medications are no longer having the same effect. When this occurs dosages will either need to be increased or medications may need to be swapped out for something stronger. Your vet will guide you through your options and hopefully help guide you when they think it is time for you to let go.

Every pet owner should have access to 24/7 vet care and this becomes absolutely imperative when you have a goose with cancer. You never know when the time will come that you will need to help them on their way, so be sure you are prepared.

Liver Disease

Black tar-like stool can be an indicator of hepatic (liver) disease. Don't be confused by a one-off pile of dark goose poop that could easily be caused by a day of eating too much mud or dark green foliage. However, consistent dark poop that does not change despite their diet should be taken more seriously.

Liver disease can be caused by medications like clindamyacin, Metacam®, Rimadyl®, Itraconazole or brought on by metal toxicity, chemicals or poisons. It can also be inherited or brought on by old age.

Vets will confirm liver disease via blood work and then offer treatment according to your goose's diagnosis.

In closing, I'm going to cover some of the "big" diseases. You will most likely *never* see these, but being an informed goose owner means it can't hurt to have at least heard of them.

For the most part, these occur in heavily populated pens and/or unsanitary conditions. Commercial hatcheries, farms and responsible breeders immunize their geese to prevent outbreaks. Many of these immunizations are given to female geese, and subsequently, their goslings hatch out with immunity.

If any of these appear in your gaggle, euthanization will most likely be in order (although not necessarily if you catch it early enough) along with close examination and extreme quarantine for the remaining gaggle. Familiarize yourself with their symptoms and then be thankful you will most likely never encounter them. I have not included treatments as these should be dealt with by a vet.

- **Duck Virus Enteritis**

Although *Duck plague* is more common in ducks than geese, geese are susceptible. Duck Virus Enteritis is caused by a herpes virus in adult geese. *Symptoms include:* lethargy, ruffled feathers, greenish-yellow and sometimes bloody diarrhea and blood coming from the nostrils.

- **Duck Virus Hepatitis**

Although more common in ducks than geese, when *DVH* does present itself, it tends to occur among goslings under a month old. It is fatal and highly contagious, which is why hatcheries immunize their geese to prevent it. *Symptoms include:* muscle spasms, which can be quite violent.

- **Riemerella Anatipestifer Infection**

New Castle Disease is a bacterial infection. *Symptoms include:* weight loss, eye discharge, listlessness, diarrhea, shaking & twisting of the head and neck.

Disease Brought on By Poor Sanitation

Poor water sanitation is the common cause of these next serious illnesses. Keep your water sources clean to avoid these deadly diseases. If they appear, vet treatment must be sought out immediately in order to save the goose.

- **Botulism**

Botulism is caused by outbreaks of bacteria in decaying organisms or more frequently in stagnant water, with food or animals decaying in it. It is not unheard of to find dead frogs or drown mice in homemade goose ponds or kiddy pools. Remove them and immediately perform a complete water change. *Symptoms include:* paralysis of neck, legs and/or wings. Death occurs quickly, usually within 1-2 days.

- **Avian Cholera**

This is very rare in the U.S. It is also caused by stagnant water. Symptoms include: loss of appetite, diarrhea, trouble breathing, and a mucus discharge originating from inside the bill.

Avian Influenza

- **Bird Flu**

Avian influenza is a naturally occurring viral infection among birds and most strains are <u>not</u> harmful. Currently, only the H5 and H7 strains are of concern. Many wild birds are carriers although they may never exhibit symptoms. The virus can be passed to other birds via saliva, nasal mucus and feces. Susceptible geese can become infected when they come in contact with these excretions, which are commonly picked up at food and water sources or on pen surfaces.

Although it has received a lot of media coverage in the past, bird flu is more common in dense, commercial populations of waterfowl outside of the U.S. It does not tend to occur among pet geese who are kept in roomy and sanitary conditions.

- **Symptoms of H5 and H7 strains**

Unusual and involuntary movements, swimming in circles, deformation of the neck, lack of interest in food or water, blindness, diarrhea and nasal or eye discharge. Death usually occurs soon after the onset of symptoms.

- **Testing**

Your vet can perform a cloacal swab, virus isolation test for the H5 and H7 strains of avian influenza. They will need to send the sample to a state approved, regulatory lab. It usually takes about five days to receive test results.

- **Prevention**

The only way to prevent outbreak is to keep your goose in a closed environment, where no wild birds have access to their food, drinking or swimming water and pen. Since most geese are not kept in a *completely* closed environment, you can achieve peace of mind in knowing that outbreaks are extremely rare among healthy pet geese kept in sanitary conditions, especially in the U.S.

Keeping wild waterfowl out of your pens helps protect your domestic geese

Considerations

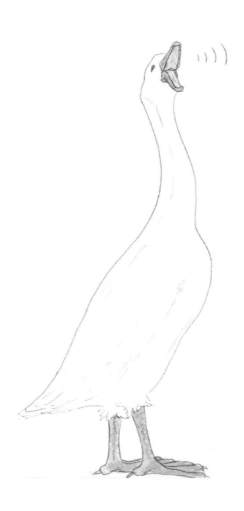

Considerations

You are now knowledgeable about the type of set up you will need for your geese and you know how to keep them safe and sound for a very long time. There are still a few important things to consider before adding a goose to your family.

Consideration #1
Life Expectancy

Geese have average life spans of 15-20 years with 25-30 years being the happy exception. If properly cared for, and blessed with good genes, your geese will likely be quite healthy throughout. If you cannot love and care for your geese for the next twenty-five years with the same fervor that you will have for them today, then perhaps you should reconsider goose ownership.

I am often advising potential adopters to take some time and think their decision through carefully because a lot can change in twenty-five years. Families with teenagers who want geese should place special emphasis on this consideration. Who will take care of the geese when they go off to college or in their own direction? Geese can't follow them to dorms or apartments. Will their parents want to devote the same level of commitment to the geese as they plan to? Geese can quickly go from a beloved pet to a neglected one.

This consideration should also be taken seriously by those renting their living space. Changing apartments often ends in homeless geese. It is not easy to find a landlord that will allow geese as tenants, and you may quickly find yourself in a terrible situation where you are welcome, but your companion is not. All too frequently this ends in owners having to relinquish their pets. Not only is this painful, but because most shelters are full or cannot accommodate geese, things often turn from bad to worse in a brief period of time. It is wiser to adopt geese when you are in a permanent living situation—or at least one that will last for twenty-five years.

Consideration #2
Gaggle Size

Geese are flock animals. This means they are most content when they are in the company of other geese. We have known many pet owners with only one goose who thought their goose could not possibly be any happier, but when they adopted a second goose they were amazed by the difference in the spirits of their pet. To avoid depriving your goose the companionship of their own kind, you should always start your gaggle with a minimum of two geese. I would not recommend starting with any more than this if you have never had geese before.

If you temporarily have only one goose, you may want to consider placing a mirror into their pen to keep them company until you can adopt a companion for them. Solitary geese will often spend a great deal of time sitting in front of their reflection, enjoying the company of their new friend. Many will sleep in front of their mirror.

If you have a solitary goose that has never seen another goose before and you'd like to know if they would enjoy a friend, add a reasonable sized non-breakable mirror to their nighttime quarters. Leave it in there for a while and see what the long-term reaction is. Keep in mind initial reactions aren't the same as long-term reactions, so give your goose time to get used to it. If they enjoy watching the other goose, that's a good indicator that they would benefit from companionship.

Many families with one goose have contacted us to adopt another goose to avoid leaving their pet alone while they are at work. The tactic of adding a mirror is a great way to prepare your goose for companionship. Even if it reacts poorly to it at first, or ignores it, it will still get them used to the fact that another goose will soon be in the pen with them.

Consideration #3
Gender Selection

Keep in mind the compatibility of your flock members. Gender selection is not as simple as you might think. There are five recommended types of gaggles regarding gender. By this I mean, the number of ganders and geese you want to keep in any one enclosure.

1) All ganders
2) All geese
3) One gander & one goose
4) One gander & multiple geese
5) Even pairs of geese and ganders

SEE **APPENDIX E** FOR "MANAGING A MULTIPLE GANDER GAGGLE"

The All Gander Gaggle

- **Benefits**

1. Ganders tend to get along very well if there are no geese in sight or earshot to argue over. We know of a number of families who keep all-gander gaggles.

2. The benefit of this type of gaggle is owners have no concerns over egg disorders, breeder rations, added calcium sources or keeping ganders out of laying formula feed. It is an easy, straightforward feeding ritual—the same for everyone.

3. Since most shelters are brimming with unwanted, homeless ganders, a gaggle of adopted ganders provides help where it is needed most.

- **Drawbacks**

1. Ganders will still have brief disagreements and pecking order disputes and they may get a little crazy in the spring, even without geese about.

2. Ganders enjoy the companionship of geese and are unable to enjoy this natural part of their lives when they only have males for companions.

The All Female Goose Gaggle

- **Benefits**

1. Provided no wild geese can get into your goose pen, you are guaranteed unfertilized eggs. This means you will have a breakfast food on hand and you are certain not to hatch out any unwanted goslings.

2. An all-female goose gaggle is a peaceful gaggle. Disputes tend to be very limited and brief in most cases. A newcomer may shake up the pecking order momentarily, but it is usually resolved relatively quickly.

3. Concerns regarding over-mating do not exist.

- **Drawbacks**

1. Unless you are adopting adults, it can be difficult to obtain a gaggle of all female geese.

2. Laying geese require more attention to their dietary needs and can be susceptible to reproductive issues.

3. In buying into the concept that an all-female goose gaggle is the best gaggle, many homeless ganders are left without options. Denying even a single gander into your all-female goose gaggle prevents one needy animal from finding a loving family.

4. Geese enjoy the companionship of ganders and are unable to enjoy this natural part of their lives when they only have females for companions.

The One Gander and One Goose Gaggle

- **Benefits**

1. Both members experience the company of the opposite sex.

2. A gaggle of only two geese requires less pen space than larger gaggles.

- **Drawbacks**

1. Over-mating can occur if you have an overzealous gander

2. Eggs must be collected to prevent unwanted hatchings

3. The gander and the goose have different dietary needs, which will require your attention.

The One Gander and Multiple Geese Gaggle

- **Benefits**

1. All members experience the company of the opposite sex.

2. Over-mating is rarely an issue with so many geese for a gander to choose from.

- **Drawbacks**

1. Eggs must be collected to prevent unwanted hatchings

2. The gander and the goose have different dietary needs, which will require your attention.

The Even Pairs of Geese and Ganders Gaggle

- **Benefits**

1. All members experience the company of the opposite sex.

2. You have the opportunity to alleviate shelter overfill by adopting homeless ganders.

- **Drawbacks**

1. Eggs must be collected to prevent unwanted hatchings.

2. The ganders and the laying geese have different dietary needs, which will require your attention.

3. Over-mating can be an issue if multiple ganders choose one favorite goose.

3. Pens will need to be spacious.

4. Large gaggles can have loud moments when they become excited or alarmed.

Gender Identification

Now that you've decided on the type of gendered gaggle you would like, you are faced with the next dilemma, which is getting the genders you want for your gaggle. Determining the gender of a gosling or goose can be quite challenging.

Gender Identification / Goslings

Although some goslings can be sexed by color, the sex of other breeds can not be guaranteed and you won't necessarily know what you have for quite a while. Many places will only sell *straight-run* goslings. This means if you order six goslings, you get what you get. It can be a bit of a crap shoot getting the gender gosling(s) you desire. This is the common reason so many ganders are dropped off on public ponds; too many ganders in a straight-run batch.

Although many sources will offer instructions on how to sex a gosling yourself, it can actually be quite harmful to the gosling if it is done too early or by someone inexperienced. This should be left to professionals to avoid permanent damage to the gosling.

Because it is so difficult to get a gender specific gosling (unless you choose a breed with a color variation that differentiates male goslings from female goslings) many families start by opting to get only two goslings. When the goslings mature their gender will become obvious. A family wishing to further increase the size of their gaggle, can adhere to the five recommended types of gender-shaped gaggles by adding sexually mature and identifiable adult geese to their gaggle rather than goslings. In this way, they can carefully control the number of ganders and geese in their gaggle.

Gender Identification / Geese

When attempting to determine the gender of geese it often helps to have multiple strategies and a very good eye and ear.

- **Sexing by color**

The great thing about selecting Pilgrim geese is you are guaranteed the genders you want. Females are grey with brown eyes. Males are white (often with black or gray speckles) and they have blue eyes.

Pilgrim Geese: Harmony & Melody are grey while their brother Egor is white with grey spots

135

- **Sexing by size/weight**

Male ganders tend to be larger than female geese by a pound or two within the breed. Males often stand higher up and appear more regal. This tends to only helpful if you can make actual side-by-side comparisons within a gaggle, and it isn't always reliable.

Chan (Left) is larger than China Girl (Right)

- **Sexing by the knob**

Some people will advise sexing Chinese geese by the size of their facial knobs, but I can tell you, it is not reliable. There is a much better way to sex a Chinese goose and that is by the sound of their honk.

Skynyrd the gander (left) has a more pronounced facial knob than Ms. Donald (right), but this isn't always the case

- **Sexing by the honk**

Adult male and female Chinese geese have very different calls. Males are very vocal, with long-winded, sing-song, high-pitched voices—especially when excited. They stand much taller than females and they stretch their necks high up into the air while they carry on. Females, on the other hand, are not as vocal and make short, low-pitched sounds.

- **Sexing by behavior**

Sexing by behavior is a pet owner's last resort, but it is often very telling if you know what to look for.

Males will commonly initiate mating behavior and attempt to mount females on water. Males will often swim more frequently in ponds while females will often stand on the shore and avoid going in because they know what will follow. Females lay eggs seasonally with eggs appearing between February and May, but older females often do not lay eggs.

A newly introduced female will commonly run away from the approach of the existing alpha gander (although timid ganders may also run away). On the other hand, a newly introduced male will often engage in a brief dual with the existing alpha gander to vie for leadership and establish the pecking order.

An existing alpha gander is more likely to only approach a newly introduced female *once* in confrontation and ignore her after she runs off. On the other hand, an existing alpha gander will sometimes approach and drive off a newly introduced gander multiple times to reaffirm his leadership and authority.

Some females will instigate fights. Females are sometimes seen "cheering on" and coaxing their ganders to fight with a newly introduced gander. Females will get close to the action, but rarely participate in these confrontations. Females tend to greet or ignore newly introduced females.

Consideration #4
Breed Options

Your next step is to do some breed research. Read up on different types of goose breeds and then choose the breed that is most appealing to you, will fit best into your lifestyle and will make you the happiest.

Breeds

Because there are already dozens of waterfowl breed books out there, I'm going to keep this rather quick and simple. There are plenty of more detailed resources out there to help you fine-tune your decision and I always advise lots of good research before welcoming in any new pet. The number one question I'm asked about geese is how loud and how friendly. Most geese will be friendly if you spend the time it takes to bond with them (and provided you remain in charge), but not all geese are quiet.

There are heavy-weight (African, Embden, Toulouse), medium-weight (Buff/Grey Back, Buff, Chinese, Pilgrim, Pomeranian, Sebastopol) and light-weight (Roman) geese.

There are two classes of geese; those who are descendants of wild Swan geese and those who have descended from wild Greylag geese. Geese with small pom-poms on their heads are referred to as "tufted." Following is a list of the *most common* breed choices available. This list is not all-inclusive, but it will get you started.

Greylag Goose Descendants

Most domestic geese are descendants of wild Greylag geese. The vocalizations of all of these geese are very similar. They tend to have loud alarm calls, but most of the time they chit-chat in more subdued voices or are relatively quiet unless something exciting is going on.

- **Pilgrim geese**

Pilgrim geese are very common. Males have blue eyes and are mottled with gray or black spots. Females have brown eyes and are gray with white underbellies. As they mature more white will often emerge around the bills and on the faces of females.

Pilgrim geese: Melody, Harmony & Charming (left) and Wilma (right)

- **Toulouse geese**

Toulouse geese are also very common. They look very similar to female Pilgrim geese except that they tend to be a little larger. Dewlap Toulouse geese have a flap of skin under their chin. Toulouse geese are usually very inquisitive making them a fun choice if you are looking for a friendly and interactive pet. Of course their personalities will also be shaped by their upbringing, so don't rely on Mother Nature to give you a friendly goose. As with any goose, you will need to bring out the best in them. Toulouse geese often have a difficult time in extreme heat due to their body size and shape. They tend to pant excessively in hot weather and may not be the best choice for you if you live in a hotter region.

There is a pitch difference between the calls of males and females, but you would have to hear it for yourself to recognize it. They also tend to be more conversational than other geese—although not enough to be obtrusive.

Toulouse gander: Duran "Moon" (left) and Dewlap Toulouse gander: Grampa (right)

138

- **Embden and Roman geese**

Embden geese are another very common goose. They are the largest of all geese and can weigh from 20 - 30 pounds. Roman geese are less common and look very similar to Embden geese except that they are smaller (12- 14 pounds) and have shorter bills. Romans also have wing feathers that (when folded up at their sides) are a bit longer than their bodies. These two breeds are often intermixed resulting in a medium-sized Embden, which are very common in some regions.

Embden goose: Fanny

- **Buff Back and Grey Back geese**

Buff Back and Grey Back geese are mostly white with either buff or powder grey colored feathers on their head, wings and hips. Those with buff coloring are called Buff Backs and those with grey are referred to as Grey Backs. We don't see as many of these as we do other breeds in our rescue endeavor.

Buff Back goose: Jetti

- **Pomeranian geese**

Pomeranian geese are mostly white with dark grey markings on their head, wings and hip feathers. They don't seem to be as common as some of the other breeds—at least not in our region.

Photo of Pom Pom Courtesy of Michael and Diane Pajak

- **Sebastopol geese**

Sebastopol geese look like big, fluffy pillows. They are harder to find than most other breeds of geese and for that reason, aren't abandoned as frequently. If you are looking to adopt a rescued Sebastopol you will likely need to keep your eye on shelters and watch closely for newcomers.

Sebastopol goose: Mademoiselle Fifi

140

- **Buff geese**

Buff geese are a fawnish-grey color with white underbellies. They almost look like a sun-bleached Toulouse or Pilgrim goose. They don't seem to be very common in the U.S.A, and we haven't run into any yet in our rescue endeavor.

Photo of Valentino Courtesy of Peter Jacobs and Andrea Heesters

Swan Goose Descendants

The remaining domestic geese are descendants of wild Swan geese. The vocalizations of these geese are very similar to each other, but different from the descendants of Greylag geese. The calls of the ganders are almost musical in nature and they are very chatty. As with other geese, they have a loud alarm call.

- **Chinese geese**

Although Chinese geese are common they are not quite as popular as the Pilgrim, Toulouse and Embden geese and the reason for this is their VOICE! Chinese ganders are very vocal and may not be a good choice if you have neighbors close by. Chinese geese can be white or grey with very long necks and knobs at the crest of their bills. Females are quieter than males and make an odd "oinking" sound.

Grey and White Chinese geese: Skynyrd and Mac

- **African geese**

African geese seem to be a little less common than Chinese geese. They are basically a larger version of a Chinese goose with a dewlap (flap of skin) dangling below their chin. Male African geese are also very loud and vocal. African geese can be grey or white.

This Grey African gander disappeared before we could rescue him

Desirable Breed Traits

Domestic geese come in many different colors, shapes and sizes. Some geese (Chinese and Africans) honk a lot (and *LOUDLY!),* others are much quieter. Some are fancy-colored, some are plain, some are very friendly, while others tend to be a little more independent.

Many sources will tell you that they are easy to care for, but you already know what to do with that advice. Do keep in mind that some exotic breeds are more difficult to care for than others (and the information provided in this book does not always apply in the case of exotics). Be sure to take into consideration any special care needs for certain breeds to be sure you can and *want* to meet these needs.

If you've never raised geese before or if it's been a long time, I would recommend starting out with some easier to raise geese, like the hearty Toulouse. Toulouse geese tend to be very friendly while still remaining on the quieter side. They are gray with white underbellies and have orange bills and feet. They are very domesticated, so they can be quite affectionate, especially if imprinted on humans as goslings. Most geese who come through our sanctuary are Toulouse, and they have all been wonderful and interactive.

Tutter is a very friendly and playful Toulouse gander

- **Mixing breeds**

You don't have to get geese of the same breed; you are not a breeder. You can pay a lot of money for a gosling that you really like, but that doesn't mean you have to commit to keeping its bloodline clean. It's your goose; you can keep it in whatever company you like. I will admit, given the choice, ganders seem to prefer the company of geese who are of the same breed as they are, but they will not hold to this rule… they are boys after all.

Consideration #5
Size Options

The size your gosling will grow up to be is also a very important consideration. There are three sizes of geese, the light-weight breeds, the medium-weight breeds and the heavy-weight breeds.

Ms. Donald the goose (left) is smaller than Skynyrd the gander (right)

It's important to make sure your ganders aren't too much larger than your geese or the girls won't stand a chance in trying to fend them off. If your geese are smaller than your ganders you may have to separate them during the mating season to protect them.

143

Consideration #6
Geese or Goslings

The Benefits of Goslings

Many people fall for the allure of a gosling and have a love-at-first-site experience when they see them in a store. Provided you can provide a lifetime of care for them, goslings are a wonderful adventure.

Skynyrd, Lynyrd, Wilma, Ms. Donald and Golly

- **The bond of imprinting is strong**

Goslings will imprint on you, and if you spend a lot of time with them during their first six to eight weeks, they will bond very closely with you. This bond will remain between you and your geese for the rest of their lives, as long as you continue to spend time with them.

Keep in mind, not all imprinted geese who were doted over as goslings will continue to appreciate this adoration as adults. In our experience there are far less "lap geese" than there are geese who prefer to be petted while both of their feet remain on the ground.

- **What exactly is imprinting?**

We often use the word *imprinted* when we discuss the connection between humans and geese, but what exactly is imprinting?

There are two types of imprinting that occur among goslings: *filial imprinting* and *sexual imprinting*.

- **Filial imprinting**

Filial imprinting is when goslings hatch and subsequently learn to recognize their parent—or the first moving object that they consider to be their parent. This commonly occurs within a day and a half of hatching.

It makes sense that goslings who leave the nest soon after hatching, have the instincts to socially bond and stick close to a parent (even if that parent is you!) for protection. These hatchlings are more likely to survive and reproduce in the long run—an evolutionary benefit.

Occasionally we are asked if goslings who were acquired at a few days old will still imprint on their new human parents. The answer is *yes*. Imprinting is not so steadfast as to have exact time lines or conditions. We have had goslings imprint on us a month after their hatch although it does require a certain level of attention and interaction throughout the day.

Our rescue endeavor frequently exposes us to formerly human imprinted adult geese who were subsequently abandoned. These geese have completely let go of their social bond with humans. In some cases, we can re-establish this filial bond. It can take anywhere from a few months to a year, but rediscovering this bond is possible.

- **Sexual imprinting**

Sexual imprinting is when a gosling internalizes those traits that will one day be attractive in a mate. As adults, geese are attracted to mates who share the appearance of their parent.

If your gosling experienced filial imprinting on you because you were their caretaker upon hatching, they will also learn that your human physical traits are attractive. When they mature, they will begin to see you in a whole new light and may court you instead of other geese.

Sexual imprinting is not necessarily permanent—especially if there are other geese around. Although goslings may sexually imprint on you in the beginning, this tends to change once they mature and encounter other adult geese. Commonly, by their first spring, most geese will figure out the birds & the bees and will appropriately redirect their impulses, although they will still hold a special place in their hearts for you.

Sexual imprinting can also induce egg-laying in geese. If you have a female goose who has imprinted on you, your presence can entice courting behavior and egg-laying.

The Benefits of Geese

As your strapping young goslings reach sexual maturity you will slowly transform from "Momma Goose" to "Hot Momma" (or Poppa as the case may be). It tends to be very apparent when it becomes time to introduce some girlfriends to your ganders. There are a few reasons to choose adult geese over goslings.

- **Guaranteed gender**

While the sexing of most goslings can be questionable, adult geese can be gender identified with 100% accuracy in some breeds. If you can't afford any mistakes, adopting adult geese is the way to go.

- **Geese require less time than goslings**

When you have goslings, you will frequently be refreshing their food and water dishes, interacting with them, taking them for swims, cleaning out tubs and changing their bedding (especially as they get a little older). A lot of your time and energy will be expended fulfilling their every need. Adult geese, on the other hand, require a lesser level of attentiveness and can be easier on the family with a busy schedule.

- **Geese and goslings don't mix**

Introduced goslings need to be kept separate from adult geese who aren't their family, especially ganders. They can easily be killed in a pecking order confrontation, premature mating or in an accident. This means, if you have an adult gaggle do not go out and purchase a gosling and just drop them off in the mix. It could prove disastrous.

- **Helping a displaced animal**

When you adopt a displaced animal, not only are you helping to provide a home for someone without one, but you are also making room at a shelter for more waterfowl in need.

Isabel says good-bye to Goliath as he heads off to his new home

Locating Goslings

In some regions goslings are relatively easy to find at grain stores in the spring or hatcheries. Many of these will only sell goslings straight-run with a six gosling minimum in an effort to help prevent impulsive one-gosling Easter purchases and to meet minimum shipping requirements.

Finding particular breeds of goslings will vary depending on which part of the country you live in. Sometimes local grain stores may know of someone in your area who raises geese. You can contact breeders in person or on the internet if you wish to explore this avenue. Local breeders will often give you the option of purchasing the exact number, breed and sex goslings you are looking for.

Locating Geese

If you would like to adopt an adult goose, you can explore your local animal shelters or check your own local ponds for drop offs and rescue them yourself. Helping an animal without a home is one of the most rewarding things you can do.

Although I highly recommend it, you don't have to adopt a rescued goose if you want an adult goose. Explore the internet, contact breeders, or put an ad in the paper. You may be able to take a day trip and go visit a breeder—just make sure you make an appointment first. Breeders will often sell inexpensive geese that they don't want to breed or show; many of them will even ship to you (at your expense).

Adult geese don't have minimum ship requirements, so you can have just one goose shipped to you via Express Mail. You will need to confirm that the goose can ship to you in one day (type in the start & destination zip codes into Express Mail's website to confirm). Some locations are two day ships, which you will want to avoid.

- **Quarantine considerations**

When adding to your gaggle, quarantine considerations are vital. You want to make sure anyone coming in will not share contagions with your gaggle. Consult with your vet before bringing in a new member. If you don't have space for quarantine, you can bring your newly adopted goose straight to the vet for a physical before introducing them to your gaggle. Have your vet check for lice and test a stool sample for parasites.

At our sanctuary we give a precautionary delousing treatment to every arriving goose and then fecal samples are delivered to our vet for examination. All geese are quarantined and watched closely for a *minimum* of fourteen days. Provided no health issues arise during this original period, they are moved over to their new pens.

- **Bio-security**

It is vital for the safety of your gaggle that any of your farmer friends do not come wandering into your goose enclosures with the same shoes and clothing they wore into their pens. This is how contagions are introduced from one property to another. Keep visitors outside of your geese pens unless they come to you with clean clothes and clean shoes. We highly recommend Virkon S ® as a foot bath for entering guests. In addition, remember to sanitize your goose pens during and after quarantine periods by adding 1-2 tablespoons of bleach to a gallon of water. Rinse and dry pens thoroughly before reintroducing birds to the pen.

Duran Duran spend their first two weeks in West Wing, our quarantine pen

- **Adopting a rescued goose**

Adopting a homeless goose from a shelter may take a little more effort on your part. You may have to make more than one trip to a shelter, fill out forms, have visits to your home, provide photos of their housing and so on. They may require medical care in the beginning or down the road. There are also shelters that will ship you a goose if you qualify for adoption. Sometimes shelters are brimming with homeless geese; other times, they have found happy homes for all of their geese (that's a good thing!). If you plan on adopting a goose, apply a few months in advance, receive your pre-approval for adoption and then be patient.

- **Determining the age of a goose**

If you adopted your goose you might not know their age, but there are a few clues you can look for to get a general idea.

A goose under a year old will have small points at the tips of their tail feathers. These points help push out a goslings fluff when they first grow feathers.

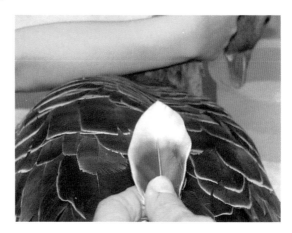

Young Rosie's pointed tail feather

The eyes of older geese are more sunk in than eyes of younger geese. You will often see heavier folds of skin over the eyelids and more elliptical-shaped eyes on older geese.

Eye Photos of a 20 year-old gander Grampa (left) compared to a 3 year-old goose Wilma (right)

- **The nature of an adopted goose**

Although geese have similar tendencies, they have very distinct personalities. Some are very affectionate, while others are a bit aloof, some are trouble-makers, while others are mild mannered, some are curious investigators, while others would rather not be bothered. We have had sleepers and geese that don't miss a thing. We have had geese of pleasant demeanor and we have had avid protestors. We have had geese that run up to greet me, honking all the while and we have had geese that stay a few feet away from me unless they see that I have snacks.

Angelo starts his attack!

It's important to know that the type of bond you will have with your adopted goose is dependent on whether they imprinted on humans or other geese, what breed they are, where they came from, what they've been through, how old they are and how much time you are willing to spend with them.

An adult adopted goose will be different from goslings who have imprinted on you and who have known you their whole lives. Adopted geese go through an initial adjustment phase, the same as any other animal. Don't get disappointed if your new goose won't come near you or runs in the opposite direction when you enter their pen. Time and patience will eventually bring most geese around.

Many of our foster geese have experienced hunger and neglect and have, quite wisely, learned to be afraid of people. When they join our sanctuary many do not want to be within ten feet of us—fifteen is better. It can take anywhere up to a year for a shy foster goose to come to terms with the fact that they are in a safe and loving place. A big bag of leaf lettuce can really help shorten that span. Most don't want to be petted or picked up, although they may come to in time. Before welcoming a goose into your family, commit to loving and caring for them regardless of how close you may become.

Although some adopted geese may never progress beyond their shyness, other fosters become some of the friendliest and most inquisitive we have ever seen. The shy and ill-tempered Ali was adopted out a year after his rescue as wonderfully mischievous. Tutter arrived fearful of humans and left with one of the most pleasant demeanors we have ever seen in a gander. They were imprinted geese who were abandoned and lost their trust in humans. Once taken into our care, and fawned over again, they reclaimed this connection.

Every goose has their own clock, but I normally tell adopting families that the goose they adopt today will be very different from the goose they have a year from now (provided the love and attention continues as it should). Although they may be adopting a very affectionate goose from us, it still tends to take a year for the goose to completely settle into their new home. They learn the daily routine pretty quickly (usually within three days) and will soon learn just where to go and will show themselves the way. Some will get right to forming a loving bond with their new family. Still, for some reason, after a year, they truly begin to realize that this change is permanent and then true happiness really begins. It's almost like a little alarm goes off in their heads telling them everything is okay now.

Close up of gentle Tutter and his protector Angelo

I think all of our adopting families would agree that the true reward of adopting a rescued goose was not only giving that goose a happy and healthy life, but also feeling the gratefulness the animal exhibited toward them. There are very few things more rewarding than having a mistreated and fearful animal come to trust and appreciate you. This bond can sometimes be stronger than raising a goose from a gosling (who doesn't necessarily know how good they have things).

- **Geese as companion animals**

This brings me to a good place to discuss a very common and peculiar question that we are asked, *"Are geese companion animals?"* When an interviewer first asked me this, I turned the question back on them and asked for their definition of a companion animal. Her reply was, *"affectionate animals able to express love and having distinct and individual personalities."* My answer was *yes!*

Photo of Allison and Skynyrd Courtesy of Wendy

One visit with our rescued gander Mac is enough to convince any of our visitors of the level of connection these birds have with humans. Mac runs over to greet every guest and will practically stand on your feet for attention. Not all geese are this overly affectionate, but I gather pleasure from all of them—even those who prefer each other's company over mine.

An experienced vet once told a good friend of mine that of all the human/animal connections he had witnessed throughout his career, the connection between humans and waterfowl is closer than any other bond. I think this is because of imprinting—something dogs and cats just don't do.

Jenn with Ms. Donald

Transporting Geese

The question of transportation of waterfowl comes up frequently. Moving geese is simple and safe if you have the right size and number of pet carriers and some cozy bedding. You can use plastic pet carriers, or pet cages with a solid floor. You don't want wire caging directly under their webbed feet.

If you are going on a long trip, use carriers that allow your geese to stand up, stretch and resettle. On the other hand, avoid carriers that are too roomy. Your goose should not have enough room to flap their wings. Too much mobility can lead to injury in a moving vehicle.

If you have multiple geese, consider who will get along for the full duration of the trip. You may want to utilize more than one carrier and just face the carrier doors towards each other so that they can see and be comforted by each other. If your geese are good friends, get a carrier that allows them to travel together.

Use hay or straw bedding inside the pet carrier. Shavings tend to spread and get messy and are less desirable. Avoid using newspaper, which can remove vital oils from your birds' feathers. Towels can get messy and toe nails can get caught in loose threads, making them a less attractive choice.

Isabel sits on our goose carrier

Geese can get car sick, and they do sometimes vomit. Be sure to keep fresh air moving through the vehicle (or a/c in hot weather) to help prevent this. A drink of water will help them to feel better and help prevent choking situations.

Tutter & Angelo

No-Spill Water Bowl

If you are going on a long trip, you can buy no-spill water dishes from the dog aisle of your local pet store and specially made for car journeys or you can make your own and save yourself a bit of money. Making your own no-spill water bowl is quick and easy.

- **First**

Purchase a disposable container that is the perfect size for your goose.

- **Second**

Carefully cut a large hole in the lid, leaving only 1 inch of plastic around the border.

- **Third**

Snap the lid onto your bowl and fill it halfway with water. It's dishwasher safe or disposable if it gets really messy.

Homemade no-spill water bowl for traveling

Shipping Geese

Although I always avoid shipping geese, you may find it necessary to have a breeder or shelter Express Mail a goose to you, especially if there is considerable distance between you and the goose you desire. Not all locations qualify for overnight shipping, so before you even consider this step visit the United States Postal Service on the internet and type in the shipper's zip code and your zip code. If overnight shipping is available from the goose's origin to your destination these steps can help ensure that your new best friend will arrive safely. Be sure to ask if your desired goose has a companion, so you can avoid splitting up a mated pair, in which case your goose will likely be distressed and call out during most of their trip (which could irritate your new goose's handlers).

1. **Purchase a shipping carton**

   If the shipper does not have access to a post office approved poultry box (which they sometimes do), you can purchase one online and have it mailed directly to them. We prefer the Horizon Micro Environments, SWAN N.E.S.T. (Natural Environmentally-Secure Transporters) purchased through: www.hm-e.net. It is ideal for shipping one goose.

Photo of shipping box Courtesy of Horizon Micro Environments

2. Shipping carton preparations

When the box arrives at the shipper's residence, they can then pack up your goose in it and ship him/her out to you. They should know, but it can't hurt to remind them, to feed and water your goose very well before putting them in the box. Before shipping a goose they should take a 1 quart plastic paint cup (found in the paint section of your hardware store), poke two holes through the side of the cup and then poke two more tiny holes through the shipping box. They can then tie-wrap (zip tie) the cup snuggly into the inside corner of the shipping box. They can fill the cup with 8-12 oz of water, so the goose will have a little drink along the way. Some people smash up wet fruit like watermelon instead. They will need to lay down a bit of hay on the bottom and then the temporary nest is ready for a goose. The SWAN N.E.S.T. box is the perfect size for a single goose.

3. List a toll free emergency number

Be sure to have the person shipping the goose list their toll free cell phone number and your toll free cell phone number on the carton and actually write "TOLL FREE CELL PH#" next to each of the numbers. Postal employees will not call you at their expense, so you need to make it free.

4. List addresses in multiple places

Always list shipping and return addresses clearly on the carton in multiple places. Avoid using labels that can peel off. Instead, write on the carton itself.

5. Guaranteed shipping

Be sure to have the shipper write "RETURN SHIPPING GUARANTEED" on the carton. If the mail system breaks down along the way and a goose becomes trapped in route, you want the postal system to know they can send the goose back and have their costs covered.

6. Ship during full weeks on Mondays

You will have to coordinate this shipment well—a life is depending on you. It is best for the breeder to ship your goose on a Monday or Tuesday during a non-holiday week; this way, if the goose is delayed in shipment in any way, they are not at risk of being locked up in a post office or warehouse over a weekend. Only ship to zip codes that have a *one day* delivery time. You can enter origin and destination zip codes on Express Mail's website to ensure a one day delivery time.

7. Never ship geese in summer, consider extremes

Never ever ship geese in the heat of June, July or August—or any time when weather conditions are extremely hot or cold during the transit route since this could lead to a horrible death for your new goose. Also take into consideration any national issues that might hold up shipping or delivery (hurricane threats anywhere along the flight route, for example).

154

8. Prepare your post office staff

Talk to your post office *before* arranging the shipment with the breeder. They will tell you what times they receive shipments, so you can arrange to be at home. Talk to them again after you make arrangements with the shipper, so they will know ahead of time that they will need to call you when your new goose shows up. Many postal workers will become so involved as to call you before or after-hours to help you get your goose out of the box and into the safety of your barn in record time.

The same goes with goslings—let your post office know ahead of time when they are coming. If you give your post office your local phone number or any number that is a "no charge" call for them (i.e. your cell phone), they will call you when your goslings arrive. You want to be available and close by when that call comes, so you can get your new family member(s) home to food and water as quickly as possible.

Consideration #7
Expense

Although geese aren't fabulously expensive to keep (hay, grain & winter veggies), there is a start up cost if you want to do it right, and if you don't do it right, predators will bring them to a quick end. The start up costs of an enclosure, feeders, heated water dispensers, buckets, kiddy pools, hay, grain and housing add up quickly, not to mention the occasional vet trip.

Consideration #8
Seasonal Timing

Keep the season in mind before you bring home goslings. You will need to keep them warm. Goslings brought home in the early spring will need to be protected from the wind and cold until they have lost their fluff and grow their first feathers. Likewise, goslings brought home in summer, will need to be protected from the heat. Extremes in either direction can be fatal.

If you're bringing home adult geese seasonal consideration is particularly important. If ganders are involved, introductions are best done outside of the mating season (February – May) after spring hormones have dropped and leveled out. This will help keep chasing and overexcitement to a minimum.

Consideration #9
Wintertime Care

Winter is often the most challenging time to care for geese unless you are in a climate where this season is obsolete. Consider wintertime care very heavily before you bring any geese into your family.

Insulating

Goose feet and bills must be kept warm. Domestic geese are not hearty enough to endure cold winters without protection. They can and do get frostbite if you don't make certain preparations. Geese should always have free access to bedded housing that will protect them from cold winds. Our barn has a thick layer (6 – 12 inches) of hay on the floor beneath them. Some days call for staying indoors. Use your best judgment.

On warmer winter days, our geese usually prefer to sleep together on an outdoor nest. I have no idea why they prefer this over their barn, but if the temps aren't dangerous, there's no need to coax them inside (provided you have a predator proof enclosure). I start and end each day with the piling of fresh hay onto their massive nest. The nest continues to expand over the winter season, leaving me a nest that could seat a dinosaur by spring—and what fun it is to pitch it all out of their pen.

Our barn has two windows. When cold weather sets in I staple some thick, clear plastic over them to keep out breezes. In colder regions, barn walls can be insulated with stacked up bails of hay. Buy plenty of hay before it becomes unavailable and get enough to use as wall insulation *and* enough to use as daily fresh bedding. You don't want to bed the floor at the cost of depleting your insulation. I tend to use 1-2 bails of hay each week to keep six geese sitting on a fresh nest. Fresh bedding is put down in the morning and at night to cover any unruly spots.

"Hey, what does that say about me?" –Mac

For those of you without barns, you want to follow the same rules of thumb in your sheds or goose houses: supply a generous layer of bedding under webbed feet and provide protection from the wind. Insulation is recommended for our Northern friends to prevent frostbite.

Keep an Open Water Source

Your geese won't care whether or not they have warm or cold drinking water available to them in the colder months, as long as they have open water. I always do a quick water temperature check to be sure that their heated water buckets are functioning well, so that I won't come home to any frozen water mishaps.

Bathing and Preening

Geese should not have unsupervised access to a kiddy pool that could freeze over on cold days. Those feet aren't as thick skinned as you might believe, and geese should not be allowed to sit in small bodies of water (which tend to be much colder than larger ponds or lakes and freeze over more quickly) for long periods of time.

Geese need to bathe and preen in order to fluff and seal their feathers and insulate them during the colder seasons. If you can escort them to a pond, kiddy pool, basin or tub, do so at least twice a week—every few days. A ten to fifteen minute session is plenty; if they want to come out sooner, that's fine.

Healthy geese can usually bathe and preen utilizing a bucket of clean water. They will dip their head and neck into the bucket and splash water over themselves and then preen. If this is your goose's only source of bathing, be sure they have access to it every day.

If your geese are shivering, they have not bathed enough and this will have to be remedied right away if you want to keep them healthy.

Heated Barns

We are frequently asked if barns (or goose houses) need to be heated. For most regions of the U.S., the answer to this question is no. If you give them protection from wind and a thick layer of bedding (*at least* 4 inches compacted) under their feet, your geese will be fine during colder temperatures. The more geese you have cuddling together, the warmer your gaggle will be.

Be wary of weather warnings in your area. Don't leave your geese outside and exposed to the cold during extreme cold or wind chills. We house all geese whenever temps drop to 15 degrees F or below to avoid frostbite. Availability of warm drinking water is always a nice way to keep your geese warm on the inside on cold days.

Some sources will say a heated barn will disrupt a goose's molting cycle, but since geese survive without any difficulty or confusion in the warmer states; we tend to believe this is a myth. What you want to avoid is heating a barn and then during the midst of winter, discontinuing the heat. You also want to avoid over-heating a barn or shed. This could cause health or respiratory issues. Whatever you decide, it must be consistent. You don't want your geese to be in a 70 degree barn one day and then outside in 20 degree weather the next. Try to keep temperature variances to a 10 degree maximum whenever possible. Geese always appreciate heat, but try to avoid using any heating devices while you are not present. If you have a heating system, be sure it is professionally installed and maintained to avoid fire hazards.

Snow on Your Aviary Net

Most people will not even think to consider their aviary net or top wire's vulnerability to snow. A wet and heavy snow can wreak havoc on your goose's overhead protection. Even the best aviary net and support structure can succumb to extreme damage if left unattended. Even a couple of inches of snow can damage or stretch top netting or wire, and it can also pull down and even break support beams and poles. If this happens, your entire goose pen can cave in on itself. Special attention will have to be placed on your goose's pen during snowstorms. You may need to leave work early or actively monitor it during your sleeping hours.

Snow piled on aviary nets can pull them down quickly

When snow storms come during the night, you will need to set your alarm and get out of bed every couple of hours to make sure snow is not piling up on top wire or aviary netting. If it is, you will need to go outside and remove it. Snow can normally be removed by using a broom handle or the like. You walk under the structure and tap the overhead netting (or wire), so the snow will fall down through it. Depending on the size of your pen this task can take minutes or hours. It is easiest to remove snow if it is done frequently. Once it piles up, it can take substantially longer to clear.

In addition, don't forget the weather's effect on other safety features such as electric fence lines. Snow and ice can disable electric fences quickly and without warning.

Icy pens are dangerous. You will need to sand slick areas to prevent your geese from spraining or breaking legs or feet. Do not use any snow or ice melting salts or chemicals in or around your goose enclosures. Keep in mind when snow melts, chemicals travel. If their pen is slippery, do not let them out in it until you make it safe for them. Again, this can take minutes or hours depending on the size of your pens.

We shovel paths in the snow for our geese to walk along

158

<u>Unsafe, Ice-Covered Ponds</u>

During freezing temps many goose ponds are partially to fully frozen. It is important to know when an icy pond is safe and when it is dangerous. Geese get excited at the prospect of water in any season and love to dive underwater and swim around. If your pond has too much ice coverage, your pet can get lost under the ice, become trapped, and drown.

This is an example of a pond that does NOT have enough exposed water.
This pond is NOT safe for geese.

This is an example of a pond that DOES have enough exposed water.
Better yet, the water is circulating. Ripples and movement on the water's surface
help geese see the open water. This pond IS safe for geese.

159

Consideration #10
Preventing Hatchings

When it comes to laying eggs, many ganders will protect a nest with more fervor and tenacity than a goose. Still, it will be your responsibility to remove eggs and prevent any unwanted hatchings. Be very attentive to how many geese you can effectively provide for before allowing any goslings to hatch out.

Think Ahead

Hatching out goslings should be taken just as seriously as when you brought your original geese/goslings home—even more so. Remember, you can't choose the sex or personality of new hatchlings.

Also keep in mind that although a pair of geese will parent their goslings together, they may need assistance protecting their goslings from other members of the gaggle. Their can be further difficulties when male goslings mature into ganders and need to compete with existing males. If you can't accommodate these changes, don't let your geese hatch out goslings.

If you do decide to let your female geese brood, be careful how many goslings you allow them to hatch out; you don't want to be one of those people creating an unwanted goose problem. You need to be responsible and avoid giving away goslings to people who do not understand the level of dedication it takes to care for a goose. Heaven forbid they become the person responsible for dumping a goose on a local pond where it can't possibly fend for itself.

- **Collect all eggs daily**

Make it a point to collect all of your eggs—especially when your goose is sitting on a nest. If you see your goose sitting in the same place day in and day out; she is most likely sitting on eggs. No matter how she protests, move her aside and remove them. You'll only hurt her feelings more later if you let her sit on them. If you have a biter on your hands, put on gloves to remove them, but *do* remove them.

If you're broody goose refuses to leave her nest and is not eating or drinking properly, remove her from her nest, remove all eggs and dismantle the nest. If you can lock her away from her nest, do so. Put her outside for a while, or use a portable playpen fence to block off the area. She may be agitated for a few hours, but she will eventually eat and drink and move on to other healthy behaviors.

- **Egg addling**

I have been contacted by many families who just couldn't bring themselves to remove the eggs from beneath their broody goose even though they didn't want goslings. At times like this it's important to provide another option. Remember, not everything that works for one family works for another.

If you can't bear to take eggs away and your goose is leaving their nest often enough to eat and drink, you can remove her daily egg and addle it (shake it vigorously). Write the date on the egg with a marker and then re-addle any prior-dated eggs one-by-one. I also advise that you candle the eggs frequently to be sure there are no signs of viable embryos. You can do this by setting them on a bright flashlight at night. Any spider-like veins forming inside of the shell are a sure sign that you've missed something.

The idea here is that sooner or later your goose will realize her eggs are not viable and she will abandon her nest. The downside is while you may be saving yourself a bit of heartache, you will also create yourself some extra work that is not entirely foolproof. Also on the downside is your goose will have put in all that effort for nothing and will have to abandon her hopes of motherhood at some point, so why not at the front end.

<u>The Mating Ritual</u>

The first time you witness a mating ritual between your gander and your goose, you may be a bit startled. Geese prefer to mate on water. A gander will use his bill to grab onto the feathers on the back of your goose's neck. He will pull himself up onto her back. Although your goose's head will sink under water, don't panic; she will soon come back up again. Experienced ganders will extend their wings to hold the goose in place as well. Less experienced ganders will do more "surfing" than actual mating.

Skynyrd mates Wilma

As long as your geese are relatively equal in size to your ganders, and you don't have more than one gander after them at one time, they will be just fine. In fact; I've noticed that it is just as often the geese initiating the courtship.

<u>Sexual Behavior</u>

I am going to include a couple of helpful hints about mating that you won't find in any other reference book (or at least not in any that I've ever read). We have fielded these questions from many families all over the world, which is a sure sign that I should include it in here, or it would be an injustice to you and your gaggle.

- **What is that thing?**

On more than one occasion I've been asked about the cork-screw looking thing dangling out of the cloaca of a gander. Frightened owners have contacted us thinking that their gander's entrails were falling out. It is an odd looking thing, but that's what it is. Rest assured, in a few minutes he'll bring it back inside again and your worries will be over.

- **Homosexuality**

Another common question we get is regarding homosexuality in geese. You may see some mating behavior between same sex geese.

Hormonal ganders will sometimes displace their over excitement and go after another gander instead of a goose. On occasion, you may need to protect your ganders from one another if they get a little bit crazy. Separations may be in order until hormone levels decline. On other occasions with same sex encounters, what you are actually witnessing are ganders vying for the alpha position in the gaggle. In either case, it is a good idea to break it up to avoid injuries.

Equally, don't be surprised when you walk out to your pens and find one of your geese "surfing" on the back of her girlfriend. You'll see her just standing there on her friend's back, holding onto to her by the scruff of the neck. You can shoo them off and take them for a swim with the ganders to get it out of their system, but you don't need to worry about this behavior. It is completely normal, especially in the spring. You can either break it up or ignore it (as long as no one is getting hurt). It means nothing, and separations are normally not needed with girls unless you have a heavy weight goose that could hurt a light weight goose by standing on her back. As with ganders, this behavior is sometimes used in re-affirming or establishing the pecking order.

- **Sex change**

We are often asked about geese transforming into ganders, or ganders suddenly laying eggs. In all of the instances we've encountered, a gender misidentification occurred. Someone thought they had a boy and then an egg suddenly appeared. The bird didn't actually change gender; it was just a case of mistaken identity. We have never witnessed or encountered a verified instance of a gander transforming into a goose or vice versa.

- **It's not aggression, it's passion**

To a gander, a human forearm and hand looks sort of like a goose's neck and head. Ganders bite and hold onto a female goose's neck feathers during mating. You may notice your ganders nibbling or biting at the backs of your hands or wrists. Be careful not to mistake this action for aggression. What you have on your hands is not an angry gander, but a bit of a passionate one. He's biting at the spot where he thinks you should have your neck feathers. Your boy is telling you that he loves you in one of the basic ways he knows how. This is just one of those habits that you are going to have to get used to as part of the ownership experience. If it gets too out of hand, try holding back a bit on some of the petting, which can sometimes stimulate hormonal behaviors and try some distraction techniques, like taking them on chaperoned walks. Avoid experimenting with hormonal drug therapies; they are un-effective and long-term studies have not been done on waterfowl to ensure their safety.

- **It's not offensive, it's defensive**

Geese will also bite if they are feeling afraid. Injured or lame geese are more vulnerable than other geese and will often bite more frequently as an act of self-preservation. Knowing how to approach a nervous goose can make all the difference in establishing a connection with them. Most geese prefer to be petted underneath the front of their bellies and then upwards towards the sides of their necks, and you'll often get a jiggle of happiness from them when you do this! Many geese do not like to be petted on their wings or back because this type of approach resembles a predatory attack. If you have a goose that is trying to bite you when you approach them, they are trying to tell you something. You will need to listen to what they're asking and then move forward accordingly. Geese thrive on routine and consistency, so for best results take small steps and practice with them daily.

Allowing a Hatch

For those who insist on hatching out goslings, avoid incubators and let your geese do the work.

- **Avoid incubating eggs**

Egg incubation requires careful attention to controlling temperature, humidity and turning the eggs. Requirements change in stages throughout the duration of incubation. We receive too many emails from people who hatched out goslings as a "fun" project and ended up with a seriously disabled gosling, or worse yet—*goslings*. This is frequently caused by improper incubation techniques. The geese are left to endure the consequences of your botched experiment.

Incubating should only be done by experienced individuals or under their direct guidance. Be careful, because many people will claim to know exactly what they are doing when they actually know little more than you do. The key to detecting these imposters is they are most likely to tell you how "simple" hatching is and will usually fail to offer any detailed information. A proficient person will be able to answer questions regarding temperature, humidity and turning rates right off the cuff—they know it. Avoid assistance from people who need to look up procedures and appear to be learning as they go.

Be proactive and ask your mentor how many times they have hatched out an abnormal gosling and what they have done with it. If you ask it in a matter-of-fact tone, some amateurs will actually admit to their faults. More often, however, these so-called *experts* will not tell you about the imperfect hatchings or the number of goslings that they have culled.

- **Let your goose do the work**

Geese are built by design to hatch out goslings, ensuring perfect temperature, humidity and knowing just when to roll their eggs. As with any animal, some geese are better at this than others.

If you are going to allow your goose to hatch out goslings, consider how many goslings you should let her hatch. Assume that every egg she sits on is viable. Do *not* account for duds. Geese often won't start seriously incubating until their nest is full, so do not remove extra eggs. As they lay them, you can remove, addle and mark them and then put them back underneath her.

For example, if you would like only one gosling, wait until she lays a couple eggs and begins nesting habits. Choose one egg for her to sit on. Remove the other eggs (one at a time), addle them, mark them with a marker and put them back into her nest. Addle each marked egg daily for 5 days and then candle them (set them on an upturned flashlight in a dark room) to ensure no red veins appear on the inner-shell surface.

Many geese will eventually push non-viable eggs out of the nest after a while, but not always.

Mating for life

While geese will frequently mate for life, ganders will still prefer options. Geese will often pair off, but if any single ladies appear on the scene, the alpha gander will pursue her and add her to his harem. Ganders will fight to protect their geese from being mated by other males, but at the same time they will often try to mate with other females if they can.

A romantic moment between Bunky and Pretty Girl

Geese crave routine and form close bonds with one another. Splitting up geese who have been together even for brief periods of time can be very stressful for them. They can mourn for long periods of time and even direct their anger towards the humans who have taken them away from each other. We've seen many cases where geese who were separated and later reunited immediately recognized each other. After witnessing so many happy reunions, we became convinced that bonded geese should stay together.

Consideration #11
Aggression

Geese really do get a bad rap when it comes to aggression. Geese are actually more protective than aggressive. It can take time to get a goose to trust you and you need to be patient as well as fearless while establishing this trust. Trying too accomplish too much too fast can have disastrous results.

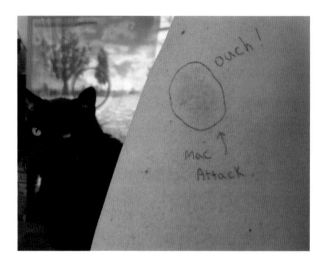

Does this photo really need explanation?

Handling an Attack:

First and foremost, protective clothing is a MUST when you have a naughty, afraid, irritated or untrained goose. Blue jeans, knee-high muck boots, a thick jacket, a pair of leather gloves and even protective eye gear can save you a lot of pain—*trust me!*

One strategy you can use to block an attacking goose who is coming towards you with an open bill is to grab them by the bill and hold it closed. It doesn't take an excessive amount of force to close a bill, so don't go crazy here. Always follow this action by saying, *"No!"* Most goose owners instinctively feel whether or not their goose will run away or come at them again upon release. If you know they have learned their lesson and will flee upon release, go ahead and let them go. When we release our geese we say, *"Up, up, up!"* in a cheerful voice. This then becomes the learned command that incites them to move along.

When Duran Duran first arrived at our sanctuary we referred to them as the *"pit vipers"* they were so misbehaved. Because they tended to tag-team us, our strategy for training them was to never enter their pen alone. When both Durans came at us, my husband and I would each take one. They were so out-of-control that we had to split them up into neighboring pens where they could be together and apart at the same time. They weren't nearly as brave when they couldn't rely on one another any more. It only took a couple weeks to teach them better manners and then they became wonderfully interactive.

One little trick I've discovered along the way is the introduction of a black broom handle with a yellow tip. I unscrewed the broom off of the end and use the handle to help me herd new geese. If I keep the yellow tip pointed towards the goose they tend to assume the pole is my neck and the yellow tip is my bill. Other times random "spooky" items can get a goose in line. I use a toilet bowl brush to scrub out heated water buckets in winter. For some reason it also acts as a magical "back up" wand when I wave it at even our bravest geese (it works on husbands too!).

- **Mounting a gander**

When blocking the attack of a goose be very careful around their wings. Most people fear the bite of a goose, but it's actually their wings, which can span up to five feet, that can do the most damage. If you close your goose's bill and they spread their wings in response, be ready with *Plan B*. This goose is not going to give up so easily. This is why it is *so* important to have the proper protective clothing on when you have a new goose that is not yet trained (or a naughty goose that you've let get out of control). Thick clothing will protect you while you get those wings under control.

Jetti flaps her enormous wings while Joop! looks on

You can control your goose's wings, by releasing their bill, doing a quick step to get behind them and then grabbing the base of their wings (at the point where they attach to your goose's back) as you move. Remember not to use excessive force when doing this—just enough to hold their wings and get them folded into place while you straddle over them and then squat down on top of them (without putting any weight on them) to teach them a quick lesson about who's in charge. Once you are in this position, gently push your goose's neck down to the ground. This is called *mounting*. Now you are communicating in their language.

Do not dismount your goose until you are sure that they have relinquished their attack and will not turn on you again when you stand up and step away with a cheerful, *"Up, up, up!"* (or whatever command you want to use to teach them to move along).

If I'm mounting a gander and don't get that feeling from him that the fight is over, I slip one hand under them from behind, slip it between his legs and then lift him up and carry him over to the pond. I've never met a gander who didn't "give" once plopped gently into the water. It just seems to break the spell.

Tony gently pins down an aggressive gander

- **Assert yourself as the alpha gander**

Some geese will relinquish alpha leadership to you immediately upon meeting you. These geese will want to be your subordinates. Others will want to push you around and vie for this heralded position. It is absolutely vital that you do not grant them this position over you or you can invite serious behavioral problems down the road. The last thing you want is a large, out-of-control gander displacing you as the alpha leader. You want to establish and maintain your position in the hierarchy.

The bottom line is if you want your geese to be well-behaved it is imperative that they respect you. To earn their respect you must embrace and demonstrate what geese see as leadership qualities. Geese want an alpha gander who is fearless, fair and generous (and fun certainly doesn't hurt either!). To be this you cannot back down from any of your geese. You must enter your pen exuding confidence and good cheer. If you are nervous or uneasy, they will know.

After learning impeccable manners at our sanctuary the Durans were quickly adopted. Their high level of inter-activeness really caught the attention of their new family. We were careful to advise the family that they would have to rule the boys with a firm and loving hand to maintain their good behavior, but unfortunately, that is easier said than done. It takes time and effort to train geese and to keep them trained.

These two Toulouse ganders know they're big and they enjoy using their size and enormous wing spans to test their boundaries and see what they can get away with. A few months into their new home their family contacted us. They were very upset that they could not keep the boys any longer, but they had become too out-of-control for handling. We arranged for the boys' speedy return and the family adopted a gentle gander from us instead.

I can't tell you how misbehaved these boys had become in those months away from us. Without continued training they reverted back to their old habits and came back to us as pit vipers—worse yet, *Duranasaurs*. They were so bad I could no longer control them on my own. My husband Tony and I had to enter their pen together in order to thwart off the barrage of attacks. The boys had learned to strike out at anyone who entered their pen—even more so if we had a bucket of food in our hands. Not good. The behavior had to be stopped. It took weeks of active intervention to establish ourselves as the alpha leaders in the pen, but eventually they got the message. They were no longer in charge.

166

The interesting thing about this story is, with all that power, the Duranasaurs weren't all that happy. They were stressed and nervous and easily agitated—conditions which can lead to health issues. Additionally, they didn't fit in with the rest of our gaggle. Their behavior was so unacceptable our other geese would have no part of them. They were ostracized for months until their behavior finally came back into check and then once they fully re-embraced the rules and boundaries again, they became relaxed and balanced geese. The reward for this was their acceptance into the gaggle, which furthered their pleasure.

The moral of this story is, if you think you are doing you or your geese a favor by allowing them to run around like tyrants, you're not.

- **Be fearless**

Whether you are adopting geese or raising them up from goslings, you may find yourself at the whim of a tyrannical alpha gander. My rule of thumb with geese is: *Never run from a goose or you will be forever running.*

When Ali and Chan first came to us, Ali was the alpha leader, and Chan was his gentle subordinate. Within minutes of his arrival to the sanctuary, Ali attempted to put me in my place with a good bite and a pretty harsh wing beating. For our own future safety, I had to set to the immediate task of establishing myself as his alpha leader. It was vital that I didn't fall into a subordinate position at the get-go, setting the pace for future interactions. The longer you are assigned to a subordinate position, the more difficult it can be to reverse the role.

After my brief confrontation with Ali, I waited for the two newcomers to settle back down, and then I re-entered the pen wearing protective clothing—a thick winter jacket, protective boots and thick gloves. Ali immediately ran over to challenge me, but I stayed in place and raised my arms out from my sides to make myself look bigger. I did not back away, nor did I step forward. I stayed confident; I leaned forward and mimicked the hissing sounds he made at me, being sure that my sounds were a little more poignant than his.

He stopped a few feet in front of me, using his better judgment and deciding that I might be too much for him to tackle. After a few seconds of stand off, I took a slight step forward, raising my knee into the air and slightly stomping my one foot down on the ground. It was a very controlled and precise movement. He held his ground and hissed again. I repeated the action with my other foot as I stepped forward again, and hissed at him with my arms still out at my sides—like big open wings. At one point he lunged forward and snapped at me, but I quickly crossed my arms in front of me in a "genie style" pose, which blocked his attempt. I leaned towards him with my still-crossed arms, an action that forced him back a few steps without me actually having to push him. My thick coat was a safety buffer between my arms and his bill if I needed it. He wasn't expecting my fearlessness. He stood there hissing at me for a moment (and I continued to hiss back) and then he relinquished and took a step back.

I continued to take small steps towards him, but decisive steps, with a good stomp to punctuate them. I kept my eyes focused on his eyes. I did not show fear. He stopped hissing and backed up again. I said, *"I am in charge"* and meant it, *"I am not afraid of you."* He turned away and quickly moved to the other side of the pen with his pal Chan. I stood in place, silent and still, for a minute and then backed out of the pen. I stood outside of the closed pen door, looking in at Ali for a moment, and then I walked away and gave him some time to think.

Over the course of the next couple weeks, I entered their pen a few times a day and went about my business with little regard for what they were doing. I made it a point to walk near them, but I showed no immediate interest in them. I would not just wander in the pen aimlessly and walk about. I would assign myself a specific task to accomplish before entering the pen; then, I would step inside and go about doing it. When my task was complete, I would leave the enclosure. Tasks can be as simple as going into the pen to refresh their hay, top off food dishes, or change out a water source. You can also enter with the mindset that you will check the sturdiness of every third fence post—an imaginary task, but any task will work, even if it's just a sham.

Lewy acts aggressively, but he's really just afraid and in need of comfort

The attitude you want to exude when entering your pen is one that is confident and determined. I say *your* pen as opposed to *their* pen because you want to think of all enclosures as belonging to you—that's part of this mindset. Be careful not to be reckless or confrontational; avoid any fast or jumpy movements. Stay in control, do not panic, and remain relaxed—never paranoid. Remember, you want to be their protector; think of yourself this way when you enter. If you seem nervous or frightened to them, they will not put their trust in you. You must be the bravest in the gaggle in order for them to relinquish their power to you and respect you.

Avoid looking at your geese when you are in the pen; pretend instead that they are not even there (do keep the alpha's whereabouts subtly in mind though… never turn your back on the ocean, I always say). Avoid focusing on any subordinate geese who have nothing to prove. This can actually draw a negative reaction from a protective alpha gander.

If you hear a gander coming toward you while you are in the pen, turn quickly and confidently, raise your arms out from your sides to make yourself bigger and hiss while making eye contact. He should stop. If he does not back away from you, then you will want to take a small step forward—with a small, but reaffirming stomp to the ground as your foot comes down. A good trick is to wear an unzipped coat when you are entering the pen. If your goose decides to challenge you, just grab the bottom zipper corners of your coat in each of your hands. When you lift your arms out to your sides your gander will take your makeshift wings very seriously and will often back down from his attack.

Be careful not to take things too far. You want to establish yourself as a trustworthy leader, not as a tyrant. You want their respect, not their fear. As soon as the gander relinquishes their challenge and moves away from you, you have done enough. There is no need to chase him off. Stand still for a moment while he backs off and then slowly go about your business again. If he comes at you again, just repeat the same tactics.

Once you have displaced the alpha goose and assumed the role for yourself, it will be time for you to become friends with your geese. The attitude you exude during your visits should slowly shift as your goal shifts. To prepare them for your first visits, find a chair that will keep you at an advantage when you are sitting in it (not too low to the ground at first). Bring the chair out to their pen and leave it there. Don't sit in it; just leave it there empty to give them time to get used to the new object. After a couple days, go ahead and relax in it. Bring them a few healthy snacks and visit with them. Geese also enjoy it when we mimic their vocalizations. Do those things which put your geese at ease and you will be on your way to a great relationship.

Consideration #12
Time Investment

If you have time in your life for trips to the vets (although they are rarely, if ever, needed with healthy birds), replenishing feeders and water dispensers, building safe havens, cleaning barns, enclosures, kiddy pools, basins and buckets, and picking up sticks and stones, then geese are for you! In addition, you'll need to save some time for all of the foraging walks, swims in the pond, walks up the stream, visits near the kiddy pool, hugs in the barn, etc. Geese are welcome members of the family when you see all of these responsibilities as part of the fun and not as an added burden.

- **Morning and evening routines for geese**

Most sources will say that geese are practically maintenance free, but this is not the case, and this myth resides at the core of the abandonment issue. It seems like a nice idea at first, but once reality kicks in, many owners will dump off their pet to free up their schedules.

You cannot appreciate the marvel of happy geese until they join your family, but if you don't have the time to dedicate to their set-up, care and enrichment, you should not acquire them. On any given day pet goose owners should not only be prepared to spend the time replenishing food, drinking water and kiddy pools, but also interacting with their pets. Geese need a quick attending to in the morning, before work, and a lengthier visit in the evening. Many pet goose owners tell us that they spend up to two hours a day with their feathered friends and more on weekends.

Morning routines at our sanctuary begin at five a.m. and entail fifteen to thirty minutes of time, depending upon the season and our number of guests. Doors are unlocked and geese are escorted from their evening enclosures to their day enclosures. Fresh hay, food and water are provided and a little time is spent saying good-bye for the day. Be wary, geese can be very adept at talking you into playing hooky for the day!

At the end of the day, follow up routines are necessary. After replenishing food, providing fresh water and touching up hay as needed, it's time to enjoy your gaggle. Geese look forward to your company, so don't deprive them or yourself of it. They are great stress relievers and provide wonderful end-of-day therapy.

Weekends will require more of your time and involvement. Keeping pens properly cleaned and maintained is best done regularly to keep tasks manageable. The longer you wait to clean out a barn, the longer it is going to take you. Depending on your pond system, you may need to set aside extra time for its maintenance as well. None of these tasks are so overwhelming as to be unmanageable, but you need to be prepared for what you are getting into before you acquire a gaggle—even a small one.

- **Continual care for goslings**

Unlike taking care of adult geese in the morning and evening, goslings need to be checked on frequently throughout the day, especially if you want them to imprint on you. Missing out on this valuable time with your goslings is passing on one of life's greater pleasures. Goslings grow fast, so enjoy them while you can! And remember the more you bond with them now, the stronger your shared bond will be as they mature.

Consideration #13
Finding a Goose-sitter

Going somewhere? Any time my husband and I decide to venture out into the world with the understanding that we won't be back by nightfall, goose consideration is needed. We need to decide whether we will arrive to the function late, whether we will lock up the geese early, whether one of us will leave the function temporarily and then return again, or whether only one of us will attend the function.

Mac carefully considers his options before choosing a good goose-sitter

When we only had a couple geese, my father used to goose-sit when we were away. I made an instructional video for him to watch, left vet phone numbers on the refrigerator and gave him a walk through of the routine. Geese are very habitual animals, so the closer your goose-sitter adheres to the normal routine, the easier it will be on both the geese and their sitter.

With the sanctuary in place, our vacations are taken separately, so one of us is always home with the waterfowl. I cannot tell you how many emails we have received from folks who have lost their geese to an irresponsible goose-sitter who either did not show up to lock up the gaggle for the night, or did an improper head count and left a member of the gaggle outside. Predators take full advantage of these types of mistakes. Be very wary of who you choose to help you out when you are away.

Consideration #14
Letting Go

As with any pet, there will come a time when you will have to say good-bye. All good things come to an end, but as my mother once said, *"This friend leaving makes a space in your home for someone else, and that someone else is out there waiting for you to find them."*

Keep in mind that your flock members will most likely choose different times to leave this world. You may suddenly find yourself with one lonely goose and you will need to consider how you will keep that one goose happy. You will need to decide whether to adopt a companion for your goose or spend a *lot* more time with the goose you have left, which could easily be a commitment of many more years yet.

Euthanasia

Although no one likes to think about it, families sometimes need to make a choice when it comes to the care of their fading goose, especially if pain or suffering (that has no hope of relief) is involved. My husband and I rely on each other's and our vet's opinion when it comes to making the decision to euthanize a goose. We only proceed if the decision is clear and all three of us are in absolute agreement.

If you're anything like me, you won't be in the proper state of mind to ask your vet questions about how they will ease your goose over to the other side, so although it may be uncomfortable to read this now, it may make things a little less stressful if you are ever faced with this later.

Most vets will use a two injection procedure when putting your pet goose to sleep. Some vets will give both injections in front of you while others will administer the first in a back room and then bring your goose to you before giving them the second injection. For the emotional sake of my geese, I prefer to be present for both injections, so that they are always with someone familiar. I just can't have any of my once-abandoned geese feeling any kind of abandonment again at the end of their life. I stay with them and talk to them and try to comfort them while they slip away.

When you and your goose are ready, your vet will administer the first injection, which is an intramuscular sedative that induces euphoria, commonly Telazol. This is a mixture of tiletamine (dissociative anesthetic) and zolazepam (sedative). Together these two drugs induce an extremely effective sedation that approximates complete anesthesia where pain is not felt by your goose. Some geese will flap their wings during this state and try to fly. They are not in pain or uncomfortable, they are just in a euphoric state. I sometimes wonder where they are trying to fly to...

The second injection is commonly administered intravenously; it is usually some type of barbiturate injection that causes rapid cardiac arrest.

Grieving

You will not be the only one to grieve when one of your geese dies. Keep in mind that some of your flock members may take it even harder than you, depending how close they were. If you have effectively established yourself as the alpha leader you can help your remaining geese through their recovery by engaging them in distracting activities.

We have witnessed depression among the gaggle when a member dies. Sometimes all flock members are affected, sometimes none, and other times just one or two. You may notice a change in diet, or witness an unwillingness to partake in usual routines or even lethargy. Some geese refuse to swim or frequent places where they used to go with their beloved companion while others refuse to leave those places.

We have witnessed geese stubbornly refusing to leave a particular location, honking in agitation—thinking that they are leaving the missing member behind. Others will become depressed and sulk in the same location for long periods of time if you do not intervene. Still other geese will actively search and call for the missing goose. We've noticed this behavior is especially prevalent if a goose was euthanized or passed away while away from home—in a vet's office. There seems to be more peace when the gaggle witnesses the death than when a flock member just suddenly vanishes. Grieving also tends to be more profound in smaller gaggles.

It can take some time for your gaggle to re-settle after the departure of one of their friends—anywhere from a few days to a few months. Their grieving will most likely worsen your grieving, but you need to get them through it by keeping their routine consistent and by providing added enrichment activities to help them endure. Be patient while they recover and resettle and consider introducing someone new if you think it will help.

Geese will mourn for their lost loved ones

Losing Ethel

Ethel was an amazing goose. She and Lucy both came to us together and were the best of friends, but when Ethel passed away unexpectedly it proved to be more than Lucy could handle. Geese will commonly call out for their missing loved ones to the point of distraction. Many will refuse to eat or drink and still others will segregate themselves in depression, which is what Lucy did.

When you're the alpha in charge of your gaggle, your geese will look to you for guidance and support when a member is no longer with them. Although you are allowed to mourn with your geese, you don't want to completely fall apart in front of them. Geese look to their alpha leader for comfort and strength during stressful times, so it's up to you to provide them with these things. You don't want to ignore that a member has been lost; you just want to reassure them that everything's going to be okay. Helping your geese cope with their loss will often help you in your healing as well.

Because Ethel and Lucy were best friends and had always known each other, Lucy took Ethel's loss the hardest. She no longer wanted to remain around the other geese and took to wandering around alone. When a goose gets depressed like this it is important to let them know that you are still being attentive to them. More frequent visits to their pen with treats is one way to let them know that they are not alone. Encouraging them to regroup with the gaggle by luring everyone in for goodies or to play with toys is another way to re-engage them. You may even want to add a new goose to your gaggle (especially if your goose is all alone now) to initiate new friendships.

Lucy & Ethel

Although it took a couple of months for Lucy to recover from Ethel's loss, with our devotion and encouragement she came to form close bonds with other geese in the gaggle and her days soon became happy again.

Enrichment

Enrichment

Once you've decided that you want geese or goslings your will want some ideas of fun activities for you and your geese to do. Geese are very intelligent and inquisitive birds, and any good pet owner will want their geese to live happy and enriched lives as opposed to sitting in a pen, bored all day.

We are often asked the difference between ducks and geese and I always respond by saying, *"If you put something new in a duck's enclosure they will fearfully avoid that section of their pen for at least three days. Geese, on the other hand, will run right over and investigate what you've brought for them."* This being the case, here are some fun ideas for you to try with them.

Enrichment #1
Water

Without a doubt, water is the greatest source of pleasure for a goose, and they don't really care what form it comes in: a bucket, a basin, a pool, a hose or a pond.

The Kiddy Pool

Some geese will sit in their kiddy pools all day long, while others will only take quick, refreshing dips. Geese who sit on their kiddy pools all day will need their water changed daily (sometimes twice daily). Geese who only dabble on their water may only need their swimming water changed every other day, except in the summer when it should be changed daily to prevent fermenting algae. The rule of thumb is: *if you can smell it, you should've already changed it.*

Geese love it when you show up to change their water and will soon recognize exactly what it is you're doing. Pools often can't be refilled quickly enough for their taste. They will commonly stand by, monitoring the progress and then with a surge of impatience, they tend to step in and sit in an inch of water, waiting for the level to rise.

Lewy makes a splash in his kiddy pool

The Garden Hose

The garden hose is not only an essential tool for refilling kiddy pools and washing the poop off the ground at the end of the day to keep your enclosure clean, but it is a wonderful way to bring good cheer to your geese. You do want to be careful of tripping your geese with the hose whenever bringing it into their enclosure—especially once the level of excitement picks up and they lose track of what they are doing. Also, be careful of spraying your geese with a hose that has been lying out in the sun; you don't want to scorch your friends.

Hot days are great days to string out the hose and stir up some excitement. Set it to a light spray and aim the cold water a foot or two up into the air. Most geese will truly appreciate this means of cooling off. Some geese prefer to be sprayed with a light shower, others will only stand under a slight misting that comes down from above, and still others prefer to stand under a hose without a nozzle that just pours out over them. Some only like their bellies sprayed while others like it when you start at the top and work your way down to their feet. You can even add a sprinkler attachment and leave it on for a few minutes of fun.

The Pond

Walks to the ponds are similar fun-filled adventures. There is nothing greater than a trip to the pond for some good water fun as well as a few tasty water plants. It's a lot of fun watching them get so excited that they dive under water and then soar up and flap their wings, actually getting a bit of lift off of the water.

Enrichment #2
Transplanting

Tall Grass, Foliage and Bushes

I always transplant interesting grasses and plants into my goose enclosure in the spring. It is a fun day for geese who just love to help explore the new greenery while you are working. I would not suggest planting anything you really care about in their pens because unless you put up protective fencing, they will make quick work of it. Also be careful that you do not transplant toxic plants into their enclosures. I highly recommend that you buy a book of your local flora to help guide you in this regard as well as consulting online sources such as the ASPCA (www.aspca.org) for lists of plants toxic to birds.

Geese love a good shade bush, especially in summer. Digging a hole in the ground to drop plants into is also a wonderful activity for curious geese who need to be a part of everything. Just be careful to keep them at a safe distance from your shovel to avoid any accidents.

Enrichment #3
Delectable Delights

Worms

Not all geese are appreciative of a good earthworm, so don't get upset if yours won't go near them or see them as invaders and attack them. At our sanctuary the geese watch the ducks feast on nightcrawlers, but turn their bills at such grotesque behavior. Even so, many of them have gone onto new homes where they have learned from other geese that these protein-filled snacks are a fine delicacy that should be appreciated.

Enrichment #4
Welcoming New Flock Members

There are few things more exciting in goose ownership than the moment when you introduce new flock members to your gaggle. You may witness different reactions each time depending on the geese. Always chaperone introductions, even if things appear peaceful at first. Once you are sure they are getting along well, check in on them frequently to ensure things are still going smoothly.

Tag

A common reaction to new flock members is what we refer to as "tag." The new goose will run over to greet your goose only to find that your goose keeps running away. This nervous curiosity can come from either direction. Eventually, they'll all grow weary from all of that running around and they will tend to settle down for a nap within a few feet of each other. It tends to only take a couple of days for things to cool down and a few weeks for both parties to become friends.

Love at First Sight

Some geese will instantly bond with a new goose, and they will all stick together right away. These meetings can result in strong friendships or everlasting love.

Mac hugs Elizabeth

Hey, That's My Man

When faced with a new gaggle, a newly introduced hen will often approach one of the ganders for protection. If that gander already has a mate, his mate may get upset about this and give the new girl a good, *"Hey, that's my man!"* Hens usually work out their issues very quickly and become fully cohesive within a day or two.

Mac gives Jenn a kiss

Aggression

It is not uncommon for pecking order rituals to arise before members become friends. This tends to occur when you welcome home a dominant gander that is not quickly put in his place. Your alpha gander may not appreciate a strong-minded newcomer, and a willful newcomer is not likely to give in easily to the existing pecking order. The more evenly matched two dominant geese are (no matter what their gender), the longer it will take them to resolve the issue.

If things get out of hand, put a divider fence (that they cannot fit their bills through) between them for a couple days. Keep them safely adjacent to each other, and let them work it out from opposite sides of a shared fence for a few days before trying to introducing them again. Spats are normal, but if it is not resolved within a minute, or if it appears to be getting too rough (beware of eye injuries), separate them and try again in another few days.

If things are strained at first, try not to worry, and just give them more time. We have had a couple female geese come through the sanctuary who were so ornery, it took months for them to successfully merge with the other geese, but on the whole, female goose troubles are pretty rare. We just waited them out and kept them in adjacent pens until they got bored with all the bickering.

There are occasions (especially between evenly matched ganders) when an existing flock member and a newcomer just can't work it out. In these cases semi-permanent separations may be in order—each goose in their own pen. Ganders who don't get along in the same pen will often enjoy one another's company when they are kept in neighboring pens. Friendships can even be formed this way—it just takes time.

Establishing Trust

If you are adopting adult geese remember that these animals have been displaced and may be very fearful of you at first (and sometimes fear is expressed as anger). This is completely normal. Allow them a couple of weeks with as little contact as possible. You want them to see you and to begin to understand that you are only there to fill the feeders and refresh the water and lay down some fresh hay. When their level of concern regarding your presence has eased off, it will become time to interact with them.

Geese model behavior, so newcomers will be closely watching the veterans. If you have your own geese who are unafraid of you, let the newcomers see you interacting with your geese. You will usually see them watching you very intently during these interactions.

Always approach a shy goose from the front. When you pet a shy goose on the back of their neck or on top of their wings you are mimicking a predatory attack, which will immediately put them on the defensive. Instead, stay well in their view, use slow movements and touch them gently with one or two fingers on the front or side of the neck. Keep these sessions very brief in the beginning. Touch the goose only once or twice while giving them a treat and then leave. Do not increase this time until the goose is a little more comfortable with it. Then, do it more than once a day and for longer durations. Just remember more progress is made when you keep your routine sessions brief and you proceed slowly. Trust does not come quickly and if you force it and push forward too fast, you may not get the same wonderful results.

If certain geese are particularly skittish, visit their barn or shed at night while wearing dark clothing. Turn off the lights and pet the geese in the dark. They can't see well in the dark, are less likely to panic and will allow more petting. Be sure to talk calmly to them during your visits, so they get to know your voice.

Not all geese want to be held, but many will get used to it if you ease into it and continue to do so regularly. One little trick is to go in their barn or shed *just before* sunrise on your day off, hold your goose on your lap and wait for sunrise. As it gets lighter, they will slowly realize what's going on. As soon as they begin to struggle, set them down.

Shy Salvadore

When working on holding your goose during daylight hours, be sure that they can see their other flock members, so they won't panic. When working on socializing more than one newcomer, switch off holding different geese on different days to avoid over-stressing your gaggle.

Enrichment #5
Walks & Foraging

Sometimes it's nice to take your geese for visits to parts of the yard that they don't normally see, provided it is safe. If you have a garden, they will love to forage through it—just keep them away from your lettuce or you won't have any left! Our geese have their own special garden that is planted just for them, and they go crazy with excitement anytime we go anywhere near it.

Safe Walks

Keep in mind that geese will often see things before you do while on their walks, so pay close attention to their body language and take interest in what they are looking at. When you see them tip their heads to look at something, take a moment to look as well. If they give the alarm honk to their fellow flock members, you need to take a good look around and figure out what is startling them.

Whatever you do, stay close to your geese and don't leave them for a minute. If an emergency comes up and you need to break away from your geese, lead them back to their enclosure before leaving them alone. Predators may be closer than you think. They are opportunistic, will wait and watch for long periods of time and they are much faster than your goose—and you.

Taking Your New Geese for Walks

Although taking a goose you've raised from a gosling for a swim can be pretty uneventful because they know the routine, new goslings should not be brought to open water where you can't protect them. Birds of prey can take a gosling away right in front of your eyes and have been known to do it, so be careful where you lead your little friend.

Taking newcomers for walks outside of their pen is entirely different from walking with a goose who has been with you for some time, and it should be done with great caution. If you are adding to an existing gaggle, don't let your new members out of their pen until you are absolutely certain they consider themselves part of your existing gaggle. You want to have no doubts in your mind that they will stick close to you or your original geese. Keep their first trip outside of their pen close in proximity and brief in time. Do this multiple times and eventually, slowly, let them build up their confidence and forage a little further away and for a little longer.

Skynyrd and Isabel hunt for muscles in the pond

A new goose can panic and run if they see or hear something out of the ordinary, so you need to slowly get them accustomed to their new surroundings before you take them on any long or distant adventures. Your new goose will eventually learn to feel safe in its new space. Once this happens, it is less likely to frighten off of your property. When my geese are frightened they tend to head straight for their pens or the pond, whichever one is closest. This is what you want. If you think your goose would run somewhere other than these safe places, you may be venturing too far for them yet.

Another helpful tool is portable playpen fencing. They are small fences that fold up and store easily and just as easily unfold into a straight fence or an octagon pen. Large commercial pet stores usually carry them, and they are a great item to have on hand. You can very easily split up a section of a barn or a pen with one of these in order to stop fighting too.

You can shape these fences to make a clear path or "run" for your newcomers to follow. It normally only takes a matter of days for them to learn their routine, provided it is done at least twice a day and occurs around the same times. We always know when it's safe to discontinue using these portable runs when the geese begin to lose site of what's off to their left and right and instead focus on the goal at the end—where you want them to go. Once they hurry straight forward to their destination at the end of the path, be it the pond, the barn or their enclosure, we take down the fencing. We continue to supervise new geese very closely during walks without fences for at least another week. We have at least one other person on hand until we are absolutely certain that we won't have any difficulties.

While walking behind a group of goose in route to a particular destination, we often follow behind with our "waddle wand." I have a black broom handle with a yellow tip that I use to guide flock members from one place to another.

Once geese learn to move according to direction given by the waddle wand, hand signals can be incorporated and subsequently substituted. It doesn't take long for geese to learn to follow directions during normal routines. I can point to most individuals in our gaggle and signal them to step forward through a gate while holding a palm up to those members who should remain where they are. Geese will associate your hand signals with expected movement, as long as you are clear and consistent.

If you have geese that already know the routine, new geese will most likely follow your geese and learn the routine that way (which is the easiest method). You will be amazed how quickly newcomers figure out the way to go especially if you keep their routine consistent.

We have very specific and timed routines for our newcomers. Within days, they master their routine without any guidance or instruction. Once this is accomplished, we can begin teaching them how to interpret our signals, so they can be directed with ease through our internal maze of pens and gates.

Taking Your New Geese for Swims

On the same note, do not let new flock members go loose on a large pond on your property or they will most likely not come back off—especially at dusk. The pond is off limits to them until they have been with you long enough to learn a routine of walking down at certain times and coming off when you call. You will know without a doubt when your geese will come off of a pond. If you are nervous about it at all, it probably means you have not arrived at that point yet.

Skynyrd prefers boating to swimming

Some geese never want to come off of a pond. We use a long pole to clear the geese off of our ponds. When the geese won't come off, we slowly sweep the pole across the surface of the pond and herd the geese off of the water. It doesn't take the geese long to realize when they see the pole, it's time to get off of the water. For larger bodies of water, you may need a kayak or canoe to round up your stubborn gaggle. Don't let them get away with their behavior, make them come off the pond when you want them off, or you will reinforce their bad behavior.

Bringing Your Goose into Your Home

Don't laugh—plenty of goose owners bring their geese inside for a walk around the house. You can actually measure your goose and purchase a machine washable diaper harness for them. All you need to do is provide a simple measurement of your goose and go online (www.indoorducks.com) to purchase a goose diaper harness. The harness snaps into place and holds a pad or baby diaper in it, so you don't have to worry about your goose pooping all over the floor.

Some people have geese who spend their entire lives indoors and are perfectly happy. Just remember to keep them on a healthy diet and avoid feeding them unhealthy table scraps. If you think a begging dog can be annoying, wait until you have a goose honking at the table for goodies.

One word of caution: don't be quick to try to save yourself the money of purchasing a harness by trying to make one yourself. We have seen make-shift harnesses that did not fit properly and resulted in broken and damaged feathers and even bald spots in some areas. Diaper harnesses need to fit properly. If you see any feather breakage or damage, you should permanently discontinue use and allow feathers to re-grow.

Skynyrd wears his diaper harness while in the house with Elizabeth

Dress Up Time

I can't tell you how many people are having fun by dressing up their geese, but there are LOTS of them! From Leprechauns to Santa Claus, from tuxedos to ballerinas, you name it, there's probably a costume (www.thegoosemother.com) somewhere online for it.

Skynyrd loves to get dressed up for the occasion

182

Goose Shoes

Goose shoes may just seem like a fun dress-up accessory, but they can also be essential in post-operative care following foot surgery. Closed-toe booties can help keep feet sanitary while holding bandages and medicine in place; they can also provide cushioning to a tender foot and even provide comfort and stability.

Photo Courtesy of www.indoorducks.com

Skynyrd sports a fashionable pair of booties

Deco Lawn Geese

Some goose lovers have discovered the fun of dressing up their plastic lawn geese. Fashion options are practically unlimited and many of the outfits will double as designs for your pet geese as well (www.lawngoosedesigns.com). Just be careful of any small parts and *always* supervise your goose while they are clothed to prevent any tripping/choking hazards.

Plastic lawn geese can be hard to find, but costumes are plentiful!

Sculpture

Another project designed more for my enjoyment than theirs is painting lawn statues. I like to purchase goose statues and then detail them with acrylic paints to look like some of our rescued geese. After that I top them off with a good clear coat and they are ready for display.

Goose sculptures can be custom painted to look more like your pet

184

Fun with Graphics

We found one website (www.bighugelabs.com) with a make-your-own movie poster option. It makes a great specialized gift for the goose-lover in your family—or someone else's. Have fun and be creative!

Skynyrd in his motion picture debut!

Letting Your Goose Swim In Your Pool

I can certainly envision the fun of having a goose swimming in my pool with me, until they poop. Although it is not for me, many owners have sent photos of themselves sharing their pools with their spoiled geese. If you want to swim with your goose, I think the best advice is: don't drink the water. This means small children should not be in the pool, since they tend to do just that. After the swimming session is complete, you may want to crank up the chlorine for a while.

Jenn shares her pool with Lynyrd, Skynyrd, Golly and Ms. Donald

If your goose is swimming in your pool, you want to be very wary of chlorine levels. I'm not sure what affect chlorine has on oiled feathers, but I'm sure long term exposure can't be entirely helpful. If you see feather issues, it is clearly time to stop this practice. Additionally, chlorine can irritate human eyes, and I'm sure prolonged exposure can equally harm your goose's eyes. Keep swimming sessions brief. The few people we have heard of who swim with their geese do not use chlorine in their pools, but have salt water systems instead.

Skynyrd floats in the pool... literally...

Enrichment #6
Fun Treats

During the winter, when grass is unavailable, geese should have greens in their diet—they love greens! Delicious fruits are another nutritious treat for your goose year-round.

Leaf Lettuce

I have found that spring lettuce mixes are a real win. I buy a few bags of the store brand every week and sprinkle it around on the hay every night and also in their water dishes. Be careful not to offer them anything with a long stem that can ball up in their gullet and cause a digestive problem. If you are going to buy a large leaf vegetable make very sure that it is served in small pieces. Scissors are a great way to cut leaves into smaller portions for your geese.

Time for salad!

A fun fall and winter activity is to hide lettuce treats around your goose's pen before letting them outside and then watch the foraging fun begin! This doesn't work as well in spring and summer when the grass has come in.

Some foods that you may think are good for your geese may actually be bad for them. Spinach is one of a few seemingly healthy treats that your geese may love, but that should actually be avoided. Beneficial calcium that your geese need for their egg-laying binds with the oxalic acid in spinach and is then removed from their system. Some other snacks that are high in oxalate and should be avoided are: beets, celery, collard greens, dandelion greens, eggplant, escarole, green beans, kale, leeks, okra, parsley, parsnips, green peppers, pokeweed, sweet potatoes, pumpkin, rhubarb, rutabagas, sorrel, squash, swiss chard, tomato sauce, turnip greens, watercress and yams.

Fruit

Watermelon, honey dew melons and cantaloupe are some favorite goose treats. In summer, serve them cold to help your gaggle beat the heat.

Mac wipes out a cantaloupe

Fanny enjoys her honeydew

188

Herbs

Another trick of mine is to go to an herbal supplement store. There are some brand names that sell herb capsules. I buy alfalfa and also dandelion roots in capsule form. I break open the capsules over their water buckets and they really seem to enjoy sucking up the ground herbs.

When giving geese winter baths, you can increase their fun by adding herbs or lettuce to their bath water. It gives them something to forage for while they're playing around in there. Bath time always kicks up a notch once the treats are introduced.

Enrichment #7
Eggs

If you have female geese, you will eventually get eggs. While I'm not a big fan of duck eggs, goose eggs are pretty good, and one crack makes a huge omelet! Be sure to collect eggs everyday, clean them well and refrigerate them immediately. If you discover a hidden egg in the pen that may have been there for an unknown period of time, don't eat it. Be careful not to dispose of unwanted eggs anywhere near your goose enclosure. You don't want hungry animals learning this is the place to find snacks. It's best to dispose of them with your regular garbage.

In addition, you should know that goose eggs should be cooked thoroughly before eating. In other words, don't eat them sunny side up. They have a higher risk of salmonella poisoning associated with them than chicken eggs. You want to clean them well and cook them thoroughly.

Wilma and Ms. Donald's eggs

Geese can be good at hiding their eggs. I have stumbled upon hidden clutches of eggs at the start of the laying season (with no one sitting on them). Consider yourself warned—if your females are laying fertile eggs and they have access to sit on them all day, search carefully before concluding that there are no eggs to find. This is a great daily adventure if you have children, but remember to have them wash their hands right afterwards. Speaking of children, in my house we color eggs all the time. We don't wait for Easter to have that kind of fun around here!

Enrichment #8
Girls, Boys & Love

Spring and early summer are eventful seasons for geese. It is the season of love. They are not the only ones having a good time; it's pretty funny to watch all the flirting going on. Occasionally a love triangle can spark some intrigue in the goose pen.

The real crack up for me is right after doing their business, the girls get right to splashing and getting cleaned up, while the boys put on a proud display that includes a good love trumpet (more on this in a minute!)

Geese Recognize Each Other

Another interesting tid-bit about the bonds between geese is although you may have trouble distinguishing geese from one another and remembering who's who, they have no difficulty telling one another apart, even after long periods of time.

We rescued Harmony and Melody a few months before finding a home for them. Their new family opted to take in the rest of their family as well, so we went back to the lake and rescued the rest of them. When Harmony and Melody were re-introduced to their parents and brother they instantly recognized each other. Unfortunately, their little brother Egor had to remain with us a while longer and missed out on that home, but he ended up finding an amazing family of his own only a couple of months later.

Enrichment #9
Naming Your Geese

Naming your geese can be a lot of fun. Angelo "The Airplane" was named after his dual angel wings. Tutter was named for his *toot-toot-toot* call. Duran Duran were named after a night of 80's karaoke fun before later earning their nickname: *The Duranasaurs.* And then there was Victor-Victoria who was named for his apt ability to hide his gender from us for so long.

Working in rescues and adoptions has taught us that other goose owners get a big kick out of the names they have chosen for their flock members as well. We quickly learned that we weren't the only ones having fun with naming our geese.

Lynyrd & Skynyrd: Cork in the water!

190

Naming Ali & Chan (a.k.a. Bites-Your-Ass & Hisses)

We rescued quite a few ducks before receiving an email about two abandoned geese. At the time we had a webmaster who loved geese, and I promised her she could name the first pair we brought in. I'll never forget that day when a rough and tumble Pilgrim gander and his gentle Chinese buddy arrived at our sanctuary. I emailed our webmaster and asked her for her decision on the names and she responded with: *Giggles and Tickles.*

Not an hour later that same Pilgrim gander got a hold of me during his routine worming and delousing and hit me so hard with his wings he nearly broke my wrist and his repeated strikes left six long bruises on my left leg. Was he supposed to be Giggles or Tickles? I remember looking at my husband Tony and saying, *"Giggles my ass. More like Mohammad Ali."* And that was how Ali got his name. So what about his charming sidekick Tickles? We decided to name him Chan after Jackie Chan.

Later that night while explaining the name change to friends, I laughed and said, *"Giggles and Tickles? More like Bites-Your-Ass and Hisses!"* And that went on to be a little inside Majestic joke.

Bites-Your-Ass (right) & Hisses (left) pose for the camera

Enrichment #10
How to Speak Goose

Chinese and African geese have a wider variety of vocalizations than other geese. Even so, it does not take long to learn the language of geese. There's happy chirping, investigative sounds, content muttering, warning honks, hissing, competitive honking and the infamous love trumpets. Geese also display their emotions in other ways including: alarm calls, love trumpets and feather ruffling.

It's fun to learn to speak goose because once you've mastered the language, you can mimic sounds and communicate with your flock members, and they will understand exactly what you mean.

When I bring geese to the vet, I often comfort them by mimicking their calmer sounds. When you vocalize that you are not afraid, your geese will often rely on your word and relax a little bit. If your vet is worth anything, they won't even raise an eyebrow.

Communication Common to All Domestic Geese

- **Alarm calls**

All geese have an alarm call. It is very loud and abrupt and is different from any other call they make. You will know this call instinctively when you hear it and you should always investigate this sound more thoroughly to make sure your gaggle is safe.

Mac sounds the alarm

Geese will raise the alarm when they hear or see anything out of the ordinary. This form of communication is by no means one way. Mimicking the warning honk is a great way for you to communicate potential danger to your gaggle.

- **General honking**

Honking is part of normal gaggle communication that commonly occurs whenever one goose has something to say to another goose. This kind of talking can be on the quiet or loud end depending on how important the message is.

192

- **Competitive honking**

Competitive honking tends to occur when either you or a goose comes within the visual range of a couple of ganders. One gander will honk and then the other, each escalating their heads higher and honking a little louder until one finally gives and the competition ends. It is a way that they verbally reaffirm who is in charge in the pecking order. Sometimes the females will get in on this as well.

- **Hissing**

Need I say more? Your goose is angry or afraid.

- **Content sigh**

Some geese will also make a content noise that is reminiscent of a sigh. While opening their bill in a yawn-like position they will let out a slight: *aaaaw* sound. Mimic this greeting back to extend the sentiment back at them.

- **Love trumpets**

Love trumpets are my favorite, and I still remember the first time I heard one and swung my head around.

The love trumpet must be witnessed to be truly appreciated. These tend to occur just after the mating ritual. Ganders will paddle their feet really fast and hoist their bodies slightly out of the water while flexing their necks upward and letting out a unique call. Chinese and African geese tend to curl their long necks into a swan-like pose during these motions. Both a display of bragging to other geese and ganders and an expression of joy, the love trumpet is a sure sign that your gander is a happy boy.

Lynyrd poses like a swan for his love trumpet

- **Head vibration**

Not all communications are vocalized. When a gander gets really excited by a goose, he will vibrate his head and neck in anticipation just before climbing on board. If your gander does this towards you, it means that he loves you, perhaps a little too much, but he loves you just the same. If you squat down in front of him and hold your hand out to touch his neck, he will step towards you and put his head over your shoulder. He's really trying to mate, but can't quite figure it out, so he will settle for a hug instead. Some geese will do this also, but we mostly see this behavior in the ganders.

Be careful! Head vibration can also be indicative of a nervous goose who may be about to bite! Once you know your goose's personality, you will know which kind of "greeting" you are receiving.

- **Feather ruffling**

Another non-vocal communication is feather ruffling. This is an *"I'm in charge"* threat display. Whenever our geese do this at me, I mimic the display back at them by shaking my body as similarly as possible. In goose lingo this follow-up display translates to: *"No, I am."*

- **The *"charge and retreat"* trait**

A couple geese have come to us demonstrating a particularly noticeable trait we call the, *"charge and retreat"* trait. Mac was infamous for this trait. I could visit him and pet him and talk to him and then the second I would turn to leave, he would drop his head and neck parallel to the ground and come charging at the back of my ankles, but when I turned on him, he would suddenly rise up and walk away like the whole thing wasn't worth his time anyway.

This infamous bluff is common among ganders who are trying to prove to themselves and others that although you are in charge they could take you out if they wanted to. *Yeah right, Mac. Whatever...* As long as they're not making actual physical contact with you, it's okay to let them do this. It helps build up their self-confidence and makes them feel important, but if it gets out of control, be sure to put a quick stop to it.

Communication Common to Descendants of Wild Greylag Geese

- **Content muttering**

Domestic geese who have descended from wild Greylag geese make a content muttering noise that sounds like: *ud-da-da-da-da.* It picks up in volume when they are excited and changes in intensity when they are upset.

Communication Common to the Descendants of Wild Swan Geese

- **Happy greetings**

Chinese and African ganders make loud and sharp: *Oy! Oy!* vocalizations that are very sing-songy in nature. They are a true expression of a content goose.

The happy honk is the greatest sound you will ever hear from your geese. It is an open bill excited honking that most often happens when you come in sight and even more so when you have a goody in your hands. Don't be afraid to mimic this sound at times of stress to reassure your geese that they are going to be just fine.

- **Investigative vocalizations**

Chinese and African ganders will make investigative *Wee-oh Woow* vocalizations that are neither loud or quiet in nature, but occur at conversational level. They make me think the goose is saying, *"hmm-mm... ohh..."* and they will repeat it cleverly as they continue to examine something intriguing.

Taking Grampa Out of the Wild

People often wonder why domestic geese cannot be turned out into the wild to live out their lives. They mistakenly believe they are hearty enough to tough it out on their own. This notion is fostered by the myth that geese are aggressive creatures fit to survive whatever Mother Nature can dish out, but this is far from the truth. In actuality, domestic geese eventually succumb to predation, injury, starvation and acts of cruelty in the wild.

Another issue that arises when domestic geese are dumped into the wild occurs when they mate with wild geese and hatch out goslings that share their inability to fly. Even though they can't migrate, these non-flying goslings are legally considered *wild* by the Migratory Bird Treaty Act, which stipulates that they cannot be removed from the wild despite their domestic origins.

Non-flying goslings that mature into adult geese and produce a new generation of offspring can further increase non-flying populations, which may interfere with pond ecology. These situations all too frequently end in bird/human conflicts that find their way to town hall and result in the mass netting and killing of geese—both wild and domestic. All this destruction is a terrible waste that can be prevented by keeping domestic geese out of the wild.

Grampa mates with a wild Canada goose and has four mixed goslings

When complaints arose about goose populations, Grampa's wild mate and four goslings were captured by authorities and relocated to unknown whereabouts. Grampa was left behind to grieve for their loss until we received written permission from the local park official and the bordering property owner to safely capture and remove him.

Today Grampa and his new mate Daisy are living together and enjoying the safety and protection of a loving home.

Enrichment #11
Arts & Crafts

Canvas Art

One project that turned out to be very rewarding was painting. I bought some non-toxic, water based kids paint at the craft store, some canvases and prefab frames. I squeezed yellow paint on a paper plate and picked up Mac, dipped his webbed feet in it and then let him walk on the canvas (with a little direction). I added red the following day and green the day after that. He didn't seem to mind, and I ended up with some really beautiful artwork.

Some geese won't have any part of this, while some of the friendlier ones could care less—especially if they are rewarded with a nice swim afterwards to clean up the paint.

Feather Art

Feathers that drop on the ground can be cleaned by dipping them in water that has been boiled and then pulled from the stove before adding a small amount of bleach. After dipping them just lay them out to dry. You can cut them, glue them, paint them, dye them… whatever! They make a fun project for kids. You can even paint *with* them—use them as a brush for interesting lines.

Greeting Cards

Photos of our geese can be digitally enhanced or decorated with feathers to make fantastic personalized greeting cards.

A caroling we go!

Photography

It can be very rewarding to invest in a digital camera with a good zoom lens. The best photos are taken during normal behaviors and when we are out of the way and the geese don't feel like we are right in their faces. Experiment and have fun. The great thing about digital cameras, as we all know, is you can delete anything that doesn't work.

Some of the best photo moments are when your geese first go out onto the water or are in the midst of a bathing routine. Water splashing takes on a whole new appearance during different hours of the day and in different seasons. Geese often open their wings like angels during their preening and this can make for some beautiful photos. Focus in on webbed feet, bills, wings and feathers. Switching photos to black and white can add extra drama. Action sequences can make great cards or framed gifts.

Black and white photographs of Fanny in the midst of a fan dance… or perhaps just preening

And then it is always fun to come up with a good caption to your beloved photos:

"Wow, who's the new girl?"

Enrichment #12
Hellos & Good-byes (Goose Greetings)

The sound of geese in our yard has truly enriched our lives. We love their greetings, and we get a good chuckle whenever we come home and hear them welcoming us.

Good Morning

Mac always chirps out a brief and profound greeting when he hears the house door open in the morning. Hearing him cheer as I come down the hill for morning rounds always puts a smile on my face. With all that happy honking, I'm sure they are saying something very important. They just get so excited. It sure is a nice way to start out my day, to see such happy geese.

Good-Bye

Be careful because leaving your goose pen can be very difficult when one of them is begging you to stay with them just a little bit longer. Mac was famous for standing on our feet and binging up at us. I'm sure he was saying, *"Please don't go yet! Won't you stay a little while longer?"*

Hello Again!

When we come home at night our gaggle will come running over to the fence to greet us. We always get out of the car to the sound of happy honking geese. How wonderful!

Good-Night

Saying good-night is always a calming close to the day. They try really hard to get me to stay with them and snuggle up with them for the night and occasionally I have commented on how tempting their fluffy pillow-like behinds are, but in the end, I'm off to the house where I watch them on camera as they gather together and wind down for the night.

Enrichment #13
Goose Scrap Book

My friends were not surprised to find that I have a baby book for my daughter and a goosey book for the gaggle. Many photos downloaded from a digital camera find their way into their goosey book. You will forget how tiny your geese once were until you go back and flip through their gosling book. I also have every email regarding bringing them into our home, every map to go pick them up, their feathers and occasionally even a newspaper article.

Get as crazy and elaborate with this as you like. It is fun to go back and see them as little peepers. They stay tiny for such a short time; enjoy it while you can and get lots of photos. It's a great project for children as well. I'm sure when my daughter gets a little older she will take over the roll of goose Record Keeper and goose Craft Project Manager.

Enrichment #14
Visitors

You're probably thinking that by visitors I mean all the people who will flock (ha!) to your house to see your amazing geese, but visitors can sometimes take other nice forms. Buster, the neighbor's dog, although an unwelcome visitor, has so far proved old and harmless and even fun to pat on the head now and then. There have been other visitors who've come to say hello as well.

Frogs

There have been many occasions where I have gone out to clean out ponds or pools and found all kinds of surprises. Some days I find little drowned mice… geese tend to attack them, by the way. Other times, I find bullfrogs. Nothing interests the geese (and my daughter) more than me pulling a six inch, live bullfrog out of one of the little ponds. Everyone wants to see a good frog.

Wild Mallards

A pair of mallards will drop by every now and again to swim on those ponds that are not inside our enclosures. The geese go crazy when their distant cousins drop in on us. I'll hear the alarm call and run outside to see what's bothering them only to find a tiny pair of ducks wandering in the yard or swimming in the pond.

Mr. & Mrs. Mallard stop by for a visit

Blue Heron

Another frequent disturber of the peace is a blue heron who visits us pretty frequently. He'll actually perch on the aviary supports or on the peak of the barn and really upset the geese. Occasionally he'll even give our rescue gear a test drive.

The Blue Heron on the sanctuary's waterfowl rescue jet ski

Wild Turkeys

Some times geese have unexpected guests over. One morning I stepped into the goose pen and saw the geese huddled in one corner, looking outside at something. I wandered over and saw something little running into the fence, trying to be with them. I went around the outside and found a baby wild turkey who had lost its mother. The little darling was trying to join up with the geese, but couldn't get through the fence. I picked him up and brought him to a wildlife rehabber where he joined a few other orphans. When they were older, they were all released together back into the wild.

Wild turkeys are common sanctuary visitors

Enrichment #15
Toys!

Providing visual stimulation for your geese is a great way to enrich their lives as well as providing you with a fun new level of interaction.

Mirrors

Acrylic (non-breakable) mirrors are a great distraction and source of entertainment for geese. Although they may fear their own image at first, eventually they will come in for the approach. Mirrors can also be used to cheer up a lonely single bird, especially after the loss of a flock mate. Your goose will be so convinced that they have a new companion that they will often settle down right in front of the mirror, gazing into their own eyes. Ganders will sometimes treat the mirror as a rival and do some pacing and pecking. If your gander doesn't settle down and the "newcomer" truly seems to be disturbing him, then do intercede and remove the mirror.

Who's that good lookin' gander?

Musical Toys

If it has buttons and makes noise they want to play with it! Toys with mirrors are all the more fun. Just be sure there are no small parts that your geese can swallow before you present them with a toy to explore.

Duran Duran play with a musical toy

<u>Tub Toys</u>

Geese are very interactive and love to pick up toys, carry them around their pens and even dunk them into buckets of water.

Playtime in the water bucket

<u>Cups of Water</u>

This kind of fun never seems to fail! Geese see in color, so use colors to intrigue them. You can partially fill a colored cup with water to interest and entertain your inquisitive goose. You can add a snack to the water for even more fun.

Tutter and Angelo play a game of "Cups"

<u>Parrot Toys & Baby Toys</u>

Some geese are entertained with parrot toys, especially if it has pieces they can nibble on, or if they include unbreakable mirrors. Avoid toys with small pieces or metal parts that can be broken off and ingested, or remove these dangerous parts before giving the toy to your goose. Don't be afraid to modify parrot toys to make them safe for your playful goose.

Skynyrd picks out his own toys at the pet store

Rio plays with his toys

203

Treat Globe

Treat globes are a fun adventure for your geese. Just stuff them full of their favorite snacks and hang them in your goose's pen. Some treat globes have small parts, so be sure to remove them before putting them out for your geese. These are best used during supervised playtimes. Treat globes are available on the internet or in the rabbit aisle of many pet stores.

Duran Rio marvels at his melon globe

Lettuce Maze

Insert leaf lettuce into a toy with holes in it, so the geese have to work to get their healthy snacks. Be careful not to make holes too small, so bills don't get stuck.

Duran Rio finds green treasure in his lettuce boat

Plush Animals

Plush animals introduced to single goslings can provide a bit of comfort and security. Be sure there are no small parts that can be plucked off and ingested.

Mac's little friend takes a ride

Goose Callers & Bird Books

We sometimes have a bit of fun playing with items that sound like geese. Goose callers or books that have sound chips in them can be intriguing for your pet.

Skynyrd reads up on his wild cousins while listening to their calls

Rotate toys in and out of play to keep things from getting dull. Remember to take care before leaving your goose alone with any toy. Avoid toys with sharp edges or breakable pieces. Consider that some toys are best used only when you are around, depending on the personality of your goose and the quality and design of the toy.

Enrichment #16
Becoming a Goose Whisperer

During the first year of rescuing geese, we learned something very interesting about them. Their behaviors tell us a lot about their past experiences, prior to their rescue. You can learn a lot about a goose; you just need to watch closely and listen.

Lancelot

Lancelot came to us one sunny spring. A couple found him wandering around a gas station in a nearby town. They picked him up, asked around town in an attempt to find his owners and then brought him home until they could find a safe place for him. A few days later they found our sanctuary.

We knew when they arrived that Lancelot was friendly because he was sitting on the wife's lap in the front seat of their truck (for everyone's safety, it is always preferable to transport even the friendliest goose in a pet carrier). The couple stepped out of the car and introduced me to Gwenovere. *Um… Gwenovere?* I took one look at the large bird in the woman's arms, the large knob on his head, and quickly broke the news that their goose was actually a gander, which was confirmed the second he spoke up and said hello.

They had fallen so in love with this gander that they asked us to keep him for a few weeks because they were in the midst of building a barn and just couldn't handle him in their kitchen anymore. The baby gates just weren't cutting it anymore. I laughed and asked what he was doing in their kitchen and they said when they set him down in their lawn, he ran up to the door of the house and honked to go inside. This boy had obviously been in someone's house before.

We agreed to take care of Lancelot for a few weeks until their barn was complete and suggested that they also think about adopting a mate for him, so he wouldn't be lonely. We could see this boy was going to be very demanding of attention and would need company when the family wasn't home.

We loved Lancelot from the moment he arrived and we had multiple families interested in adopting him if his circumstances happened to change. We would walk Lancelot around the yard and each time he would make a break for the house, running up towards the door. We knew he was far too friendly and far too accustomed to indoor living to have been abandoned. He was lost. Still, despite efforts made by the family who found him, no one claimed Lancelot, so they came back a few weeks later and brought him home to his new barn and soon after, his new mate.

A couple of years later, the husband re-enlisted into the military and the family had to move. They asked us if we would take both geese and we said we would, but they later ended up finding someone else with geese who kept their flock very safe and well-cared for, so Lancelot and Gwenovere went there instead. A few months after that, we received a phone call from a local family who had visited our sanctuary's website after hearing about us and immediately recognized Lancelot from our "adopted" photos. As it turns out, Lancelot was once there gander. He had been raised indoors and had been adored and fawned over by his family, but one day when they brought him outside to meet the rest of their gaggle, one of their other ganders chased him out of their lawn and into a nearby river. The family had been unable to intercept him and Lancelot floated away.

Despite all the family's efforts, Lancelot drifted out of sight and later climbed up onto shore in a neighboring town. Unfortunately, despite their asking around, they didn't connect with any of the same people that his rescuers had inquired with. And to make matters worse, we did not have the address of the family who took in Lancelot and

Gwenovere after their rescuing family moved away. To date we have still been unsuccessful at reuniting Lancelot with his original family. Still, they were at least relieved to find out he ended up in a safe place.

While Lancelot's family learned a valuable lesson about what can go wrong in a free-range situation, we learned something entirely different. What we learned from Lancelot is a lesson that has been repeated over-and-over in our endeavor to rescue waterfowl. If you pay close attention to a goose, you can discover *a lot* about their past.

Mac & Fanny

Mac and Fanny were abandoned on a river where they floated downstream until they found a house with a nice backyard. While the home owners enjoyed the new arrivals, the neighbors were not so pleased because whenever they went outside Mac (a Chinese gander) would chase after them. The neighbors called Animal Control and the DEP to have them removed, but neither agency would get involved for different reasons. Meanwhile, the home owners worked on finding the pair of geese a more viable option, and they soon stumbled upon our website and found their answer. We agreed to come rescue the geese, but we had to wait a couple of weeks for our quarantine pen to open up. In the meantime we advised them to tell the neighbors to stop running away from Mac because it was only encouraging his naughty behavior. We gave them a few tips to help them assert a little dominance and control his behavior until we could arrive.

A couple of weeks later, we showed up and easily captured Mac and Fanny and brought them back to our sanctuary. It only took a few minutes to understand Mac and Fanny's story. Whoever raised them from goslings underestimated how intelligent they were and never taught them any rules or manners. While Fanny (Embden goose) was a typical mild-mannered hen, Mac grew way out of control. He was a human-imprinted, fearless gander who wanted to be so close to people that he would actually climb right up on top of them. He had no sense of personal space and he was BIG. It was obvious that he had grown to overwhelm his family and not knowing what else to do they set him loose and turned their backs on him.

Once rescued, it took hours and hours of sitting with Mac and nudging him backwards when he tried to climb over me to teach him a sense of personal space. When he got too out of control, I would pick him up and plop him into his pond to calm him down.

The home owners who had contacted us to rescue Mac and Fanny kept in touch with us and even came in for a few visits. When they came for their first visit Mac's behavior hadn't changed at all, but the following year we invited them back again and they were thrilled to discover how gentle and loving he had become. In fact, he was always loving, just a little *too* loving.

Anyone who visited our sanctuary while Mac was here was greeted by him. He ran up to welcome everyone and honk a big hello. Many adopters fell in love with him, but were not a good match due to their inexperience with geese. Without a fearless alpha leader to look up to, Mac could easily revert back to his overbearing behavior again. We had to be very conscious of finding him a forever-home with someone who would both love him and keep him in line.

In the end, my best friend Jenn and her family adopted Mac and Fanny because they were looking for a friendly gander who could also inspire cohesion within their own flock. One thing Mac is good at is keeping his minions in line.

Golly

Golly was a Toulouse gander who was removed from a location where he had been kept in a wire cage that was so small he could barely stand up without bumping his head on the ceiling. He and his mate had originally come from a farm before being turned over to their new owners. After arriving, his mate was sold off separately from Golly never to be seen again. As if Golly's mourning wasn't enough, whenever his new owners would fill his feeder or water dish, they would torment him by banging on his cage with a stick to get him to back away from the door or to stop him from making noise.

After removing Golly from this situation he surprised us by instantly curling up beside women and finding reprieve in our arms. He truly craved the touch of other beings, provided they were female. This told us that he had originally imprinted on a woman before changing hands. When it came to men; however, Golly was not so kind. Not only had he been abused by men before, but he also saw men as a threat because he saw them as his competition.

Golly recovered from the loss of his mate by instantly bonding with and becoming extremely protective over young Lynyrd, Skynyrd and Ms. Donald. While the goslings enjoyed swimming, Golly had a fearful reaction to any bodies of water—including kiddy pools. This clearly told us that he had never been exposed to any water other than what was put in his drinking bowl. We relied on the other geese to ease him over this hurdle, and he eventually learned to follow them into their pools and out onto the pond.

Golly runs over to greet Pancho

Golly continued to bond with the gaggle and us, and he eventually came to tolerate men. Then one day something very interesting happened. A friend of ours began speaking in his native language around Golly. For some reason Golly was drawn to the Spanish language and instantly bonded with the first male figure he'd met since his abuse. This bond was so impressive, we were sure that it had to do with his original imprinting. It was likely that Golly's first family spoke Spanish.

Golly's story is just further testament to how much you can learn from your new feathered friend.

Enrichment #17
Happy Geese = A Happier You!

It is commonly accepted that having pets around reduces stress. Take time out of your day and sit with your geese. Relax and enjoy. If you keep your geese happy, your geese will make you happy. I guarantee it. If you spend a good amount of time with them, you are going to love them. I have never had pets that were so intriguing and fun. It's hard to have a bad day when they are around. I just go out and visit them, and they cheer me right up.

Lynyrd and Jenn inspire happiness

Time Investment

For the ultimate experience and enjoyment, you should be trying to spend at least two hours a day in the presence of your geese (this includes *any* time in their presence, which includes replenishing their feeders, water buckets etc.).

I enjoy a nice visit with the Duranasaurs

APPENDIX A

Protect Your Waterfowl; Get To Know Your Predators:
Your best defense is a good fence…

Your local Conservation Office is an excellent source of information regarding the types and numbers of predators in your area. Be careful not to make the mistake of assuming you know of all of the predator threats in your area. Some predators keep a very low profile. I have lived in Connecticut my entire life. Without any warning, I lost my nine year-old cat to a coyote attack. Coyotes were reintroduced, grew in numbers, moved into the area and were witnessed predating pets like cats and small dogs. We simply were unaware of them until it was too late. The same happened with fisher cats and bobcats. Without any warning, they began popping up all over the state. With no natural predators, these apex predators make it unsafe for anyone in the area to let their cats or small dogs outside unescorted, so it is definitely unsafe for geese too. Just because you've never seen your predators, doesn't mean that they aren't there.

I also recommend that you imagine the worst circumstances your predators may face. A hungry or starving predator (or one with little mouths to feed) is incredibly dedicated to the task of finding food. If this exceedingly motivated animal is outside of your pen, looking in at your geese it is not likely to move along quickly if no one is around. Your enclosure needs to be strong enough to withstand their attempts to break in, and that could be hours if you are not at home or if you are sleeping.

This list of predators is by no means comprehensive. I have chosen sample predators to give you a starting place of things to consider. For example I list the American Black Bear as an example of one type of bear you may have in your area. You may live where there are grizzly bears or brown bears, so keep them in mind as well. I list the Black Rat Snake, but this is an example of only one of a hundred snakes that may be a threat to your goslings. This list should give you a working idea about the types of animals that could be of danger to your goslings or geese. Use it as a tool to get you to brainstorm of other potentially dangerous predators in your own area. The rule of thumb is, if it eats meat, it will eat a goose.

You will soon discover that your goose pen will need to keep out jumping, climbing, flying, squeezing and digging predators of many sizes, and there are a lot of them. Your best strategy against them is to build a secure pen using high galvanized wire that is thick and of a tight weave. You are also wise to employ underground barriers that prevent digging and some sort of aviary structure to protect your gaggle from flying predators. Electric fencing is an added plus—especially around your top perimeter if you have an aviary net that can be chewed through. This will prevent predators from climbing on top to do so. Unless you have an *impenetrable* enclosure that will keep every kind of predator outside (including humans), it is always a good idea to lock your geese up in safe structures with flooring for the night. Some added protection never hurts.

AN IMPORTANT WORD ON RABIES: Whenever dealing with wild animals, be it the animal itself, or the remains of its kill, ALWAYS wear protective clothing. DO NOT touch wild animals or prey animals (either living or dead) with your bare skin. Thoroughly clean or discard any clothing or items that have touched the wild animal or prey animal.

The Coyote

- **Digging**
- **Jumping**

A Northeastern Coyote weighs in at about thirty pounds for a female and forty pounds for a male. They will hunt nearly any animal that they can overpower. Coyotes are opportunistic predators, so if they see something easy to catch, they will attack it and they usually do it without a trace. For pet owners, coyotes are a real danger. They will eat cats and small dogs. They are also infamous for killing chickens, ducks and geese. Coyotes are nocturnal and are most active at night, at dawn, and at dusk.

Coyotes can often be heard yipping and howling near our sanctuary as soon as the sun goes down and then well into the night. Although some people will say they prefer to avoid areas inhabited by humans, we have not found this to be true.

We have seen hungry coyotes gazing through our goose enclosures on a few occasions, usually during the dawn hours, but not always. When hungry, coyotes can be relatively fearless, especially when they're running with a pack. We have heard stories of them snatching geese on one side of the yard while their owners watched from the other side, so stick close to your geese when chaperoning them.

The first time I saw a coyote, it was the middle of the afternoon. I thought I was looking at a dirty golden retriever with a bushy tail until I saw the profile of its muzzle. Even when I barreled down the hill to chase him off, he only moved away as far as the edge of the lawn. He didn't leave the premises until my husband joined me outside and he was clearly outnumbered.

If your goose enclosure/housing is inadequate and you have coyotes, you will soon be without your feathered friends because the coyotes will continue to return until there is nothing left to take. In our area, packs come through, wipe out all the wild prey (squirrels, rabbits, foxes) and then move on, only to return later when prey animals have replenished themselves.

Coyotes can jump upward over four feet, and like many dogs have been known to actually scale fencing, so your fence should be at least six feet tall. You want a fence strong and tight enough that a forty-pound coyote can jump up on it, with paws up on the wire, without causing any damage. Large guard dogs can be a good deterrent, but remember to protect your geese from your dogs.

The Timber Wolf /Gray Wolf

- **Digging**
- **Jumping**

The average weight of a Timber Wolf (or Gray Wolf) is sixty pounds for a female and seventy-five pounds for a male. As with coyotes, they will eat anything they can take down, so your best defense is a good offense. The same kind of precautions taken to prevent a coyote attack should be utilized, if not increased, if you have wolves in your area.

Large Wolf Hounds or Anatolian Shepherds are known to be good dogs to keep a wolf at bay.

The Gray Fox & The Red Fox

- **Digging**
- **Jumping**
- **Squeezing**

A fox tends to weigh between seven and fifteen pounds. Although they are primarily nocturnal, it is not uncommon to see them during dawn and dusk hours. Some people mistakenly believe that a fox is too small to attack a goose, but this is definitely not the case.They are expert and stealthy hunters who tend to remain unseen even when close by. They often live very close to people without ever being discovered, so don't assume you don't have any around just because you don't see them.

Foxes tend to grab their prey and run off with it without leaving a trace. If you have a sudden and unexplained goose disappearance with no remains left behind, a fox is a likely suspect, and it will be back.

Because foxes are shy and prefer to remain unseen, motion sensing lights around your goose house may help deter them. A good guard dog is an excellent deterrent. Often the scent markings of a dog will keep a fox on its toes, but not necessarily away. A hungry fox will watch and wait diligently for an opportunity to seize an unprotected goose. We've heard stories of the family dog going in the house, goose owners turning their back for a minute and the fox seizing the moment. You may not see them, but they see you.

The Bobcat

- **Climbing**
- **Digging**
- **Jumping**

Bobcats can be anywhere from fifteen to thirty pounds (males 20-30 pounds, females 15-25 pounds) and can jump up as high as *twelve* feet. Bobcats are solitary animals who, like the fox, are very adaptable and can live in very close proximity with humans without being detected. If you do come in contact with a bobcat, they can be provoked to attack, so use extreme caution.

Motion sensing lights around your goose pen can be helpful, but a large guard dog can be of greater assistance if this predator is a known trouble-maker in your area. Human scent can also be a deterrent, which is why I send my husband around our pens on "urinary errands."

The Raccoon

- **Climbing**
- **Digging**
- **Reaching**

Raccoons weigh around thirty pounds. They prefer to do most of their dirty work in darkness; however, they can sometimes be seen during the day.

The number one thing that raccoons do is look for food, so do not underestimate the determination of this crafty predator. They are lured in by goose food and the geese themselves. They are very good problem solvers and excellent lock picks. I can remember a few occasions as a youngster when a raccoon let our chickens out while getting at the grain. Padlocks, thankfully, are beyond their capabilities.

Raccoons are capable of tearing and biting through aviary netting and poultry fencing to get at your geese. A raccoon will employ every tactic at its disposal to get at your gaggle. Worst of all, raccoons have been known to eat a goose right through the fencing if they can get their paws on any part of the sleeping bird.

Avoid luring raccoons into your yard by keeping attractive food items out of their reach. Predator urine (available at your local grain store) applied often around your enclosure may help keep raccoons away, but don't rely on this measure alone. You may have some added success by keeping motion lights around your barn at night, but once they grow accustomed to this, it will lose its effectiveness. A dog is not necessarily a good idea to keep raccoons away from your pens since a confrontation will most likely end with your dog in a vet office. As with any wild animal, be extremely cautious of rabies when dealing with raccoons. They are known carriers in many regions.

The Fisher Cat

- **Climbing**
- **Digging**
- **Squeezing**

A female Fisher Cat tends to weigh around eight pounds and males around twelve pounds. The Fisher Cat is a ferocious nocturnal predator. They will kill anything they can overtake. Fisher cats are very fast and extremely agile. They can elongate their bodies and squeeze into small holes and gaps.

These solitary predators are designed by nature to climb over, dig under and gnaw through obstacles, so be very wary of them. Locally we have heard of one animal breaking into a turkey farm and wiping out dozens of birds during a bloodthirsty rampage.

The Long-Tailed Weasel

- **Climbing**
- **Digging**
- **Squeezing**

The Long-Tailed Weasel only weighs about a pound and like the fisher cat, it is a ferocious and blood-thirsty predator. They can squeeze through holes as small as an inch and are notorious for killing entire coops of geese if uninterrupted. They tend to do most of their work at night, but can occasionally be seen during the day.

Healthy rodent populations and access to a water source tend to lure in weasels. Keep rodents under control to avoid fostering an environment suitable for weasels. If you have a lot of hawks, owls and other birds of prey in your area, they will help keep rodent, and therefore weasel, populations under control. Cats are an excellent deterrent; not only do they hunt rodents and weasels, but their scent also act as a deterrent. Remember to protect your geese from your cat. Spreading bobcat scent around the outside perimeter of your pens is another preventative option.

The American Black Bear

- **Climbing**
- **Digging**
- **Breaking and entering**

Do I need to tell you how big a bear is? BIG! An American Black Bear can range anywhere between 100 and 650 pounds. Bears have been known to wander through many areas where they have never been seen before.

There is no protection against a bear other than extremely strong, fully enclosed pens and a sturdy barn to lock your geese up in at night. If bears are a threat in your area, be careful not to lure them toward your geese. Don't make food sources available to them. Unless you are allowing your geese to hatch out goslings, pick up daily eggs and store or dispose of them properly. Don't allow unfertilized eggs to linger in nests and tickle a bear's nose, and don't throw old eggs into the woods. Be mindful of where you store your grain; it should be locked up in a building where a bear cannot gain access. You may even wish to store it in a separate building from your geese.

The Snapping Turtle

- **Swimming**

The common Snapping Turtle can grow anywhere between 10 and 35 pounds. Snapping turtles will eat goslings and have been known to do a great deal of damage to the feet and legs of swimming adult geese.

Do not let your geese swim on your pond if you have a snapping turtle in it. The tricky part is, you may not know if a snapping turtle is living there. Snapping turtles have been known to travel long distances, so a newcomer could join your pond's ecosystem at any time without your knowledge. The best thing you can do is keep your eye on your rocks, logs and shores, so that you will detect an unwanted guest early on and can take care of removing it (hopefully with some help).

The Alligator

- **Swimming**

The American Alligator can weigh up to 800 pounds. They will eat geese and goslings and, like the snapping turtle, can also cause serious leg damage during close encounters. As with snapping turtles, do not let your geese swim on your pond if there is any chance an alligator could be in it.

The Northern Pike

- **Swimming**

Yes, even a fish can be dangerous. The Northern Pike weighs in around eight pounds. Pike lurk in the water, in the vegetation near shore, and they have been known to eat goslings.

Your best defense is to keep your goslings off of water inhabited by the Northern Pike.

The Opossum

- **Climbing**
- **Digging**
- **Reaching**
- **Squeezing**

The Opossum weighs in anywhere between 4 and 12 pounds depending on gender. Opossums are nocturnal and are generally interested in eggs, but they will take a gosling.

Opossums are nocturnal and can often be deterred with motion sensor lights or a good dog. Pick up eggs daily to avoid luring them in.

The Skunk

- **Digging**
- **Squeezing**

A Skunk weighs in at about fourteen pounds and they will eat eggs or goslings.

As with opossums, motion sensor lights are helpful, but I am NOT going to recommend a good guard dog…

The Norway or Brown Rat

- **Climbing**
- **Digging**
- **Gnawing**
- **Jumping**
- **Squeezing**

Brown Rats weigh in at about eleven ounces. In prime conditions, where there is plenty of food, rats will multiply very rapidly. They can have up to fourteen young every twenty days, and they are able to reproduce within two months of being born. They can fit through an opening the size of a quarter, leap up to three feet in the air and climb walls.

Rats eat eggs, can kill small goslings, harass larger geese and spread diseases. Despite all this, it is nearly impossible to build a rat-proof enclosure. They will literally burrow under and around enclosures and barns and chew their way through and into buildings to get at stored grain. They will literally tear down the barn around your geese in order to get inside (which can create passages for other predators). Every effort should be made to eliminate them the instant they are found on the premises.

Discourage rats by storing your goose grain in metal containers. Metal flashing can be mounted over base boards to keep rats from chewing through them, but ultimately, the aid of a few good cats is your best deterrent.

The Black Rat Snake

- **Climbing**
- **Squeezing**

The Black Rat Snake can grow up to eight feet long and they can climb trees. They are constrictors who wrap around their victims and suffocate them before consuming them and goslings are in high risk of predation.

Although they are rarely known to cause trouble, keep all native species of snakes in mind when building your enclosures, especially if you have eggs or goslings. Digging predator barriers will keep rodents from digging tunnels into your pen, which will also keep snakes from moving into tunnels and finding a way inside. Cats, dogs and the presence of large predatory birds can be good snake deterrents.

There are laws protecting native snakes, so before you react to any on your property, it would be wise to first check your state's legislature on the matter.

The Domestic Dog

- **Digging**
- **Jumping**
- **Climbing**

Domestic Dogs can weigh anywhere from 2-200 pounds. They are found in close association with humans nearly worldwide. If you don't have a dog, one or more of your neighbors most likely does, so you will need to keep this potential predator in mind when building your enclosure.

Dogs range in temperament from gentle to ferocious depending on nature and nurture; that is, their breed type and their training. However, even the kindest pet dog, can turn in a moment of excitement and cause harm to your goose, even if there has never been a problem before. For this reason, you should NEVER leave your dog alone in the company of your goose. We have heard many stories of wonderful and friendly family pets suddenly deciding a chase would be fun. When the goose makes a break for it, the dog gets overly excited and bites at the goose.

When introducing a gosling to a *trained* and *friendly* dog, be extremely cautious (aggressive dogs and geese don't mix, so don't even try it). It is often wise to allow the dog to smell the gosling from the other side of their pen. Be sure the dog is in a calm state of mind before the introduction—as opposed to an excitable or hyper state of mind.

Dogs are often known for their jealousies, so be extremely cautious with your very fragile gosling. As the goose matures and the dog becomes accustomed to your new gosling, the two should begin to become friends. Puppies or young dogs should never be allowed near geese or goslings because their playfulness can easily cause serious injuries or even death.

Keep in mind, a goose pen that allows predators inside is merely a trap for your geese. If you are going to put up a fence, you best put one up that keeps predators out, or you will just be doing them a favor. A fence that is not high enough will only trap your geese inside, at the mercy of the predator. Build a pen, not a trap for your gaggle, and never leave your geese exposed and unprotected when you are not right there to chaperone.

The Domestic Cat

- **Climbing**
- **Digging**
- **Jumping**
- **Reaching**
- **Squeezing**

Domestic Cats weigh in anywhere between 5 and 16 pounds, although some breeds can weigh as much as 25 pounds. The temperament of a cat will depend on its breed and socialization. Cats are very high jumpers, excellent hunters and catch their prey much more frequently than they miss it.

Cats and kittens are deadly to a gosling or small goose. However, a full grown, heavy weight goose will most likely not be of any interest to your cat.

The Diurnal Birds of Prey… The Hawk, The Falcon & The Eagle

Hawks, falcons and eagles are all diurnal raptors—birds who hunt during the day. If your geese do not have top cover, they will be at the mercy of these predators. Most attacks occur on free range geese, especially when they are in open areas with no bushes, trees or houses to provide shelter.

If you see one of these flying predators near a kill site, it does not necessarily mean they brought your goose to its demise. You will need to examine the area carefully in order to determine if the raptor was the culprit or if they are just a scavenger. Diurnal raptors pluck out a goose's feathers before consuming it, so their beak marks can often be found on the shafts of the plucked feathers. In addition, if the base of a plucked feather is smooth and clean, the bird was plucked while warm, which means the raptor is your problem. If the feathers have small amounts of tissue clinging to their bases, they were plucked from a cold bird that died of another cause and the raptor was just scavenging. Take a look around the site; raptors will often defecate in the immediate area of a kill they've made.

The best defense against raptors is a well-built enclosure with sufficiently strong aviary netting on top. Hawks will attack through netting if they can push down on it far enough to get to your geese, so choose your top cover carefully. Guinea fowl will sound an alarm when any large bird flies overhead, so they can help warn the gaggle of incoming trouble. Raptors are commonly seen being chased away by families or flocks of crows, so another strategy to deter them is to put out food for your crows to encourage them to settle nearby. This is a great way of keeping your skies clear of trouble.

All hawks, falcons and eagles are federally protected under the Migratory Bird Treaty Act, which prohibits their possession or destruction. No permits are required to merely scare them off with your presence unless they are nesting or are an endangered or threatened species, as is the case with bald and golden eagles. Check your own state's laws and regulations prior to taking any action against these birds.

The Red-Tailed Hawk

- **Flying**

Red-Tailed Hawks weigh anywhere between 2 and 4 pounds, females being larger than males. They are very aggressive raptors.

We frequently see these hawks in our area and they are impressive. I have no doubts that they could take a small goose, although they seem to be scanning for goslings.

Red-tailed Hawks will take one of two tactics to catch their prey. They will sit on a branch and scan the surrounding area for prey or they will make flight patterns, back and forth over an area in search of prey.

The Northern Goshawk

- **Flying**

The Northern Goshawk weighs anywhere between 1 ½ - 3 pounds, and they are ferocious killers. They are mostly a concern if you have goslings.

While most hawks hunt over open areas, goshawks tend to hunt within forests, flying beneath the canopy in pursuit of prey.

The Chicken Hawk or Cooper's Hawk

- **Flying**

Chicken Hawks normally only weigh between 8 and 21 ounces. Although not nearly as large or aggressive as many of the other raptors, we are commonly asked about them (largely because of their name, I suspect), so I am including them on the list. They are really only a concern if you have goslings.

The Peregrine Falcon or Duck Hawk

- **Flying**

The Duck Hawk weighs between 1 and 2 pounds. This falcon is a brutal bird killer, making prey of birds as large as Mallard ducks or as small as goslings.

The duck hawk can easily overtake a fast flying bird. If its prey is not too heavy, it will actually seize it mid-air and fly away with it. They strike their prey with such power that it either kills them on impact or sends them tumbling to the ground.

The Bald Eagle

- **Flying**

The Bald Eagle weighs between 8 and 14 pounds, with females being larger than males. Bald eagles actively prey on waterfowl, both ducks and geese. In active areas, it is not uncommon to see them preying on Canada Geese.

The Golden Eagle

- **Flying**

The Golden Eagle weighs between 6 and 13 pounds, with females being larger than males. We have seen a golden eagle perched on one of the corner posts of our aviary. I had never seen or heard of anyone in Connecticut seeing one first hand prior to that day, which just goes to show you that uncommon predators can pass through your property and take advantage of an easy meal. A strong aviary net will protect your gaggle from this formidable hunter.

The Nocturnal Bird of Prey... The Owl

Protect your gaggle from owls by providing them a safe nighttime lock up. Barns or sheds are preferable to aviary areas. Guinea fowl will sound an alarm when any large bird flies overhead, but if they are left out to roost, owls can easily pick them right out of the trees. Strobe lights have been used as a night deterrent against owls with varying degrees of success.

All owls are federally protected under the Migratory Bird Treaty Act, which prohibits their possession or destruction. No permits are required to merely scare them off with your presence (unless they are nesting) except in the case of an endangered or threatened species, as in the case of the great-horned owl. Check your own state's laws and regulations prior to taking any actions against these birds.

The Great-Horned Owl

- **Flying**

The Great-Horned Owl is found throughout North America and weighs between 2 and 4 pounds, with females being larger than males. Four pounds may sound small, but if you have ever seen one of these magnificent creatures first hand, with its wings open, it is astounding.

Owls are nocturnal raptors and notorious goose hunters. They have been known to herd geese into aviary nets and then eat them through the netting.

The Barred Owl

- **Flying**

The Barred Owl is found in the Eastern U.S., Oregon and Washington state. They weigh between 1 ½ and 2 pounds. Although they primarily hunt rodents, they will hunt small geese and goslings if they are not properly protected. We have many of these owls in our forest and can hear them in the late afternoon. Occasionally we have even been lucky enough to spot one high in the trees.

The Spotted Owl

- **Flying**

The Spotted Owl weighs between 1 and 1 ½ pounds. Although found in our Western-most states (Oregon, Washington, California), their ranges within these states are limited. Spotted owls are also found in Colorado and in some regions of Arizona and New Mexico. As with the Barred Owl, they are mostly a threat to small geese and goslings.

Great Gray Owls

- **Flying**

In the U.S., Great Gray Owls are mostly seen in the states of Washington, Oregon and Alaska. They weigh between 1 ½ - 3 pounds. They are dusk and dawn predators and will do most of their hunting during these half-light hours. Like the Barred Owl and Spotted Owl, they are mostly a threat to small geese and goslings.

APPENDIX B

Helping Your Goose Survive a Predatory Attack

Unfortunately, waterfowl rescue includes getting heart-breaking and frantic emails from pet owners whose geese have just been the victim of a predatory attack. For those families who have not lined up their 24 hour emergency vet care, the next few hours are critical while they find one. We are not qualified vets and, quite likely, neither are you! This information is in no way a substitute for actual vet care. Your goose needs a qualified veterinarian as soon as possible. This information is only to help your goose stay alive until you can get them the help that they need. Geese are very resilient and will often survive a predatory attack if you can get them safely through their first few hours and get them on antibiotics relatively quickly.

Bring your goose inside to a quiet and calm room. Most people use the bathroom because a makeshift nest can be set up in the bathtub. Running water makes it easy to keep clean and the shower curtains or doors make it a quiet retreat.

If you have other geese, have another family member make sure they are all safe and accounted for. Expect that the predator will try to return (they normally do… it's usually just a question of when).

Once your other geese are in a safe place, start making calls to find a vet who can help.

- **Bites and lacerations**

If your goose has any lacerations or bite marks, you are going to want to use a saline solution (contact solution) to do a quick flushing of the wounds. Then use gauze pads to apply direct pressure to stop the bleeding. Once bleeding is controlled, you can lightly spray the area with a non-stinging wound wash.

Once major emergencies are tended to, you also want to gently clean any bleeding scratches. Again, do a quick flush with some saline solution and then spray the scratch with wound wash.

If your medicine cabinet is fully stocked and you have Baytril® on hand, give your mature goose one 68 mg antibiotic pill to help prevent infection. If your goose survives the original attack, fighting off infection will be their next battle.

- **Bill injuries**

Treat any lacerations/scratches on a goose's bill following the same instructions and cautions listed above.

Wound wash and saline solutions are harmful if swallowed. Do NOT use these products anywhere inside your goose's bill or mouth. Flush these regions briefly with clean, cold water to help prevent the risk of infection.

If your goose's bill is broken, save any pieces you can find or send a family member back outside to look for them and then pack them in ice. Control any bleeding using direct pressure.

- **Broken feathers**

Don't worry about broken feathers unless they are blood feathers and they are bleeding. If any of their feathers are bleeding from the break points, they will need to be plucked out to stop the bleeding. Refer to the "blood feather" section of this book for detailed instructions.

- **Swelling**

Injuries often swell and having an anti-inflammatory like Metacam® or Rimadyl® on hand will help keep this under control. Use as directed. If you don't have either on hand, you can try using a cold compress to control any swelling. Be very careful to monitor your goose to ensure they do not become too cold and go into shock.

- **Eye injuries**

Eye injuries can range from scratches in or around the eye socket to the loss of an actual eyeball. Vetropolycin® antibiotic eye ointment is great if you have it on hand. First flush out the eye (or empty socket) with saline solution (preferably a *sensitive eye* formula) and then apply a small amount of eye ointment to the eye, or if the eye is missing, enough to fill the eye socket.

- **Pain management**

Unfortunately, until you get to a vet there is not much you can do to manage your goose's pain. Metacam® or Rimadyl® will take down any swelling and help control pain, but it does not alleviate it entirely. You will need to keep your goose as comfortable and relaxed as possible until pain medications can be obtained.

- **Water and food**

Try to keep your goose hydrated once they are stable. A goose needs 60 ml of water for every 2.2 pounds of their body weight every 24 hours. This means a 16 pound goose needs approximately 430 mls of water per day. Keep water in front of them continually throughout their recovery, and if you don't see them drinking, use a syringe and gently administer 18 mls of water (or water with electrolytes if you have it) every hour.

If your goose doesn't tolerate these frequent disturbances very well, you can spread out the administering of fluids a little bit. So instead of administering 18 mls per hour for a 16 pound goose, you can give them 36 mls of water every 2 hours, but let them take a few breaths; do not squirt all 36 mls down their throat at once. You don't want to choke them.

You commonly do not need to force feed a goose while waiting for vet assistance to become available. Your goose will not starve in a few hours. If your goose is injured on a Saturday night, however, and you can't get to a vet until Monday morning, feeding becomes necessary. Do not start feeding until your goose has rested for quite a few hours and is no longer in risk of going into shock if disturbed.

If your goose is not eating, at some point you may want to grind up their food (using a food processor) and mix it with just enough water to make it a liquid and then suck the mixture up into a syringe and administer 1-2 mls every 3-4 hours to help keep their energy up. Use your best judgment to decide if your goose should be disturbed to eat or if they should just be left to rest. Another option to getting your goose eating is to give them their favorite treats. A good watermelon, cantaloupe or honeydew melon can get some vital water and sugars into your recovering goose.

If your goose has any bill injuries, grind up their food to make eating easier. Put a small bowl of powdered food beside their water bowl. If you don't see any evidence of them eating, you can try floating some of the powdered food in the water to see if they will sift through it. If they still aren't eating you can syringe feed, but do so very carefully.

APPENDIX C

How to Build an Outdoor Enclosure

These directions are generic in nature. All construction needs to be carefully planned to ensure adequate weight support and structural integrity.

<u>Perimeter Fencing</u>

Your perimeter fencing must be strong. Dogs, weasels and raccoons can bite through poultry wire, so it is best not to use this material as the only barrier between predators and your gaggle.

For human comfort and pen accessibility, we suggest a six foot high perimeter fence. This will also discourage most jumping predators from gaining access. Your enclosure should measure a minimum of 250 square feet per goose.

Ideally, ½" PVC coated, welded wire mesh should be used as perimeter fencing. Weasels can squeeze through a hole that is 1" or larger, making ½" wire mesh a wise choice.

If welded wire mesh is out of your price range, you can make a perimeter fence using PVC coated galvanized wire. The tighter the weave of wire, the safer your gaggle will be. If you can't find a weave small enough, you can back this wire with a layer of 1" hex poultry wire. Simply fasten the two layers together using zip ties. **Do Not** leave your gaggle unattended in a pen of this construction during dawn, evening or dusk hours when weasels tend to hunt.

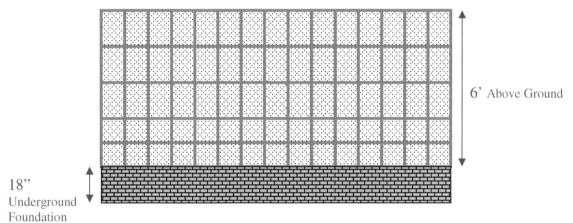

6' Above Ground

18"
Underground
Foundation

Double-layered fencing mounted to an in-ground foundation

<u>Foundation</u>

Fencing should go at least 18" below the ground **- OR -** you can put a cement foundation into the ground.

Foundations can be constructed by pouring cement into trenches measuring 18" deep x 6-8" Wide. Or you can place cement blocks (holes facing DOWN) into these trenches.

The perimeter fencing is then mounted to this foundation.

<u>Fence Posts & Gates</u>

Fence posts and support beams should be placed *no further* than 10' apart and should be mounted firmly in place. Cross beams provide added support.

Avoid dangerous gaps between your gate and your door frame. The fit must be snug. Gates should be padlocked; raccoons are excellent latch picks (as are neighbors).

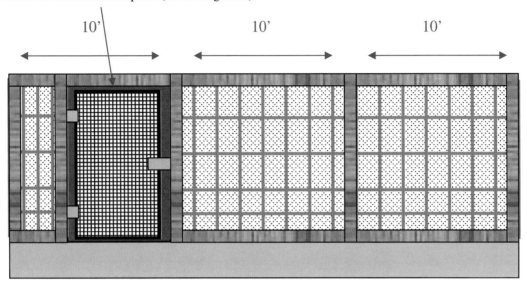

Fencing with posts, door frame and gate…avoid gaps in the red zone

Electric Fencing

Energy efficient, solar powered, electric fencing can be safely installed around the top perimeter of your pen. This added feature will prevent predators from climbing up on top of the enclosure's aviary net or top fencing. You can purchase a back-up rechargeable battery and plug-in charger (which may be needed occasionally in winter).

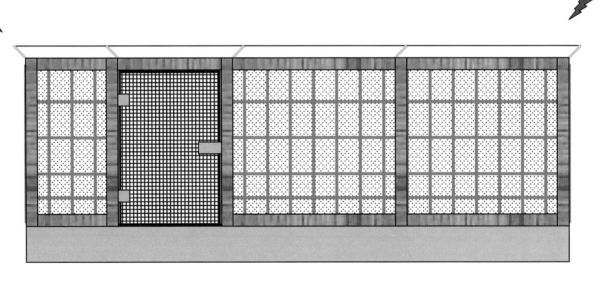

Electric Fencing around top perimeter

Homemade mount for electric fencing alongside our solar powered fence charger

Aviary Net

An aviary net or ceiling fence needs to be raised over any pen where your gaggle will remain unmonitored. We purchase our nets through Louis E. Page (www.louispage.com).

Netting/top fence support posts should be placed every 10 square feet throughout the enclosure. Be sure that these posts are high enough to allow comfortable entry into your pen.

Aviary nets are not effective enough to protect flock members during dusk, dawn or dark hours. Raccoons can climb up and gnaw through them *unless* you utilize electric fencing.

The weight of snow can bring down netting or top fencing with inadequate supports. Braced crossbeams offer added strength, but during heavy storms, you still may need to do some clearing.

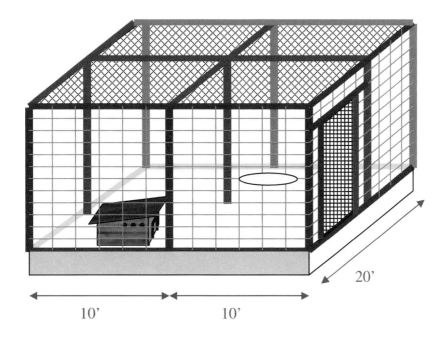

Aviary support posts should be placed a minimum of every 10 square feet

Homemade Aviary Wire

You can weave your own aviary net very inexpensively and very easily. Purchase one-inch hex, galvanized poultry wire and cut it to the size of your enclosure, then fasten sections together using tie wraps.

For Example: If your enclosure will measure 20' wide by 25' long, you would need to buy a single roll of 4'x 100' galvanized, one-inch hex poultry fence and a single roll of 4'x 25' fence. Cut the rolls into five sections, each measuring 25' in length. Lay the five lengths of fence out in a giant 20' x 25' square and then tie wrap the sections together. Place a tie wrap about every 4-5 inches apart to sew your five sections together. It's easy to do and it moves along fairly quickly.

Night Housing

Always lock up your gaggle at night, during prime predatory hours. Place a floored house inside your enclosure for extra protection. The door must latch securely for maximum effectiveness. Houses also provide shade, a break from the rain and a nesting place during the day.

Include adequate ventilation holes. Each hole must measure less than ¼" diameter to prevent weasels from entering. *Minimum* overnight housing for a pair of geese: 4' W x 4' L x 4' H

Our 4' x 4' x 4' two-goose house with open doors

Digging Predator Barriers

Digging predator barriers should be inserted under the ground around the entire perimeter of any pen—like a skirt. Standing outside of your perimeter fencing, dig a trench that goes 6" down into the ground and 2' out and away from the perimeter fencing.

Lay a 2 ½' wide strip of welded wire mesh into the trench (length to be determined by the length of your perimeter fence).

Secure one side of the welded wire mesh to the bottom of your perimeter fencing and then push it 6" down into the trench. Then bend the wire outward, so the remaining 2' of wire lies in the trench you've dug out.

Some cutting and folding will need to be done at corners to ensure you have good protection in these areas.

Refill the trench, placing dirt over the top of the welded wire mesh—burying it.

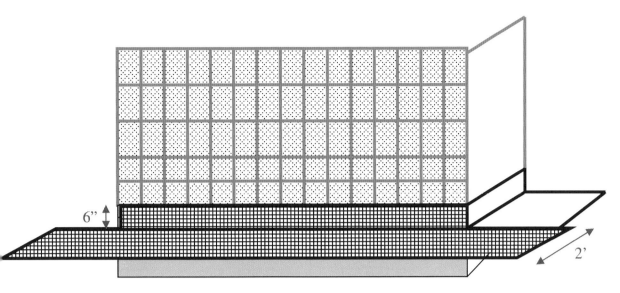

Underground predator barriers

How do predator barriers work? A predator approaches your perimeter fencing and tries to dig its way in at the base of the perimeter fencing—at the point of their obstruction. They hit the underground wire mesh and move to the left or right, along the baseline of the perimeter fence. Unable to get in, they give up. Predators are not crafty enough to back up two feet to try to dig in under the barriers.

Motion Sensor Lights

Mount motion sensor flood lights around your pens to alarm predators and alert you.

Abby's Goose Run is protected by electric fencing, digging barriers, aviary netting and motion lights
It also has cat ramps for rodent protection and weasel aversion

Louisville is one of our most impressive predator proof pens to date
This enclosure resides further into our forest than our other pens
and was subsequently built of even stronger materials

APPENDIX D

How to Give a Goose a Pill

It may sometimes be necessary for you to give a pill to your goose. Administering a pill to a goose is easy once you know how to do it. You can easily do it alone once you've had a little practice at it.

<u>Option 1</u>

Some geese will be fooled by the age old trick of hiding the pill in the treat. Count your blessings if you have one of these! You may want to wear leather gloves during the exchange if you have a biter on your hands. If your goose is too bright for this trick, then join the crowd and read on…

<u>Option 2</u>

- **Lay out a blanket**

It is very easy, especially while mastering this technique, for you or the goose to drop the pill you are trying to dose. To prevent you from digging through the hay (Baytril® is light brown) or having to go back to your vet for a replacement pill, lay an expendable blanket or towel on the ground for you and your goose to sit on during the procedure.

- **Catch the goose**

In order to avoid injuring your goose, it is important to know how to catch and handle them. Geese have fragile hips and legs. *Never* catch them by the feet or legs or you risk breaks, sprains and dislocations that can lead to permanent lameness. If your goose is accustomed to being handled, you can just pick them up by placing your hands over their body—one hand on each side, the way you would pick up a cat. Once in your arms, you can support their feet. If you have a shy or aggressive goose, it will likely take a little more effort. Still, you should be able to catch and hold any member of your gaggle at any given moment. This is imperative in case of an emergency.

Although imprinted geese tend to be easy to handle, shy or aggressive geese can be a bit of a challenge to pick up. Toenails can cause deep scratches and an occasional wing not held properly in place can give you a nasty punch if it hits you right. The inside of their bills have serrated edges rather than teeth, but they can still break the skin and cause some damage. Proper handling and protective clothing, including a thick, long sleeved coat is a wise choice if you prefer to avoid these kind of battle scars.

If your goose is not used to being handled, you will need to corner them in their pen. When doing this, be very careful not to run them over or through any obstacles (the edge of their pool, for example). Slowly ease them to the section of their pen that will allow for an easy and safe capture.

A real handy universal trick of grabbing a goose is to FAKE LEFT AND GRAB RIGHT. Use this technique more than once if you need to, and trick them into your own or your partner's hands. Never rely on your partner to catch the goose. Both of you make your best attempt. The most common goose catching mistake is, *"I thought you were going to get him."* If one of you grabs the goose, the second person needs to jump right in and help you secure the goose. The second most common goose rescue mistake is, *"I thought you had him."*

Once cornered, scoop up your goose from the back by sliding one hand under their body and between their legs. Do not support their legs to avoid toe nail scratches and wing flapping (it is more difficult for them to flap their wings when you are not supporting their feet, which provides them with leverage). Keep one wing pressed against your torso and gently, but firmly restrain the other with your free hand.

Safe goose handling

Now that you have your goose, you can carry them to a well-lit area where you already have your blanket set up and waiting.

- **Hold the goose in place**

Kneel down on the ground and set your goose down keeping your hands on each side of their body. Use your hands to hold your goose's wings in place and to keep them from flapping. Depending on the goose, this is not always as easy as it sounds and can take some practice. Goose wings are strong and can sometimes be tricky to keep in place, especially if your goose is particularly excited or defensive. If your goose is a biter, you made need to use one hand to keep them from turning on you.

Demonstration of the holding technique.
After getting your goose in this position,
slowly bring your knees together to hold the goose and his wings in place.

228

- **Sit over the goose**

Ease yourself over the goose, so that they are between your legs. Gently bring your legs together until the goose is held just snug enough to prevent him from flapping his wings.

Keep one of your hands in front of his chest to keep him from darting forward. Keep your legs and feet together behind you to prevent the goose from backing out.

- **Take out the pill**

While your goose is being held in place, remove the cap from the prescription bottle and *recap* it. Always recap the bottle because if anything goes awry, the goose will usually manage to spill the pills.

Hold the pill tightly between your thumb and forefinger of your *dominant* hand. First-timers can set the pill down on the blanket next to them where it will be easy to grab.

- **Open the bill**

There is more than one way to position your hands and fingers during this procedure. You will quickly learn the way that is most comfortable for you and your goose.

Place your *dominant* hand over the top of the bill and hold the bill in place. Cup your *non-dominant* hand beneath the bill and then curl the tips of your thumb and forefinger up on either side of the base of the bill, pushing your fingertips between the upper and lower bills. Most geese will react by opening their bill for you, but if not, use the very tips of your fingers, or a tiny edge of your fingernail to *gently* pry their bill open. Once open, slip your fingers further into the bill, so your goose can no longer close it. Now, with your goose's bill slightly pried apart, you are ready for the next step.

Keep in mind, even though you have pried your goose's bill apart, the edges of their bill can be a little sharp. If they exert pressure on you, it can range from a mere pinch to breaking skin. When working with a particularly ornery goose, I usually opt to wrap the portion of my index finger and thumb that will end up between their bill with a couple band-aids or some gauze tape to prevent them from breaking any skin.

In this photo, my dominant (right) hand is holding the upper bill steady.
My non-dominant (left) hand is cupped beneath the lower bill.
I have curled the thumb and forefinger of my left hand into my gander's bill to hold it open.

- **Tilt the head backward**

Tilt the goose's head gently backwards, keeping your fingers in place, so that the back of the goose's head is close to your chest.

- **Push the pill down**

Release your *dominant* hand from your goose's upper bill and reach for the pill. Keep your *non-dominant* hand in place holding the bill apart.

I use my right hand to reach for the pill
while continuing to hold his bill open with my left hand

Take the pill that is pinched between the two fingers of your *dominant* hand and put it down inside the bill just over the tongue so it drops into the hole of the goose's throat. Follow this action by quickly using your forefinger to push the pill barely into the goose's throat.

I push the pill down over his tongue with my right hand

230

I always stroke the goose's throat to help ease the pill downward and then watch for a couple of seconds to be sure the pill isn't reproduced. Once the pill is down, carefully stand up and step away from the goose (be careful dismounting if you have an ornery goose or you may get snipped at). I like to have a bucket of water right nearby, so the goose can have a drink as soon as I release them.

Geese as Pilling Patients

Giving a goose a pill may sound tricky at first, but once you master the maneuver, it is very quick and pretty simple. In my experience there are three types of goose personalities when it comes to taking their pill:

1) Those who take their pill without difficulty.
2) Those who bite and pinch you as often as they can through the entire procedure.
3) Those who clench their bills tightly and refuse to open them up.

The first type of goose patient is always preferable and pretty self explanatory.

Although the *Biter* can be a nuisance, they are not the most difficult of the three types to give a pill to. Be sure to wear leather gloves and a thick, long-sleeved coat to protect your arms. When he bites at you, just grab his bill, hold him steady and pop the pill down.

The *Clenchers* are the most difficult geese to give a pill to. A clencher will stubbornly refuse to open their bill, but they can be outsmarted. Geese tend to open their bills when you dribble water on the tops of their bills. Reach into his water bucket, dribble a bit of water on his bill and when he opens his bill, get any finger in there as quickly as you can. Once you have the bill pried open, follow the steps above. It can take a few tries to get them to open up or to successfully get your finger in between their bill.

If the water trick doesn't work try giving them a little tickle on their breast feathers. This sometimes will give them the urge to try to bite you, depending on their personality. Hurry up and put a finger into that open bill and continue with the procedure. If none of these tactics work, you will need to rely on your patience and perseverance. Eventually your goose will either open their bill or you will get it open. Just remember to keep your cool and remain gentle.

With practice, administering pills becomes a very simple and painless procedure that is as quick as the slide of a hand, but with any luck, you won't ever need to master this skill.

Remember that hint I told you earlier when finding a vet? One sign that they are not experienced with geese is if they cannot easily pry a bill open. An inexperienced waterfowl vet who is faced with a stubborn goose will often attempt to pry open the bill at the *tip* of the bill instead of the base. This is a sign that they have not had many geese as patients. It is a parrot strategy. Once you get good at administering a pill to a goose, you will recognize in a second when a vet isn't doing it properly.

APPENDIX E

Managing a Multiple Gander Gaggle

Although commonly uneventful, managing a multiple mixed-gendered waterfowl gaggle has its occasional hiccup. This is especially true of a newly introduced group of geese who have not fully bonded together yet or geese penned in too small of an area. In either case, things tend to be worse in the spring and early summer—during the mating season.

The myth that ganders do not make ideal pets or that multiple ganders are not a viable gaggle option is simply untrue. The situation just needs to be handled responsibly. It is extremely rewarding to have more than one gander in your gaggle, so you can experience a whole new level of group dynamics.

There are definitely some guidelines to consider before welcoming multiple ganders into your gaggle, but with a little forethought and planning, ganders make a wonderful addition to your family.

1. Be sure to maintain a healthy ratio of ganders to geese in your gaggle. Having one gander for every goose will help prevent fighting. This ratio will also prevent over-mating issues with your female geese.

2. It is highly recommended to have female geese that are *equal to* or *larger* in size than your ganders. This gives them a better ability to thwart off unwanted advances.

3. Never allow multiple ganders to mate with the same goose at the same time, especially on water. An improper gander/goose ratio (or oversized ganders in comparison with geese) can result in goose drowning. If one gander is trying to mate with a goose and a second gander swims over to interrupt, it may become necessary for you to quickly break things up.

4. If you are seeing irritated bald spots on the backs of any of your goose's necks, they are receiving too much attention from your ganders. Affected geese should be separated from overzealous ganders to allow the area to heal and their feathers to re-grow.

5. Spacious pens are a very good means at maintaining group harmony. Cramped spaces tend to foster misbehavior and territoriality, so consider carefully how many birds can comfortably fit into your barn and enclosures before adding new members.

6. Whenever possible, introduce new flock members in the fall when hormone levels are at their lowest and mating season is on the decline. Many ganders get along very well from July – January, especially in colder regions. Be careful that they don't mislead you into believing that it will always be this harmonious, though. Many new owners have been fooled by how well their ganders get along during their first year, only to discover that things aren't nearly so peaceful the following spring.

7. All introductions should be carefully monitored to ensure flock member's safety. Keep a close eye on pecking order disputes between any of your flock members. It is completely normal to see temporary squabbling among members as pecking orders are established and reaffirmed. The introduction of any bird, gander or goose, can cause the entire gaggle to suddenly have to rehash things out. Fighting should be considered excessive if the squabbles appear to be getting too rough, too frequent, or they simply do not subside. When these conditions exist, separations are definitely in order.

Your geese have personalities, moods and feelings. Some conditions lead to resentment among members, others lead to contentment. There are a number of combinations of separations available to you and varying levels of effectiveness depending on when they are used, so remember not to limit yourself to only one remedy.

To stop fighting among your ganders, a few good options are available to you:

- Separate pairs of geese and ganders from one another.

1 Gander & 1 Goose	1 Gander & 1 Goose	1 Gander & 1 Goose	1 Gander & 1 Goose

- Separate out one of the pairs involved in the fighting; that is, one pair in one pen and everyone else in another.

1 Gander & 1 Goose	3 Ganders & 3 Geese

- Separate out more than one pair of fighting ganders.

1 Gander & 1 Goose	1 Gander & 1 Goose	2 Ganders & 2 Geese

- Try other combinations, depending on the personalities and genders of your flock members. Remember, the object is to find the arrangement that best works for you and your geese. Don't be afraid to try different arrangements to determine which solution produces the best behavioral results.

2 Ganders	2 Ganders	4 Geese

OR:

2 Ganders & 2 Geese	2 Ganders & 2 Geese

Think Before You Hatch!

Preventative care is a vital part of maintaining a healthy gaggle. As tempting as it may be to allow geese to hatch out a clutch of eggs, consider carefully before you proceed. A sudden overload of ganders in your pens can cause an imbalance in your goose/gander ratio that can result in more fighting the following spring. You may soon have a serious problem on your hands. Irresponsible hatching is one of the root causes behind waterfowl abandonment—on ponds and at animal shelters.

Addling eggs is not always reliable. It is best to search out and remove all eggs from their pens every day in order to avoid future heartache. This small effort on your part does wonders for the homeless domestic waterfowl population.

Have no fear, ganders are here!

Most people will limit themselves to only one gander while others prefer to keep only geese. Many people fear the safety of their geese with a gander around, but ganders don't have any intentions of hurting your geese. Although the mating routine can be quite distressing to owners who have never witnessed a gander forcing a goose's head below the surface of the water before, it is all quite normal and natural and owners' fears soon subside (provided that geese are not too small for their ganders and there are no obstacles in the water for them to get trapped under).

Having a gander in your gaggle opens owners up to experience a whole new world of goose behavior. Courtship consists of a wide new array of honking, trumpeting, flirting and bathing. The interrelationships among all members are heightened and your geese live more enriched and normal lives.

Multiple ganders are a very viable option provided you prepare ahead of time. As long as you have the means to separate them if things get touchy and don't mind some extra time and effort on your part they are great fun. Nature has provided a few helping factors:

1) Ganders don't tend to fight if they have been raised from goslings together, especially if they are the same breed.

2) Many ganders get along wonderfully once they get past their initial alpha struggle.

3) Most ganders get along without a hitch from July – January (outside of the mating season)

4) As ganders bond and age, fighting commonly wanes off between them.

The only word of caution regarding multiple ganders is to consider your housing situation before you take them in and weigh whether or not you can accommodate separations. If you can spaciously divide your enclosure, you can successfully care for more than one gander.

If you give your gaggle a lot of room and introduce new ganders one at a time, the pecking order tends to be established very quickly.

APPENDIX F

Wild Waterfowl Rescue

Majestic receives many inquiries regarding wild waterfowl in need of assistance, but we choose to focus all of our efforts on domestic waterfowl who have significantly fewer advocates. All healthy wild waterfowl can fly while most domestics cannot.

It is <u>illegal</u> to keep wild waterfowl without state and federal wildlife permits!

The Migratory Bird Treaty Act (MBTA)

The U.S. Fish and Wildlife Service created this Act to provide protection for migratory birds. Among other things, the Migratory Bird Treaty Act stipulates that it is unlawful to capture, buy, sell or own any migratory bird or their eggs. Individuals who do not adhere to this Act may be fined or can even face jail time. In addition, any animals will be confiscated, making this even more painful.

This means, leave the wild gosling, goose and un-hatched egg where it is *unless* it is an emergency and the animal's life is in immediate danger. Then you may remove it from danger and arrange for its *immediate* transfer to a licensed wildlife rehabber.

Let go of any grand ideas of removing a wild gosling (or un-hatched egg) from its nest so that you can raise it as a pet. Wild animals belong in the wild; you need to leave them there. For more information about this Act visit www.fws.gov.

<u>What to Do In an Emergency</u>

As a preparative measure, begin to take notice of business cards of licensed wildlife rehabbers in your area. Often times they are available at your vet's office, humane society or pet supply stores. Take their card, or copy their information, so that you will have their contact information on hand in the case of a wildlife emergency. Usually, the card will indicate the types of animals they are licensed to handle, but in an emergency don't be afraid to call them regarding a type of animal that they do not handle. Rehabbers are known for having a wonderful network of connections. They may be able to direct you to someone who can help in your particular situation.

If a wild goose or gosling is in immediate danger, you may carefully and humanely capture it and arrange for its immediate transfer to a licensed wildlife rehabber. If the bird is not in immediate danger, but you are concerned about it, contact a wildlife rehabber for advice <u>before</u> intervening. Don't assume that goslings or eggs have been abandoned just because you do not see their mother nearby. Avoid the temptation of disturbing a nest until after you've discussed the situation with a licensed rehabber.

I know how darling those little goslings are, but you must keep their best interests in mind, and set your own desires aside. Wild goslings need to be taught to forage for natural foods and they need to learn to exercise their wings and learn to fly. It is vital that wild goslings do not imprint on humans (that means YOU!). If a wild gosling imprints on a human rather than a goose, they won't fair well in the wild. They may not act appropriately around other geese and become outcasts, or they may seek out other humans once released, which could prove very harmful. A licensed rehabber has the training to take care of a wild gosling and ensure that it can be released safely back into the environment.

Do not feed a wild goose or gosling until you have received advice from a rehabber (if you can't find one right away contact a vet who is experienced with waterfowl care). Place the goose in a protective container (or pet carrier if you have one on hand) with an expendable dry towel free of any loose strings that might cause tangles. Make a small water source available—nothing that can spill and make a big mess. You want your temporary guest to be warm and cozy, but not hot—remember an adult goose's feathers are excellent insulators. Goslings should be kept warm and draft free. Avoid using newspapers for bedding. They can remove precious oils from a goose's feathers.

Try not to disturb the goose. Let it rest quietly in its container in a safe and closed off room until you can arrange for it to be delivered to a rehabber. Be extremely cautious that neither children nor family pets have access to the goose.

Once you have the goose or gosling resting safely in a protected location, your highest priority is to contact a rehabber. Upon delivering the goose to a rehabber, remember to make a healthy donation. Caring for animals is very costly and most rehabbers do it without any funding, so your donations are needed and appreciated. Ask them how much it will cost to care for the goose until it can be released and then donate as much of that as you can, or donate extra to help the other animals in the rehabber's care as well.

INDEX

**A portion of the proceeds from the sale of this book
Are being donated to
Majestic Waterfowl Sanctuary**

Made in the USA
Charleston, SC
02 October 2010